EDI DEVE[illegible]ENT [illegible]ES
An[illegible]al C[illegible]

Successful Development in Africa

Case Studies of Projects, Programs, and Policies

Contributors
Rundheersing Bheenick
Edouard G. Bonkoungou
Catharine B. Hill
Earl L. McFarland, Jr.
D. Nelson Mokgethi
Katundu M. Mtawali
Morton Owen Schapiro
Stephen Wainaina
Stephen D. Younger
Jean-Baptiste Zongo

The World Bank
Washington, D.C.

Manufactured in the United States of America
First printing March 1989
Second printing October 1989

The Economic Development Institute (EDI) was established by the World Bank in 1955 to train officials concerned with development planning, policymaking, investment analysis, and project implementation in member developing countries. At present the substance of the EDI's work emphasizes macroeconomic and sectoral economic policy analysis. Through a variety of courses, seminars, and workshops, most of which are given overseas in cooperation with local institutions, the EDI seeks to sharpen analytical skills used in policy analysis and to broaden understanding of the experience of individual countries with economic development. Although the EDI's publications are designed to support its training activities, many are of interest to a much broader audience. EDI materials, including any findings, interpretations, and conclusions, are entirely those of the authors and should not be attributed in any manner to the World Bank, to its affiliated organizations, or to members of its Board of Executive Directors or the countries they represent.

Because of the informality of this series and to make the publication available with the least possible delay, the typescript has not been prepared as fully as would be the case with a more formal document, and the World Bank accepts no responsibility for errors.

The backlist of publications of the World Bank is shown in the annual *Index of Publications,* which is available from Publications Sales Unit, The World Bank, 1818 H Street, N.W., Washington, D.C. 20433, U.S.A., or from Publications, Banque mondiale, 66, avenue d'Iéna, 75116 Paris, France.

Library of Congress Cataloging-in-Publication Data

Successful development in Africa : case studies of projects, programs, and policies / contributors, Rundheersing Bheenick . . . [et al.] .
p. cm. -- (EDI development policy case series. Analytical case studies ; no. 1)
ISBN 0-8213-1163-8
1. Economic development projects--Africa, Sub-Saharan--Case studies. 2. Africa, Sub-Saharan--Economic policy--Case studies. I. Bheenick, Rundheersing. II. Series.
HC800.S83 1989
338.967--dc19 88-36905
CIP

EDI Catalog No. 405/032 ISSN 1013-333X

Contents

Preface v

Introduction 1
Earl L. McFarland, Jr.

Part I. Micro Studies

1. Burkina Faso: The *Projet Agro-Forestier* – A Case Study of Agricultural Research and Extension 11
Stephen D. Younger and Edouard G. Bonkoungou

2. West Africa: The Onchocerciasis Control Program 27
Stephen D. Younger and Jean-Baptiste Zongo

3. Malawi: Lessons from the Gravity-Fed Piped Water System 57
Catharine B. Hill and Katundu M. Mtawali

4. Kenya: A Case Study of the Production and Export of Horticultural Commodities 79
Morton Owen Schapiro and Stephen Wainaina

Part II. Macro Studies

5. Mauritius: A Case Study of the Export Processing Zone 97
Rundheersing Bheenick and Morton Owen Schapiro

6. Ghana: Economic Recovery Program – A Case Study of Stabilization and Structural Adjustment in Sub-Saharan Africa 128
Stephen D. Younger

7. Botswana: Macroeconomic Management of Commodity Booms, 1975-86 174
Catharine B. Hill and D. Nelson Mokgethi

Conclusions 207
Earl L. McFarland, Jr.

Abbreviations

CIDA	-	Canadian International Development Agency
cif	-	charged in full
CPI	-	consumer price index
EEC	-	European Economic Community
FAO	-	Food and Agriculture Organization of the United Nations
fob	-	free on board
GDP	-	gross domestic product
ICRISAT	-	International Crops Research Institute for the Semi-Arid Tropics
IMF	-	International Monetary Fund
OPEC	-	Organization of Petroleum Exporting Countries
OXFAM	-	Oxford Committee for Famine Relief
UNDP	-	United Nations Development Programme
USAID	-	United States Agency for International Development
WHO	-	World Health Organization

Preface

This collection of case studies examines a variety of successful development projects, programs, or policy actions undertaken in a number of African countries. By successful, we mean that the policies achieved their intended objectives and that the economic benefits outweighed the costs. We recognize, of course, that success has many dimensions and that there is always room for disagreement about how successful any particular policy or project has been.

Each study analyzes the problems that a specific development activity addressed, the experience in carrying out the activity, the degree of success, and possible implications for similar activities in other settings. All the studies come from Sub-Saharan Africa. We selected this region because, in general, its economic performance in the 1970s and early 1980s was poorer than that of any other region and because its failures and disappointments have attracted much attention. Bleak generalizations are, however, too sweeping. The region has also had many successful activities, and we can learn from them.

All but one of the case studies are collaborative efforts by a faculty member in the Department of Economics of Williams College and an African professional working in each country. An advisory committee, consisting of Henry J. Bruton, Paul G. Clark, and Richard Sabot of the Department of Economics, participated in planning the research and offering critiques of earlier drafts. The studies were carried out with the cooperation and financial support of the Economic Development Institute of the World Bank. They are intended for use in courses and seminars offered by EDI or by EDI in cooperation with other training institutions. They should also be of interest to officials and scholars concerned with effective activities for promoting economic progress in other developing countries.

Earl L. McFarland, Jr.
Williams College

Introduction

Earl L. McFarland, Jr., Department of Economics, Williams College

The seven case studies in this book differ in various dimensions, as well as in their country settings. Four of them analyze development projects or programs, namely, (a) a project for controlling the runoff of rainfall in semi-arid areas of Burkina Faso; (b) a multicountry program to control the serious endemic disease of river blindness (onchocerciasis) in West Africa; (c) a program to organize gravity-fed piped water systems for rural villages in Malawi; and (d) a program to develop horticultural commodities for export in Kenya. The other three studies analyze macroeconomic programs or policies, namely, (e) a trade strategy based on the creation of an export processing zone in Mauritius; (f) a balance of payments and structural adjustment program in Ghana; and (g) macroeconomic management of commodity booms in Botswana.

A brief introduction to each case study follows. The final chapter suggests some wider implications that emerge from the studies.

The *Projet Agro-Forestier* in Burkina Faso

This agricultural research and extension project in Burkina Faso, initiated by Oxfam, started very small, but as it grew, those involved learned and adapted the project accordingly. The technique, imported from Israel, of using earthen basins to catch rainwater for trees turned out to be of no interest to local farmers. Yet a local adaptation of that technology using rock bunds to slow the runoff of rainfall from terraces proved very effective in reducing soil erosion and retaining moisture in the soil, thereby increasing the yield of foodgrains.

The technology involved is very simple. Farmers can readily understand the technology, see the results, and do the basic work and maintenance themselves with locally available materials. The technology involved has all the desired attributes of being simple, cheap, and visibly effective.

The extension services involved are also simple. Few extension workers can help many farmers. An elaborate network of government extension services is not needed. The benefits are so obvious and the costs so minimal that farmers readily undertake the improvements on their own. Farmers are not required to move, to grow crops they are unfamiliar with, to borrow money to purchase a new technology, or to do anything very different from what they have been doing all along. For a minimal investment of time and effort on their part, they can increase output and reduce risk at the same time. Explaining why the "new technology" has spread so quickly is not difficult—it has all the basic ingredients for success.

From the national point of view, this project has two limitations. The yield increases that the bund technology makes possible are modest rather than dramatic, and the technology has spread too gradually to have had a large effect on national foodgrain output as yet. Finding ways to stimulate a more rapid and widespread adoption of this kind of low-cost method to manage rainfall runoff in semi-arid areas could increase benefits at the national level. However, the search for "green revolutions" must not lead us to overlook the smaller but valid gains from techniques that are simple, inexpensive, and easy for small farmers to implement.

The Onchocerciasis Control Program in West Africa

This is a program to control onchocerciasis (or river blindness) in West Africa by aerial spraying of the river sites where the fly that carries the disease-causing parasite breeds. At the technical level, the program has special characteristics that make its direct replication elsewhere unlikely. Yet the program's outstanding managerial efficiency allows us to draw some interesting conclusions that may well be relevant for a broader range of development activities.

The program's most distinctive characteristic is that even though it directly affects many rural people spread across a number of West African countries, it does not demand any significant change in behavior on the part of the program's beneficiaries.

The means of dramatically reducing the incidence of this endemic disease had only two dimensions, a technical dimension and an institutional dimension, without the sociological complications that make so many development problems difficult.

Modern science is quite effective in solving purely technical problems. Given sufficient funds for research, scientists can often find technical solutions. In the case of onchocerciasis, researchers not only solved the technical problems, but found they could control the disease at a low cost per capita. Thus, one implication of this experience is that for some problems, a technical solution can be very powerful at modest cost.

Implementation of the program required a unique international institution, and involved cooperation among a number of national governments in West Africa, the World Health Organization, and an international staff of technicians. Its central task, once researchers had developed the appropriate sprays, was to carry out systematic aerial spraying of widespread river areas, and to monitor the results carefully.

The effective management and operations of this institution were greatly facilitated by having few, but clearly defined, objectives. The program's central objective was simply to kill the flies that carried the parasite. A few clear targets greatly facilitated conduct of operations, assessment of performance, and organizational morale. The focusing and sharpening of operating targets can be pertinent even for projects like large irrigation schemes, which often have a wide range of potentially conflicting objectives.

The Gravity-Fed Piped Water Program in Malawi

This study examines a program in Malawi based on piping water from higher elevations to villages, where it is distributed by a simple network of pipes and standpipes.

A number of important aspects of the gravity-fed piped water program have contributed to its success. The basic system was devised in cooperation with the local residents who benefit from it. The technology involved is easily understood and maintained by local residents. The benefits are readily apparent to the beneficiaries. The design of the gravity-fed system had time to evolve as a single project grew into a national program. The costs to the government are low compared to alternative village water systems.

The first gravity-fed water project in Malawi was born out of cooperation between a local project committee and a perceptive government engineer. Since that time, projects have been based on strong community support from the construction phase all the way to maintenance of the completed systems. The obvious benefits of a clean and convenient water supply that villages can largely construct and maintain themselves has made villagers with a project eager to show residents of other villages how it works.

The technology of supplying reliable clean water throughout a village distribution network calls for an engineered design, use of manufactured components, and continuing maintenance. However, the villagers can do most of the construction and maintenance themselves. In addition, the robustness of the design and the ready availability of the components make the system very reliable.

In common with the Oxfam project in Burkina Faso, the gravity-fed water scheme began small. The government took a while to realize how effective the system really was, and it was not prepared to put massive resources into making the program a national program at an early stage.

The program's gradual expansion over time reduced the number of government extension workers and engineers required, stimulated much learning from experience, and permitted improvements in project design and an important shift to domestically produced pipe that was both better and cheaper. The program also attracted financial contributions from international agencies, which lowered the costs to the government.

The success with village water projects has eased the way for public health workers in Malawi to introduce a complementary health program. Evaluation studies indicate that the combined benefits of these complementary projects are greater than the sum of the parts. Moreover, indications suggest that villagers involved in such projects have widened their appreciation of how they can organize themselves to improve their environment and work with the government to obtain benefits that they want.

Production of Horticultural Commodities for Export in Kenya

The subject of this study is a program carried out in Kenya jointly by the government, a parastatal, and the private sector to stimulate the production and export of horticultural products.

The growth of horticultural production and exports in Kenya since 1968 has been impressive. In 1967, Kenya did not export any fresh horticultural products. By 1986, horticultural exports had reached 3.3 percent of total exports, and ranked third among agricultural exports behind coffee and tea. The story is largely one of what the private sector and the public sector can accomplish when they work together rather than at cross purposes.

It was only in the late 1960s, after some encouraging private initiatives, that the Government of Kenya began to put resources into promoting the growth of the horticultural sector. In 1967, the government established the Horticultural Crops Development Authority (HCDA) and endowed it with broad and sweeping powers over virtually every phase of horticultural production. Thus, one of the most interesting aspects of this study is what the HCDA did, and also what it did not do, that encouraged horticultural production and exports.

The mix of activities that the HCDA became involved in is fairly standard: research, training, extension services, provision of basic infrastructure, distribution of seeds, and help in marketing. Many foreign nations also contributed funds and personnel to horticultural projects.

An important function of the HCDA, however, as participation by small producers expanded, has been to maintain the high standards of quality required to satisfy the export market. The HCDA's record suggests that a parastatal can perform this function well.

The main power that the HCDA did *not* use was its power to control prices. These were left largely to be determined by market forces, and the resulting profits induced substantial investment and an impressive expansion of production and exports. Farmers' responsiveness to economic incentives was demonstrated once again in this experience.

A final lesson comes from Kenya's success in penetrating highly competitive export markets for horticultural produce. Both government support and the knowledge of foreign markets provided by foreign investors contributed to this success. But the main lesson is not to underestimate the scope for expansion of nontraditional exports.

The HCDA did not have to face the policy dilemma of wanting to keep prices high for producers, but low for consumers, that is common with basic foodgrains. Furthermore, horticultural production in Kenya was so small in the late 1960s that all the HCDA's efforts could be concentrated on a relatively small number of farmers. The HCDA was able to grow with the horticultural sector and learn its job as it grew. Nevertheless, the responsiveness of farmers to market incentives and the positive impact that government support can have when it focuses on those activities that government performs best are lessons that should be transferable to the production of basic foodgrains.

The Export Processing Zone in Mauritius

This case study analyzes the benefits, in terms of increased employment in industry, higher real wages, increased export earnings, and a decline in the birth rate that can be attributed to the export processing zone (EPZ) in Mauritius. This is a zone created by the government within which firms enjoy a wide range of incentives to produce manufactured goods for export. As the EPZ evolved, the government noted shortcomings and adapted its policies to deal with them. This learning from experience and policy flexibility is a key part of the story.

The first lesson is that economic incentives have a powerful effect on how an economy develops. The annex to the study lists 24 different incentives initially granted to EPZ firms, of which some of the most important are complete exemption of import duty on capital goods, raw materials, and manufactured inputs; a 10- to 20-year corporate tax holiday; free repatriation of capital and remittances of profits and dividends; favorable access to loans; speedy government processing of licenses; and guarantee against nationalization. The response was an increase from a base of zero in 1971 to value added equal to 54.5 percent of total manufacturing value added, exports equal to 52.8 percent of total exports, and more than 78,000 jobs in EPZ firms by 1986.

The second lesson is that the package of incentives enabled Mauritius to attract a substantial amount of investment and to break into a highly competitive export market. In so doing, the country was able to reduce greatly its extreme dependence on a single primary export (sugar), and escape the limitations on manufacturing development posed by the small size of the domestic market.

The third lesson is the importance of investment in human capital. The supply of competitively priced semiskilled labor was an important factor in attracting both foreign and domestic investment to the EPZ. Even more important, the transition of the EPZ from its present relatively low technological base to a higher technology base will depend heavily on the skills acquired by the existing industrial labor force and continuing improvements in the educational system.

The last lesson is one that is stressed throughout this volume—the importance of learning from experience. The flexibility of Mauritian policymakers in adapting policies as conditions changed has been a crucial ingredient of success. When EPZ expansion hit a period of relatively slow growth in 1977-82, policymakers responded with a package of institutional and policy reforms that (combined with macroeconomic stabilization and structural adjustment programs and improving international markets) strengthened economic incentives and accelerated EPZ growth.

Similarly, when the government realized that EPZ concentration on a few products and a small number of export markets was potentially dangerous, it provided incentives that encouraged diversification of both the product mix and markets. The government has also encouraged backward linkages with the domestic economy and reformed the tax system in such a way as to reduce the differences in tax incentives that EPZ firms and import-competing firms faced. The authorities have undertaken tariff reforms to stimulate greater efficiency in import-competing firms and greater linkages between EPZ firms and the domestic economy.

Each step along the way has revealed the need for further policy changes. Policymakers have learned from experience and have adapted policies to achieve their desired objectives.

The Economy Recovery Program in Ghana

This study focuses on the economic recovery program that the Government of Ghana initiated in 1983, and examines some of the major macroeconomic and microeconomic policy changes that have begun to put the economy back on a satisfactory growth path after many years of economic stagnation.

The story of Ghana from the late 1960s to 1982 is one in which political instability and the rapid turnover of policymakers contributed to misguided economic policies, which governments adhered to despite their realization that these policies were crippling the national economy. The inability to change policies that were driving the economy farther and farther down is perhaps the most striking element of Ghana's history during that period.

In fairness we should recognize that when a country's political situation is chaotic and the economic situation is already bad, policymakers will be understandably reluctant to implement any unpopular policy changes. As the economic situation worsens, the economic "medicine" required will be even more painful in the short run, and the policymakers' political support will be even weaker. Failure to take unpopular policy actions when they are first required can lead to a deadly downward spiral in which it becomes harder and harder to turn the economy around again.

However, the study focuses on something more positive. Starting from a desperate economic position, how were Ghanaian policymakers able to get the economy moving forward again? The government that came to power in 1982 became committed to carrying out economic reforms, and by then the economic crisis was so profound that virtually everyone agreed that drastic action had to be taken. Once the economic recovery program began, policymakers continued to learn from experience and adjusted their policies as needed to achieve the objectives that they had set.

If much of Ghana's earlier woes can be traced to getting the prices wrong and then keeping them wrong (or even making them worse) for a long time, Ghana has worked hard to get the prices right since 1983. Key prices, such as the exchange rate and cocoa prices, were so wrong that even finding out what the right price ought to be took considerable trial and error. From its level of 2.75 cedis/dollar in April 1983, the cedi was devalued many times during the next several years, reaching 90 cedis/dollar in January 1986. Later that year, Ghana moved to a foreign exchange auction system that resulted in marginal rates of 150-160 cedis/dollar. Cocoa prices were raised in several stages from 12,000 cedis/ton in 1982 to 85,000 cedis/ton in April 1986. During the same period, other key agricultural prices and other controlled prices were also raised significantly, and most prices were decontrolled.

A worsening of the drought in 1983 kept the agricultural sector from responding to the price changes, but in 1984 and 1985 agricultural production and exports surged in response to normal rainfall and greatly improved economic incentives. Growth in real GDP was a strong 8.7 percent and 5.1 percent, respectively, after three consecutive years of negative growth rates.

The message is not, however, that getting the prices right is the whole story. Ghana's infrastructure had deteriorated to such an extent that many producers in key sectors (such as timber and minerals) were unable to take advantage of the improved prices until the infrastructure had been restored enough to move commodities to markets again. Thus, another important observation from the Ghana study is that its structural adjustment program required substantial resources from international organizations. The country would not have been able to increase its foreign exchange earnings, a necessary first step toward recovery, without external resources to help restore the most essential components of a deteriorated physical infrastructure and to purchase essential inputs for its export sector.

Ghana's experience with the economic recovery program is compatible with the view that an orthodox structural adjustment program can turn around even a worst-case situation, if sufficient external resources are forthcoming, and if the program can be maintained long enough for some positive effects to show. An important political-economic implication is that when an economy has become severely repressed and disorganized, a government that aims to turn the economy around needs strong political support, an understanding of strategic economic changes, and a pragmatic approach to making policy adjustment as it gains experience.

Macroeconomic Management of Commodity Booms and Busts in Botswana

This study looks at the diamond boom and bust in Botswana in the early 1980s to determine how Botswana was able to avoid both the excesses of the boom period, and the shocks to the economy of the subsequent bust that have had such negative impacts on the growth performance of many other exporters of primary products in the developing world.

Since the early 1970s, Botswana's earnings from diamond exports have exhibited a generally rising trend. In the early 1980s, however, diamond prices fell sharply and diamond exports came to a standstill. This situation is similar to that faced by many primary exporting countries, notably, petroleum exporters. Botswana's macroeconomic policies during the earlier boom, and then in the acute bust, allowed the country to avoid or ease many of the serious problems often associated with commodity booms and busts. How and why was Botswana able to manage the boom and bust relatively successfully?

During boom periods, the policies adopted by Botswana have included avoiding excessive increases in government expenditure, instead building up international reserves and government balances at the central bank to be used when the boom ends. In addition, by management of the nominal exchange rate, the government avoided real exchange rate appreciation.

When the bust occurred, its severity and duration were quite uncertain. The government did not try to ride through the bad times just by using the country's reserves and ability to borrow externally. It adopted a variety of adjustment policies that affected the exchange rate, bank lending, interest rates, and public sector wages. It adopted cuts in expenditures, although their impact turned out to be small. The cushion built up during the boom, reinforced by corrective policies during the bust, minimized the setback to the economy.

What features of the political economy in Botswana may have contributed to this relatively successful experience in macroeconomic management of boom and bust? The case study suggests four interesting aspects.

First, Botswana's cultural tradition of open discussion of issues facing the community has helped the government reach a consensus on longer-run policies. Major policy decisions are taken only after extensive consultation at different levels in the bureaucracy, culminating in discussions at cabinet level and in Parliament. Policies agreed upon therefore have some staying power.

Second, there has been considerable continuity of leadership in the government since independence. Many key policymakers have remained the same, and have participated in a long-running series of debates on economic issues. Many government leaders recognize the importance of the economic dimensions of problems they face, and are experienced in weighing economic objectives against other considerations.

Third, although a number of political parties freely compete for voter support, the electoral support for the ruling party nationwide has never been seriously threatened. The government's political security and authority have made it more likely to pursue policies for their potential longer-run benefits, and less likely to adopt policies purely for their shorter-run political appeal.

Finally, as a cattle country subject to highly variable rainfall and pasture, and as an exporter of other primary products besides diamonds, Botswana has had considerable experience with short-run economic instability. The costs of instability and the benefits of risk-reducing tactics are widely recognized. Moreover, the earlier trials and tribulations of a number of other mineral exporting countries have offered some object lessons that have not gone unnoticed by government.

Part I. Micro Studies

1

Burkina Faso: The *Projet Agro-Forestier* A Case Study of Agricultural Research and Extension

Stephen D. Younger, Department of Economics, Williams College
Edouard G. Bonkoungou, Institut de Recherche en Biologie et Ecologie Tropicale, Burkina Faso

This paper is a case study of the *Projet Agro-Forestier* (PAF) in the Yatenga region of Burkina Faso. Oxfam, a private development organization, funds and manages the project, whose aim is to prevent soil erosion and increase crop yields through water conservation. The Yatenga region has a history of overuse of land resources, which has decreased the arable land surface and caused severe degradation of the environment. Past efforts by government and international organizations to improve the situation have largely met with failure, while traditional methods of adapting to soil erosion have been insufficient.

Over the course of four to five years, the PAF has developed a simple, inexpensive, labor-intensive technology that successfully collects water and holds it on the fields, preventing erosion and increasing the land's absorption of water. The PAF has also acted as an agricultural extension service to teach the region's farmers about the technology. Thousands of farmers now use the technique, and the number is growing rapidly as people observe its success.

The key to the PAF's success lies in the way it has carried out its research and extension work. The program has been extremely farmer oriented, and the participation of local farmers has been an important factor in both the development of the technique and in its rapid adoption in the area.

Background[1]

The Yatenga region of Burkina Faso is located in the sudano-Sahelian area that borders the southern edge of the Sahara desert. The region is dry, with average annual rainfall of 680 mm, and is subject to drought; less than 400 mm of rain fell in both 1982 and 1983. Nevertheless, subsistence agriculture is the dominant occupation in the area. Incomes are very low, US$40-75 per capita in 1978. To survive, many families depend on remittances from relatives who have migrated to the Côte d'Ivoire.

We would like to thank Peter Wright and the participants from Williams for their helpful comments. We are especially grateful to the Oxfam and PAF staff in Ouagadougou and Ouahigouya, Tony van Zutphen, Michael Butcher, and Mathieu Ouedraogo for their kind cooperation in providing us with data on the project and comments on an earlier draft.

1. This section draws heavily on Wright and Bonkoungou (1985).

Traditional agricultural techniques cause considerable soil erosion and depend on long fallow times to restore the soil's productivity. Yet strong population pressure—each square kilometer supports an average of 75 to 100 people—forced farmers to shorten and eventually eliminate the fallow periods. Continuous cultivation has led to dramatic soil erosion; most of the region's upper slopes have been destroyed. Marchal (1983, p. 225) estimates that by 1973, 11 percent of the land surface in central Yatenga had been degraded beyond use, and that the amount was growing by 0.35 percent per year.

The PAF began in 1979 as a response to the environmental degradation. The project borrowed from techniques developed in the arid regions of Israel (see Shanan and Tadmor 1979). Low earth walls were used to enclose a one square meter runoff surface called a microcatchment. At the microcatchment's lowest point, a basin was dug to collect water from the surface, and various trees species were planted. The hope was that the trees would help prevent soil erosion.

The PAF persuaded eight village "groupements" (cooperatives) to try out this idea. The farmers were skeptical, as farmers usually are with new extension schemes, so they volunteered their worst pieces of land for the experiment. They became more interested, however, when they observed the large amounts of water that built up in the microcatchments. Several decided to plant upland rice in the basins, and sorghum was introduced by accident (through manure) in some cases. These crops did very well. Thomson (1980, p. 5) notes that the sorghum "...had massive heads relative to the best in adjacent fields."

Discussions between PAF staff and participating farmers at the end of the first season confirmed that the farmers were much more interested in planting crops rather than trees, and the PAF agreed to shift its focus in accordance with the farmers' wishes. Further, as the farmers began to appreciate the potential benefit of water harvesting, they shifted their attention from group plots to their own individual land. The PAF also accepted this change in focus.

Two more years of experimentation led to further changes in the project. The participating farmers decided that construction of the complete rectangular microcatchment required too much labor. Instead, they had begun to construct one-sided barriers of rocks or branches placed perpendicular to the water flows. This was basically a reintroduction of a traditional technique that farmers had abandoned. While this technique did save work, water could easily flow around the ends of the barriers, creating two new water courses. To solve this problem, the PAF realized that the barriers should be longer and that, for maximum efficiency, they should follow the ground's contour lines (figure 1.1). In response to this need, the PAF developed an inexpensive (and rather ingenious) device: the water-tube level. The level accurately identified the contour lines on the gentle slopes common to the Yatenga, and the PAF found that they could train an entire village in its use in two or three days. By 1982, experimentation with the elongated barriers, "diguettes" or "bunds," yielded the technique that is used today.

The technique as currently practiced involves determining the contour line with the water-tube level, digging a small trench on the contour to anchor the rocks, and building a barrier 10 to 50 centimeters high and 10 to 100 meters long (depending on the size of the field). Spacing of the bunds depends on the slope of the field—steeper slopes require more closely spaced bunds—and on how much time the farmers can spare. Wright (1985) notes that many farmers spaced the bunds far apart in the first season and then added intervening bunds later. Farmers also tend to treat their more degraded fields first since water runoff is greater and the marginal benefit of erosion control is higher.

Rocks are now the overwhelming material of choice because the bunds must be semipermeable. Solid bunds, for example, the earthen ones originally used, tend to be washed out by heavy rains and therefore require continuous repair, while the rock bunds allow enough water to pass through to avoid their own destruction. An interesting observation is that in the region around Ouahigouya, rocks are no longer free: in 1986, a cartload of rocks cost about CFAF 600.

Figure 1.1 Bunds Criss Cross a Field

In the short run, the technique works to improve crop yields in two ways. The most important advantage is that the bunds hold rainwater on the fields rather than letting it run off. This is the water harvesting aspect of the project, which increases the absorption of water by the land and thus by the crops. In a semi-arid region like the Yatenga, this is an important advantage. The second short-run advantage is that fertilizer (usually manure) and organic material applied to the fields are more effective since they are less likely to be washed away. Further, the presence of manure in the fields attracts termites that bore into the ground, helping to aerate it.

Over the long run, the principle advantage of the bunds is erosion control and an increase in soil quality. Wright (1985) notes that as much as 20 mm of soil had accumulated behind some of the barriers after their first year of use. This makes the soil directly behind the bunds relatively rich, allowing the growth of some specialized crops and, ironically, given the origin of the project, bushes and trees.

With the water-tube level and the bund technique perfected, the PAF began an extension campaign to encourage their use in the Yatenga. Sticking with the principle that farmers' participation should be voluntary, the PAF worked to convince farmers that the bund system would benefit them directly by improving their crop yields and controlling erosion. Their most effective tactic has been to bring potential participants to visit current participants who explain and promote the technique themselves. Soil erosion is discussed and demonstrated using a model. Appropriate forms of community organization for the construction of bunds are also discussed. Finally, the new participants return home where the use of the water-tube level is demonstrated.

The success of this approach to extension is shown by the growth of participation and the current excess demand by farmers in the area for PAF training sessions. Despite a field staff of less than six people, the PAF had trained 500 people by 1984, with 546 hectares of land treated. By 1986, the number of hectares treated rose to 2,500, and the amount of new land treated roughly doubles every year.

Measuring the Success of the PAF

The clearest way to measure the economic success of the PAF would be a cost-benefit analysis that compared the total cost of research and development, training, materials, and labor to the market value of any increases in yields. However, because the PAF is a small project, no one has yet done this, and the dearth of accurate cost data make it a rather crude exercise. Nevertheless, annex 1.1 reports our attempts to piece together enough data to estimate the internal rate of return to the PAF.

Some data have been collected on the project. In 1985, ICRISAT carried out a careful cost-benefit analysis of an agricultural package that included rock bunds along with a low dose of fertilizer, an appropriate sorghum variety (ICSV1002), and tied ridges. This package was evaluated in farmer trials and in ICRISAT-controlled test plots.

The farmers' trials are perhaps the most interesting because they are realistic, but they test only the package as a whole. No controls were used to evaluate the individual components of the package or their interactions. The results show that yields were an average of 67 percent higher on the test plots, with the most striking gains being made in the sudan-savanna regions where yields were 300 percent higher, compared to improvements of 34 percent in the areas with better "guinean" climates (ICRISAT 1985, p. 10). This difference is probably because the Sahelian regions are drier and also receive more sheet flow of water from higher slopes that have been denuded. Thus, water harvesting was both more effective and more necessary in the sudano-Sahelian zone, which has a climate similar to that in which the PAF operates. In general, the percentage increase in yield increased with the amount of water runoff from uphill. ICRISAT also notes that the farmers in the Sahelian zone took more care to construct higher and less permeable bunds, which ICRISAT's experiments found were more important factors than simple regional dummy variables (ICRISAT 1985, p. 10).

ICRISAT then calculated the annual yield increment necessary to cover the costs of the package, most of which are for fertilizer. Using a conservative discount rate of 15 percent, they found that 67 percent of the farmers in the Sahelian region exceeded the breakeven yield, while only 19 percent in the guinean zone did so. This again emphasizes the importance of placing and constructing the bunds so that they capture a fairly heavy runoff (ICRISAT 1985, p. 10). Thus, in the Sahelian region at least, the water harvesting package seems to have a good rate of return. What is more, this is likely to be understated since all data come from the first year of application only. Yet 90 percent of the farmers in the test reported substantial accumulation of soil and organic matter behind the bunds, with soil depths increasing more than 20 mm in the first year in some instances. So future yields should be even better.

In the researcher-managed trials, ICRISAT was able to separate the effects of the bund system from those of the fertilizer and tied ridges. These results show a yield increment of 40 percent due to bunds alone in the Sahelian zone and of 9 percent in the guinean, with only the latter being statistically significant (ICRISAT 1985, p. 14). ICRISAT notes, however, that participating farmers criticized ICRISAT's choice of plot sites, since none received sufficient runoff from uphill.

In less formal tests, Wright (1985) reports yields for plots with and without bunds as shown in table 1.1.

Table 1.1 Effects of Rock Bunds on Crop Yields

Year	Rainfall (mm)	Control plots No.	Control plots Yield (kg/ha)	Treated plots No.	Treated plots Yield (kg/ha)	Z*
1981	692	3	510	14	857	n.a.
1982	421	45	442	47	495	1.26
1983	413	37	295	63	418	3.01
1984	383	72	153	74	292	3.89
1986	n.a.	33	612	33	972	1.13

n.a. = not available
*Test statistic for the difference between the two means. The critical value for a 95 percent confidence interval is 1.96.
Source: 1981-84 : Wright (1985)
1986 : Ouedraogo (1987)

These data must be interpreted carefully since the treated plots may differ from the control plots in more ways than simply having bunds. For example, bunds make added organic matter or fertilizer more effective because it is less apt to be washed away by the rains—this makes its application more likely: of the treated fields, 60 percent received manure, though only 2 percent received chemical fertilizer. (Data for the control fields are not available.) In addition, 33 percent of the treated fields used small water collection holes. Note also that the soil in 70 percent of the fields treated was poorer than average, and fully 45 percent had been abandoned prior to the experiment. Thus the control yield for those plots ought to be zero. Nevertheless, Wright uses productive control plots in all his calculations.

Not only are the yields of the treated fields generally higher, the highest yield differentials occur in years with low rainfalls. This makes intuitive sense since the marginal value of a unit of water saved is likely to be higher when rainfall is lower. If this is the case, then risk-averse farmers are likely to value the bunds more than the expected value of yield increases. This is because the marginal utility of an extra kilogram of yield is higher, perhaps much higher, at low yields where it may help prevent malnutrition or starvation.[2]

2. This result must be treated with some caution, however, since it is likely that soil quality is increasing on at least some of the test plots—those that have had bunds for more than one year—at the same time that rainfall is decreasing through the four years of Wright's sample. Ouedraogo (1987) provides evidence for the importance of this factor. He reports that in the 1986 season for plots of similar quality, yields were 1,112 kg/ha for plots treated in 1984, 883 kg/ha for those treated in 1985, and 873 kg/ha for those treated in 1986.

Based on ICRISAT's cost assumptions, the staff and materials costs of Oxfam, and the yield data provided by Wright (1985), we have calculated the internal rate of return to the PAF project in annex 1.1. We find that under very conservative assumptions, the internal rate of return to the project is 37 percent, while under a slightly more optimistic set of assumptions, the rate is 42 percent. In addition, we find that when treating sunk costs as sunk, the return to treating a new hectare of land is very high, 147 percent. Therefore these calculations suggest that the return to the PAF is at worst quite respectable and at best extraordinary.

Wright (1985, p. 5) analyzed his data somewhat differently. He estimated that a farmer needs about 90 kilograms of grain to eat while treating one hectare of land. Since the average annual yield increases are higher than this, at least the subsistence labor cost can be covered in only one year. The results of an Oxfam/Cathwel-sponsored revolving food bank program that lent farmers enough food to "pay" neighbors to help construct bunds support this argument. After two years, 55 percent of the villages involved had at least replenished the original stock of grain provided by the program, and another 23 percent had partially done so (Ouedraogo 1986). On average, the stocks were almost exactly replaced with a 1 percent increase.

Since the farmers in Yatenga are adopting the technology at a rapid rate, in most cases without any incentive or subsidy other than the expected increase in yields, they obviously believe that bunding has an acceptable rate of return.[3] This is all the more convincing in light of the fact that some of the initial participants were considered crazy by their peers (Wright 1985, p. 7).

Learning from the PAF's Success

What accounts for the success of the PAF, and what can we learn from it? To some extent, the success merely reflects the ingenuity and hard work of the farmers and extension workers involved (and the luck of finding an interesting innovation). Our interest here, however, is in drawing lessons for civil servants rather than farmers, so we will concentrate on Oxfam's role in the PAF's success. Of course, Oxfam employees are not civil servants, but the role they have played is essentially that of agricultural researchers and extension agents. As such, they could just as easily have been employed by the government extension service as by Oxfam. Oxfam's personnel have been particularly effective and offer us several lessons about good agricultural research and extension.

Communication, Flexibility, and Patience in Extension Work

Many authors have written about agricultural extension in developing countries (for example, see Murphy 1983, Perraton et al. 1983). For the most part, evaluations of extension services are rather pessimistic. Orivel (1983, p. 16), for example, notes that "... the literature is extremely discouraging." Benor and Harrison (1977, p. 6) claim that "...it is difficult to find many developing countries with a really effective service." Indeed, dissatisfaction with agricultural extension has run so high that the World Bank has developed its own approach, the training and visit

3. Oxfam has provided villages with water-tube levels free of charge, and occasionally lends donkey carts for hauling rocks. It also funds the program staff, of course, providing a type of research, development, and extension service subsidy. However, there is probably a positive external benefit to erosion prevention that the farmers are not taking into account in their own calculations.

system, to try to overcome many of the problems. (See Benor and Harrison 1977 for a description of the training and visit system, and Feder et al. 1983 for an evaluation of its effectiveness in India.)

The most commonly cited problems with agricultural extension in developing countries are (a) poor organization, with extension agents having no clear line of technical support or administrative control; (b) diffuse responsibilities, with agents being expected to perform many nonextension (even nonagricultural or bureaucratic) functions in addition to extension work; (c) poor training of extension agents; (d) lack of ties between the extension service and agricultural research, both from researchers to the service and vice versa; and (e) sporadic contact between agents and the farmers they are supposed to serve. (See Benor and Harrison 1977 or Orivel 1983 for a more detailed discussion of these problems.)

The PAF has managed to avoid or solve all of these problems. Because it is a small organization (two Oxfam resident representatives in Ouagadougou and a few field staff in the project area), the project has not encountered the organizational problems of large extension services, nor have the field staff's responsibilities been too diverse. Further, because the bunding technology is fairly simple, training has not been a problem. The real lessons to be learned from the PAF's extension campaign, then, pertain to points (d) and (e) above. Three important factors contributed to their success: good communication, flexibility, and respect for participating farmers' opinions and preferences.

Communication between agricultural research and the extension service is good because in the PAF, the researchers are also the extension agents—all research has been carried out "on the farm."[4] Equally important, however, is the good communication between farmers and the research/extension agents, which has been facilitated by high levels of contact between the PAF field staff and farmers. The staff live in the project area and frequently visit the treated plots. (This was especially true in the early, experimental stages of the project.) Further, the staff has taken the farmers seriously, encouraging their feedback on the project.

Such two-way communication is rare. Even though it has become commonplace, especially among economists, to pay lip service to the wisdom, skill, and profit-maximizing ability of peasant farmers, most agricultural extension pays little attention to the inputs of peasants. For the most part, experts working in the capital or abroad conceive and test projects and techniques in idealized laboratory conditions. These experts then pass on their packages to the agricultural ministry where extension agents, acting as subordinate experts, deliver them to farmers. The communication here is all top down. The government views the information that the experts provide as the information that matters, and sees the role of extension as one of dissemination to producers. Little room is left for feedback or input from the producers to the experts. (Summarizing a World Bank/UNDP volume on agricultural extension, Pickering (1985, p. 168) argues that: "At the present time in most countries farmers' participation in the identification and subsequent follow-up of production problems is more or less inadequate.") Many of these projects and

4. The obvious analog for larger research and extension organizations is the field test/demonstration plot, which also integrates research and extension functions. The USAID has recently emphasized the importance of field testing by farmers (as opposed to extension agents) under realistic conditions (see Murphy 1983). As we have seen, this approach has been quite successful at promoting farmer participation in the PAF and has also improved the PAF staff's credibility with farmers.

techniques fail, and the farmers on the receiving end of this process have become skeptical about the experts' expertise, making extension work all the more difficult.

The PAF has been an exception to this pattern. It has encouraged feedback from farmers both through more frequent contact with farmers and, frankly, a less arrogant attitude about the worth of farmers' inputs, and has allowed for it in the project. This has paid off by establishing a high degree of credibility for the PAF extension service among farmers, and by redirecting research efforts in response to farmers' inputs.

The most striking evidence for this proposition is the project's evolution. Remember that the initial idea was to encourage reforestation by planting trees in microcatchments. After the first trial of this technique, farmers were not sold on the idea, but were very keen to use the catchments for crops. This was an important turning point in the project's history: not only was the PAF receptive to the farmers' suggestions, it was sufficiently flexible to respond to them, thereby significantly altering the project's focus.

This degree of flexibility and responsiveness to farmers is unusual. Where most projects would have forged ahead with the original tree planting as planned, or perhaps abandoned the idea altogether, Oxfam changed course at the farmers' behest. This is the feature that makes Oxfam's approach to extension service stand out. Effective communication from the farmers to Oxfam allowed the project to change dramatically from a transplanted idea to the rather "home grown" project we observe today. Of course, many other refinements and modifications came in time, some from outside (notably the water-tube level), and some from the farmers themselves. The point is that the give and take between extension agent and farmer has been extremely valuable in the success of PAF.

Cooperation from farmers is not automatic. Indeed, many extension projects fail and many extension workers are frustrated precisely because farmers are skeptical and uncooperative. Nevertheless, recognizing that skepticism about new techniques is a rational response on the part of farmers who face hunger or starvation if an experiment fails is important. To its credit, the PAF has understood and respected subsistence farmers' position, and rather than trying to tell them what is good for them, the PAF has concentrated on letting the farmers themselves decide whether or not to try the bund technique. This requires a great deal of patience and a great deal of respect for farmers' opinions, but it is clear that both of these have helped the PAF gain the farmers' cooperation.

Further, the fact that participation in the program has been voluntary, with the only incentive for participation being expected increased crop yields, builds a kind of insurance into the program. It could not have proceeded if the farmers had judged it a poor bet on its own merits. It is, of course, possible to get farmers to try an experiment even if they think it is a stupid idea if a sufficient subsidy or external incentive to participate exists. But as soon as the incentive is withdrawn, the project is no longer profitable and farmers abandon it. By avoiding such incentives, the PAF guarantees that one group of experts, the farmers, believe the project has a reasonable expected rate of return.[5] Equally important, this structure also gives the PAF agents an incentive to pay attention to the farmers since the fate of their project depends on the farmers' evaluation.

---

5. There is a place for subsidizing farmers' participation in extension projects in the experimental (rather than implementation) stages of the project to encourage realistic field tests of a technique. This is particularly true when the technique is new and unusual so that farmers would be disinclined to try it without some subsidy to encourage participation.

In this context, a useful comparison is available. From 1962-65 the Groupement Européen de Restauration des Sols undertook an anti-erosion project in the Yatenga. This group constructed earthen embankments, small dams, and rock barriers over 120,000 hectares of the region. The project was designed and executed by expatriates, using modern equipment, such as bulldozers, that is quite expensive locally. The group neither consulted the local farmers nor encouraged them to participate. Consequently, the farmers did not understand or maintain the system. As a result, the system quickly deteriorated, and by 1965, the project was officially described as "an unfortunate experience" (Wright and Bonkoungou 1985).

The project described above has much in common with the PAF project. They both addressed the same issue and used similar approaches to soil conservation. Yet one failed while the other succeeded. The important difference between the two appears to be the degree to which the local population was involved in the evolution, design, construction, and maintenance of the project, that is, each organization's approach to extension work.

A Place for "Low Tech" Advances

In addition to the way in which the PAF has developed and disseminated its technical innovation, we would like to draw attention to the innovation it has focused on, that is, a low tech, low cost, low risk technological improvement. Quite often governments, international organizations, and experts hope that a technological change will have dramatic, widespread effects—a technological revolution. Yet technological changes that are less grand in scope and scale, changes that involve small projects or apparently minor alterations in techniques, also have a role. These changes are not dramatic, and are therefore not very attractive to experts or bureaucrats. After all, scientists gain acclaim for breakthroughs, not refinements, and bureaucrats make points supervising large, expensive projects. But more humble technological progress, while less glamorous, can be both significant and profitable.

The PAF is an example of this kind of technological change. It has proved profitable and has contributed significantly to agricultural production in the Sahelian region of Burkina Faso. This has been accomplished at very low cost—a key feature of "minor" technological improvements—and without substantial inputs from outside the existing production system, such as machinery, chemicals, or special seeds. As Benor and Harrison (1977) note, this approach to introducing agricultural changes is likely to be more successful in terms of effective extension because it does not require farmers to take large initial risks or make large initial investments to try out an idea. Should it work, it improves the extension agent's credibility. Should it fail, it will not be a spectacular disaster so that resentment about the failure is less likely. In subsistence agriculture, where the consequences of a large failure are extreme, the more cautious approach would appear to be more attractive. Active farmer participation is much more likely in projects that do not involve high risks.

A second important feature of the type of technique that the PAF has pursued is that it has a very small minimum efficient scale compared to a project like that of the Groupement Européen de Restauration des Sols, which employed significant amounts of sophisticated (and expensive) equipment, and which must be undertaken on a large scale to be cost-effective. This allowed the project's initial research and development stage to proceed at very low cost, and it also allowed farmers to test the technique on an efficient scale for low cost, thus increasing the likelihood that they would be willing to try it out.

Of course, once a technique is proven (to both researchers and farmers), it must be reproducible on a much larger scale. Here, too, the bunding technology is quite appropriate. Individual farmers can expand the area covered at their own pace and get roughly proportional returns for their efforts—the technology has constant returns to scale. As for the PAF project as a whole, it is now at the point where rapid expansion is appropriate. After the initial experimentation stage, when only tens or hundreds of hectares were treated, it became clear that the PAF had developed a profitable technique and that much wider extension was appropriate. Thus, the PAF is hiring more of its own extension agents and coordinating its efforts with the government extension service. Because of this growth and coordination, and because of the large excess demand for training from farmers who have recognized the value of bunding, the prerequisites for a rapid dissemination of the technique are now in place. As our cost-benefit results show, the returns to such an expansion could be outstanding.

Conclusion

The PAF's most important and unusual feature is its approach to agricultural extension work. The project has been extremely farmer oriented: at each stage, the farmers have been actively encouraged to participate and their opinions have been respected. This respect, and the appreciation of the problems farmers face, are unusual in agricultural extension work, yet the approach has paid off handsomely.

To gain the farmers' cooperation, the PAF staff have been unusually patient and flexible in both the research and extension phases of the project. They have allowed things to proceed at a pace and scale agreeable to the farmers, and they have altered the project significantly in response to their input. This patience and flexibility has not only gained the cooperation of the farmers, but has also lent credibility to the PAF staff, which should make cooperation in future extension projects easier.

In addition to these lessons on extension service, the PAF also demonstrates that a project that proceeds with a low budget and pursues a low tech method can yield significant returns. Of course, this does not imply that all agricultural research should follow such a strategy—many high tech projects have also yielded high rates of return—but it does suggest that a place exists for simpler technological changes, and that planners should not forget them when working on an agricultural development strategy.

Annex 1.1 Calculating the Internal Rates of Return to the PAF

The estimates of the internal rate of return given here are rough because the data available are not extremely accurate. Nevertheless, the exercise is worthwhile to get a "ballpark" figure.

The project's major costs are Oxfam's expenditures on staff for research and development (in the early years) and for extension service. Later on, when large amounts of land were involved, the costs of constructing bunds—labor costs and the cost of a donkey cart to bring stones to the field—became significant. We have also added a maintenance cost for existing bunds. The major benefit, of course, is the value of the increased yields on crops planted on treated fields.

We took the costs of the Oxfam staff from Wright (1985) for the years 1981-84 and from Ouedraogo (1986, 1987) for 1985 and 1986. These costs also include Oxfam's relatively minor expenditures on equipment and materials for the water-tube levels. For the years after 1986, we have assumed that the cost per hectare for Oxfam support remained constant at the 1986 level of (1984) CFAF 7,964 per hectare. As table A1.1 shows, costs fell dramatically during the project's initial years, and with the increased use of Burkinabe extension agents and widening farmer participation, the PAF's cost per hectare could continue to fall, making our assumption somewhat conservative.

Table A1.1 Oxfam Costs for the *Projet Agro-Forestier,* 1981-86

Year	Annual cost (real 1984 CFAF)	Surface area treated (ha)	Cost/ha (CFAF)
1981	6,870,446	7	981,492
1982	6,134,938	62	98,950
1983	14,256,049	150	95,040
1984	13,345,000	327	40,810
1985	13,021,876	642	20,283
1986	7,016,284	881	7,964

Source: Wright (1985) and Ouedraogo (1986, 1987)

We took the labor and donkey cart costs from ICRISAT (1985). ICRISAT assumes a dry season wage of CFAF 15/hour, which is half the cropping season wage. Estimates of the time needed to gather stones and construct bunds are based on observations of the farmers who participated in the ICRISAT field study.

We have seen no figures on the cost of maintaining existing bunds. These costs are likely to be quite low, both because they involve only labor and because the bunds are sturdy constructions. For our purposes, we have assumed that the yearly maintenance costs are 10 percent of the labor costs necessary for construction of the same bunds.

The benefits are more difficult to estimate. For the years 1981-84, we have used the yield differentials cited in Wright (1985) and Ouedraogo (1987) for control and treatment plots. For the remaining years, we use the weighted average of the 1982-84 and 1986 yield differentials, namely, 144 kg/ha. If anything, this is a conservative estimate, and perhaps very conservative since, even though 45 percent of the treatment plots in Wright's study had been abandoned so that the appropriate control yield for them is zero, he (and Ouedraogo) attribute a positive yield to all control plots. The sample for 1981 is very small, and we have therefore omitted it. No data are available for 1985. For the record, the 1981 yield differential is the largest that Wright reports, so this omission will bias our return estimates downward.

The number of hectares treated is based on Wright (1985) for 1981-84 and Ouedraogo (1986, 1987) for 1985 and 1986. For the remaining years, we have used the 1986 figure (881 ha) and have either assumed that construction stops at that time, or continues on to 1990. These too are likely to be conservative figures, since construction is currently continuing and the program seems to be expanding rapidly beyond the 881 ha/yr figure. (Current plans are to treat 1,200-1,400 hectares in 1987.)

Finally, we took the price of output from ICRISAT (1985), that is, CFAF 90/kg, the official government price for the 1984 growing season. This too is a conservative assumption since many farmers grow millet on the treated fields, which usually fetches more than sorghum.

Based on these data and assumptions, our most conservative calculation assumes that the program would cease to develop any further fields after the 1986 growing season, but that already treated fields would be maintained until the year 2000, giving us a 20-year horizon for the project as a whole. Insofar as this assumption does not allow the project to defray the very heavy initial research and development and extension costs that Oxfam incurred, it is quite unfavorable. Nevertheless, the internal rate of return under these assumptions is 37 percent (table A1.2).

Our second run (table A1.3) assumes all of the above except that construction continues at the rate of 881 ha/year up to 1990, at which time it ceases. Again, we run the project out 20 years, yielding an internal rate of return of 42 percent.

Finally, we note that if the proposed coordination with the government extension service works well, the area of land treated will be much larger than the current area. If the expansion is dramatic, then Oxfam's initial research and development costs would become trivial relative to the size of the project, and a calculation of the internal rate of return should exclude those costs. Performing this calculation with a time horizon of 20 years, yields an internal rate of return of 147 percent.

Table A1.2 Data for Assumption of Construction to 1986

Internal Rate of Return: 37 percent

Year	PAF cost per hectare (constant CFAF/ha)	New hectares treated (ha)	Cumulative hectares treated (ha)	Yield differential (kg/ha)	Total benefits per year (constant CFAF)	Total costs per year (constant CFAF)	Net benefits per year (constant CFAF)
1981	981,492	7	7	347	218,610	7,021,121	-6,802,511
1982	98,951	62	69	53	329,130	7,471,959	-7,142,829
1983	95,040	150	219	123	2,424,330	17,509,156	-15,084,826
1984	40,810	327	546	139	6,830,460	20,460,982	-13,630,522
1985	20,283	642	1,188	144	15,396,480	27,033,664	-11,637,184
1986	7,964	881	2,069	360	67,035,600	26,399,131	40,636,469
1987	0	0	2,069	144	26,814,240	730,357	26,083,883
1988	0	0	2,069	144	26,814,240	730,357	26,083,883
1989	0	0	2,069	144	26,814,240	730,357	26,083,883
1990	0	0	2,069	144	26,814,240	730,357	26,083,883
1991	0	0	2,069	144	26,814,240	730,357	26,083,883
1992	0	0	2,069	144	26,814,240	730,357	26,083,883
1993	0	0	2,069	144	26,814,240	730,375	26,083,883
1994	0	0	2,069	144	26,814,240	730,357	26,083,883
1995	0	0	2,069	144	26,814,240	730,357	26,083,883
1996	0	0	2,069	144	26,814,240	730,357	26,083,883
1997	0	0	2,069	144	26,814,240	730,357	26,083,883
1998	0	0	2,069	144	26,814,240	730,357	26,083,883
1999	0	0	2,069	144	26,814,240	730,357	26,083,883
2000	0	0	2,069	144	26,814,240	730,357	26,083,883

Note: Base year for constant CFAF index is 1984.

Table A1.3 Data for Assumption of Construction to 1990

Internal Rate of Return: 42 percent

Year	PAF cost per hectare (constant CFAF/ha)	New hectares treated (ha)	Cumulative hectares treated (ha)	Yield differential (kg/ha)	Total benefits per year (constant CFAF)	Total costs per year (constant CFAF)	Net benefits per year (constant CFAF)
1981	981,492	7	7	347	218,610	7,021,121	-6,802,511
1982	98,951	62	69	53	329,130	7,471,959	-7,142,829
1983	95,040	150	219	123	2,424,330	17,509,156	-15,084,826
1984	40,810	327	546	139	6,830,460	20,460,982	-13,630,522
1985	20,283	642	1,188	144	15,396,480	27,033,664	-11,637,184
1986	7,964	881	2,069	360	67,035,600	26,399,131	40,636,469
1987	7,964	881	2,950	144	38,232,000	26,710,124	11,521,876
1988	7,964	881	3,831	144	49,649,760	27,021,117	22,628,643
1989	7,964	881	4,712	144	61,067,520	27,332,110	33,735,410
1990	7,964	881	5,593	144	72,485,280	27,643,103	44,842,177
1991	0	0	5,593	144	72,485,280	1,974,329	70,510,951
1992	0	0	5,593	144	72,485,280	1,974,329	70,510,951
1993	0	0	5,593	144	72,485,280	1,974,329	70,510,951
1994	0	0	5,593	144	72,485,280	1,974,329	70,510,951
1995	0	0	5,593	144	72,485,280	1,974,329	70,510,951
1996	0	0	5,593	144	72,485,280	1,974,329	70,510,951
1997	0	0	5,593	144	72,485,280	1,974,329	70,510,951
1998	0	0	5,593	144	72,485,280	1,974,329	70,510,915
1999	0	0	5,593	144	72,485,280	1,974,329	70,510,915
2000	0	0	5,593	144	72,485,280	1,974,329	70,510,915

Note: Base year for constant CFAF index is 1984.

References

Benor, Daniel, and James Q. Harrison. 1977. *Agricultural Extension: The Training and Visit System.* Washington, D.C.: World Bank

Blade, Arlene. 1979. *Microcatchment Project.* VOL 093, Six-Month Report. Oxfam.

Cernea, Michael M., John K. Coulter, and John F.A. Russell (eds.) 1985. *Research, Extension, Farmer: A Two-Way Continuum for Agricultural Development.* Washington, D.C.: World Bank.

Feder, Gershon, Lawrence J. Lau, and Roger H. Slade, 1985. *The Impact of Agricultural Extension: Case Study of the Training and Visit System in Haryana, India.* World Bank Staff Working Paper no. 756. Washington, D.C.: World Bank.

ICRISAT. 1985. *Annual Report of ICRISAT/Burkina Economics Program, 1985.* Ouagadougou: ICRISAT.

Marchal, J.Y. 1983. *Yatenga Nord Haut-Volta—La Dynamique d'un Espace Rural, Sudano-Sahelian.* Paris: ORSTROM.

Murphy, Josette. 1983. *Strengthening the Agricultural Research Capacity of the Less-Developed Countries: Lessons from AID Experience.* AID Program Evaluation Report no. 10. Washington, D.C.: USAID.

Orivel, François. 1983. "The Impact of Agricultural Extension Services: A Review of the Literature." In Perraton et al. *Basic Education and Agricultural Extension: Costs, Effects, and Alternatives.* World Bank Staff Working Paper no. 564. Washington, D.C.: World Bank.

Ouedraogo, Mathieu. 1986. *Rapport d'Activités de la Campagne 1985.* PAF/Burkina Faso, (Oxfam). Ouagadougou: Oxfam (processed).

Ouedraogo, Mathieu. 1987. *Rapport d'Activités de la Campagne 1986.* PAF/Burkina Faso (Oxfam). Ouagadougou: Oxfam (processed).

Perraton, Hilary, Dean T. Jamison, Janet Jenkins, François Orivel, and Lawrence Wolff. 1983. *Basic Education and Agricultural Extension: Costs, Effects, and Alternatives.* World Bank Staff Working Paper no. 564. Washington, D.C.: World Bank.

Pickering, Donald C. 1983. "Sustaining the Continuum." In Perraton et al. *Basic Education and Agricultural Extension: Costs, Effects, and Alternatives.* World Bank Staff Working Paper no. 564. Washington, D.C.: World Bank.

Shanan, L., and N.H. Tadmor. 1979. *Microcatchment Systems for Arid Zone Development: A Handbook for Design.* Jerusalem: Hebrew University.

Thomson, James T. 1980. *Oxfam Microcatchment Project: Preliminary Evaluation.* Ouagadougou: Oxfam.

Wright, Peter. 1985. *Water and Soil Conservation by Farmers.* Ouagadougou: Oxfam.

Wright, Peter, and Edouard Bonkoungou. 1985. "Soil and Water Conservation as a Starting Point for Rural Forestry: The Oxfam Project in Ouahigouya, Burkina Faso." ***Rural Africana.*** **Nos. 23-24.**

2

West Africa: The Onchocerciasis Control Program

Stephen D. Younger, Department of Economics, Williams College
Jean-Baptiste Zongo, Socioeconomic Evaluation Unit, Onchocerciasis Control Program

Onchocerciasis is a parasitic disease that affects 20 to 30 million people and is endemic to parts of Africa, Latin America, and the Arabian peninsula. The disease is most common in West Africa, where researchers estimate that ten million people carry the parasite. The parasite's most important effect is blindness, although it also causes severe skin irritation. For the most part, the disease affects small, isolated, rural communities. In some villages, especially those close to rivers, 10 to 13 percent of the population may be blind.

The parasite, *Onchocerca volvulus*, is a worm that spends part of its life cycle in humans and part in one of several blackfly species of the *Simulium damnosum* group. This second part of the worm's life cycle led several field studies undertaken in the 1960s to conclude that onchocerciasis might be controllable in West Africa. Blackfly larvae need aerated water (such as river rapids) to develop, and in West Africa, which has generally gentle terrain, these sites are both identifiable and relatively few. Thus, interruption of the parasite's life cycle might be possible by attacking the larvae in river rapids (larviciding), thereby reducing the blackfly population.

With this strategy in mind, seven West African governments approached the international donor community to gain their support for a control program based on aerial larviciding of the blackfly breeding sites in river rapids. The donors accepted the proposal, and the Onchocerciasis Control Program (OCP) was formed in 1974. The OCP is a semi-autonomous branch of the WHO (the executing agency) and is sponsored by the WHO, the UNDP, the FAO, and the World Bank. These institutions, as well as several other bilateral and multilateral aid agencies, provide financial support for the program (see annex 2.1 for a list of contributors to the OCP).

The OCP's larviciding strategy has been very successful, interrupting transmission of the disease after ten years in over 90 percent of the program area, and showing good progress toward its goal "...to eliminate onchocerciasis as a public health problem and an obstacle to socioeconomic development and ensure that there is not subsequent recrudescence of the disease" (WHO 1985, p.88). This chapter examines the factors behind the OCP's success.

Background[1]

O. volvulus is a small worm—adult females are 50-70 mm long and 0.04-0.06 mm in diameter. Adult worms live in fibrous cysts in human skin. Each cyst contains one or more pairs of worms. Fertilized adult females give birth to 500,000 to 1 million microfilaria a year for about 12 years. The microfilaria can migrate through the body and sometimes arrive at the eye, where they cause the formation of scar tissue or lesions. If enough microfilaria invade the eye, the victim goes blind.

The microfilaria also reside in the skin where they can be ingested by female blackflies, which need human blood for their eggs to mature. The blackfly digests most of the microfilaria, but a few manage to pass through the intestinal wall and develop in the thoric muscles. After they have grown into infective larvae, the worms migrate to the fly's mouthparts, where they can be retransmitted to humans and develop into mature adults (see figure 2.1).

At the outset of the OCP, the only drugs effective at killing either the microfilaria or adult worms in humans had very serious side effects, so the only viable approach was to attack the parasite indirectly by controlling the blackfly population.

Nevertheless, controlling insect populations is a very difficult task, and other attempts to eradicate diseases by eliminating their insect vectors have not fared well (the most notable example is the attempt to control malaria by killing mosquitos). However, the OCP's strategy had three advantages. First, the blackfly larvae must live in well-aerated water, usually river rapids, and these sites are easily and completely identifiable. Second, the larvae are vulnerable to larviciding since they filter particulates from the water for nutrition, and an effective and ecologically safe larvicide, temephos, was available. Third, onchocerciasis, unlike malaria, is a cumulative disease. One fly bite, or even several, is unlikely to transmit sufficient infective larvae to produce enough microfilaria to cause blindness. Thus, complete elimination of the fly population was not necessary for effective control of onchocerciasis.

From the start, the program recognized that blackflies were capable of migrating considerable distances, so that control efforts would have to be widespread to cover most of the blackfly's habitat in West Africa. Indeed, earlier attempts to control blackfly populations in smaller regions of West Africa had failed in some areas because flies from outside the control area migrated into it. The program's organizers also thought that the adult parasites could live and reproduce in humans for up to 18 years (although later research established that their reproductive life is actually only 12 years), thus the OCP would have to be long-lived—initial plans called for 20 years—to prevent retransmission of microfilaria from already infected people to blackflies at the end of the period of blackfly control.

The OCP is headquartered in Ouagadougou, Burkina Faso, and employs about 800 people. The staff is international, but predominantly African. All the employees from the level of sector chief down are African, and 57 percent of the senior management and professional staff, including the director, are African. The treatment area is divided into 7 geographic sectors and 24 subsectors that covered about 875,000 km^2 in 1985, with approximately 18,000 km of rivers. In addition to the blackfly (vector) control unit, which receives about 70 percent of the OCP's budget, the program has an epidemiological evaluation unit, a socioeconomic development unit, and an administrative services unit (see figure 2.2).

---

1. This section is based on WHO (1985), chapters 1-3.

Figure 2.1 Life Cycle of Onchocerca Volvulus

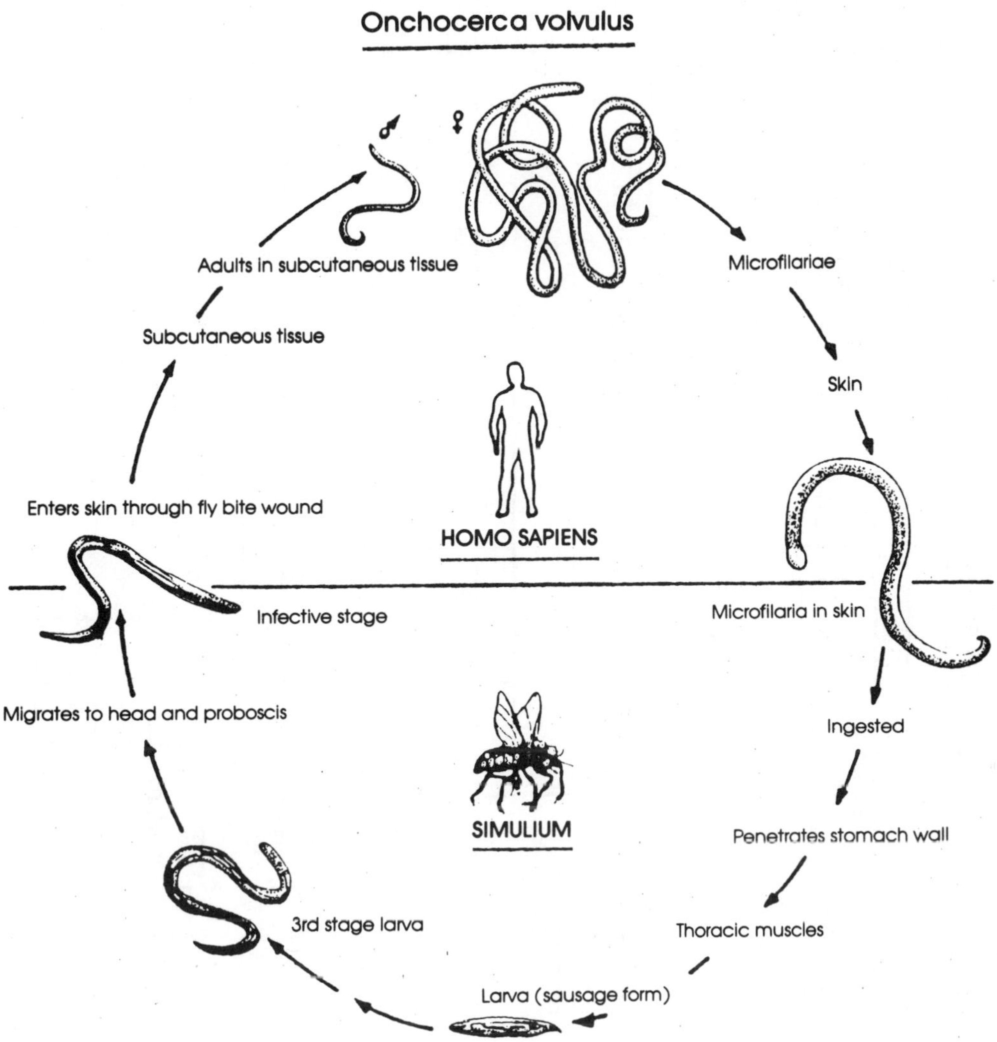

Source: WHO (1985)

Figure 2.2 Organizational Chart of the Onchocerciasis Control Program (as of January 1, 1988)

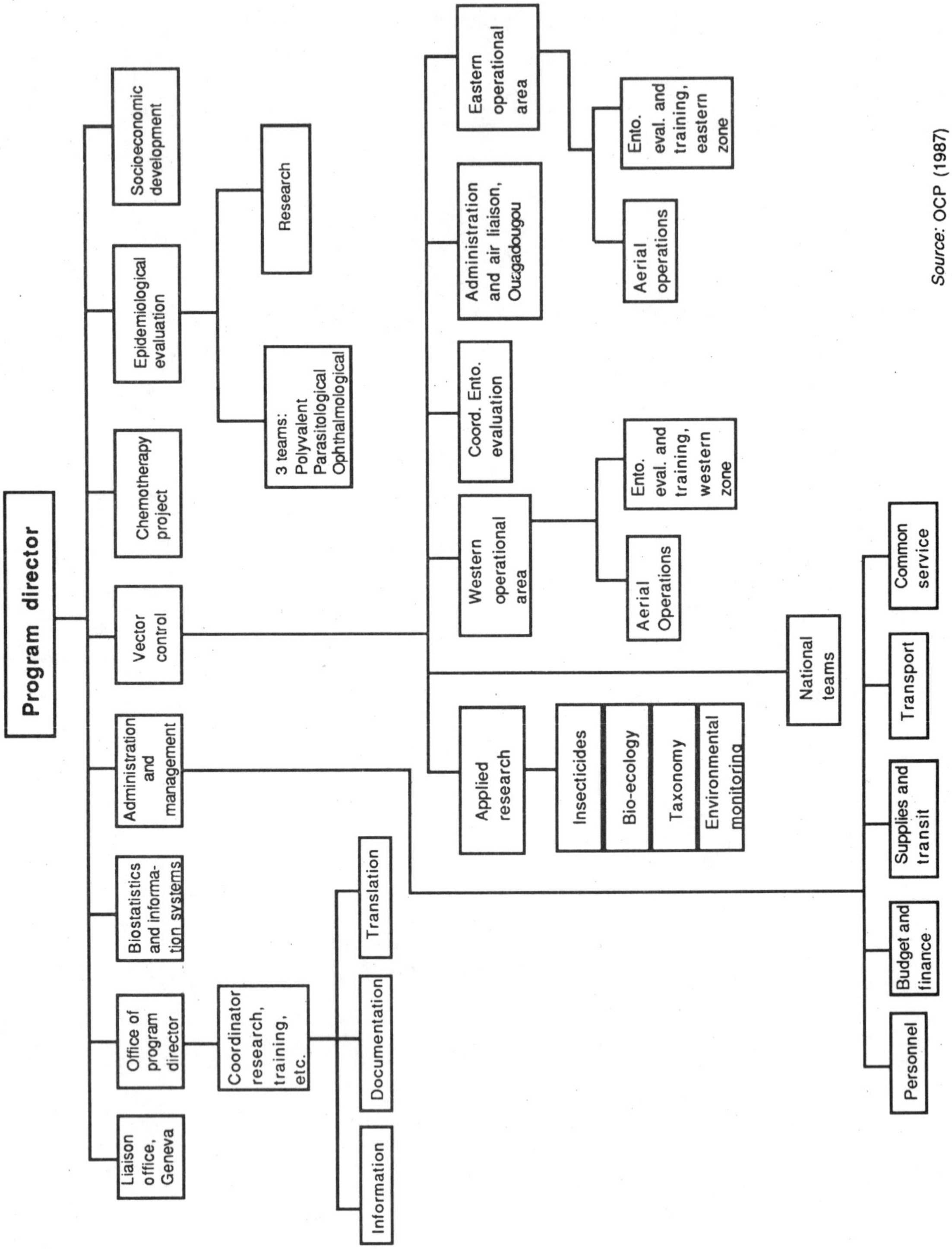

Source: OCP (1987)

While the OCP has pursued scientific research on blackflies, larvicides, and potential drugs for use in humans, its most important operation is larviciding. This work has two key parts: monitoring and treatment. The monitoring system employs many local people to record the number of times that flies try to bite them in a given period of time and to trap flies and deliver them to sector headquarters. There, staff test the flies for the presence of infective larvae and send the results to OCP headquarters, where a vector control team identifies areas that need larviciding. The actual larviciding is done by airplanes and helicopters stationed at two aerial operations bases whose activities cover the entire program area. The OCP headquarters radios the 7 sector and 24 subsector stations with directions on when and where to larvicide.

The larviciding system depends on an unvarying and continuous routine of information collection, evaluation, and response that has gained wide praise for its efficiency. This efficiency is absolutely necessary for the success of the OCP, since a failure at any point in the system, even a temporary one, could allow a resurgence of transmission of the parasite from humans to the blackflies, restarting the parasite's life cycle and frustrating the control attempts. Research has shown that blackflies can recolonize an untreated area within a month.

Measuring the Success of the OCP

The most obvious way to measure the success of the OCP is to perform a cost-benefit analysis of the program (see annex 2.2), but as is often the case with health projects, the results are inconclusive. Even though the project's costs are well defined, obtaining accurate estimates of the benefits is difficult. Consequently, we turn to indirect evidence of the OCP's success. In particular, we can show that (a) the OCP is well on its way toward achieving or even surpassing the goals originally set out for it, and (b) the OCP has done this on or under budget. Thus, we can conclude that the program has been executed successfully, and we shall focus on the execution in drawing lessons from the OCP's experience.[2]

Entomological Results

As mentioned earlier, the goal of the OCP is to eliminate onchocerciasis as a public health problem and an obstacle to socioeconomic development, and to ensure that no new outbreaks occur subsequently. Evidence that the OCP has indeed attained this goal is striking. In the original program area, the transmission of the *O. volvulus* parasite was almost completely interrupted in the program's first eight years. Entomologists at the OCP calculate the annual transmission potential (ATP) for onchocerciasis, which is the theoretical number of infective larvae that a person would receive at a particular place (capture point) in one year. Places with ATPs greater than 800 are considered hyperendemic, that is, more than 60 percent of the population carries the parasite, blindness rates are about 10 percent of the total population, and up to half of all males over 40 are blind (WHO 1985, p.12). ATPs of less than 100 are considered tolerable.

Figure 2.3 shows that before the OCP, 56 percent of the capture points had ATPs greater than 800, while only 9 percent had ATPs less than 100. As early as 1976, only

2. The fact that OCP has achieved its goals on budget still leaves open the possibility that its rate of return is not very high, but only if the program as originally conceived did not have a high rate of return (see annex 2.2).

two years after larviciding began, the figures changed dramatically: the ATP was below 100 at 65 percent of the capture points and remained above 800 at only 2 percent. By the eighth year of the OCP, 85 percent of the capture points in the original OCP area had ATPs of less than 100, and only 1 percent had an ATP greater than 800 (see figure 2.4). The few zones where the ATP remains high are affected by reinvasion of blackflies from outside the OCP area. This problem, which now appears solved, will be discussed later.

In sum, the figures show that the OCP succeeded in killing enough fly larvae that the number of bites a person is likely to get by a fly carrying the *O. volvulus* parasite has become too small to be infective. Indeed, a USAID evaluation team reported that in 1986, it was unable to collect any blackflies at OCP-controlled sites, while the team collected 18 in 20 minutes at an uncontrolled site in Togo (USAID 1986).

Figure 2.3 Annual Biting Rates in the Onchocerciasis Control Program Area Before Operations Began

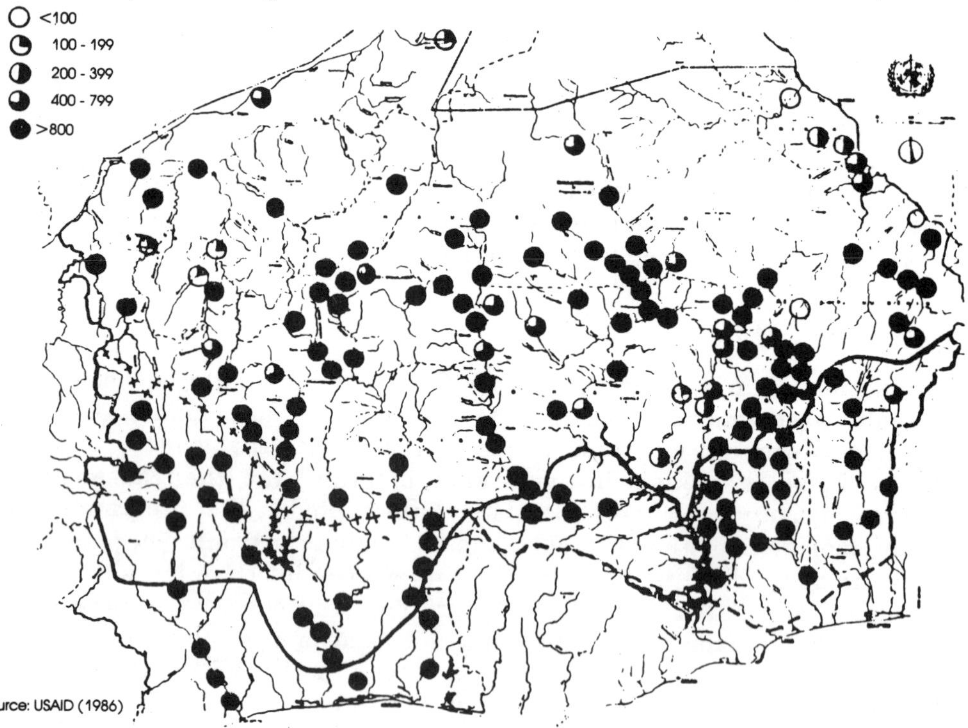

Source: USAID (1986)

Figure 2.4 Annual Transmission Potential in the Onchocerciasis Control Program Area, November 1983 - October 1984

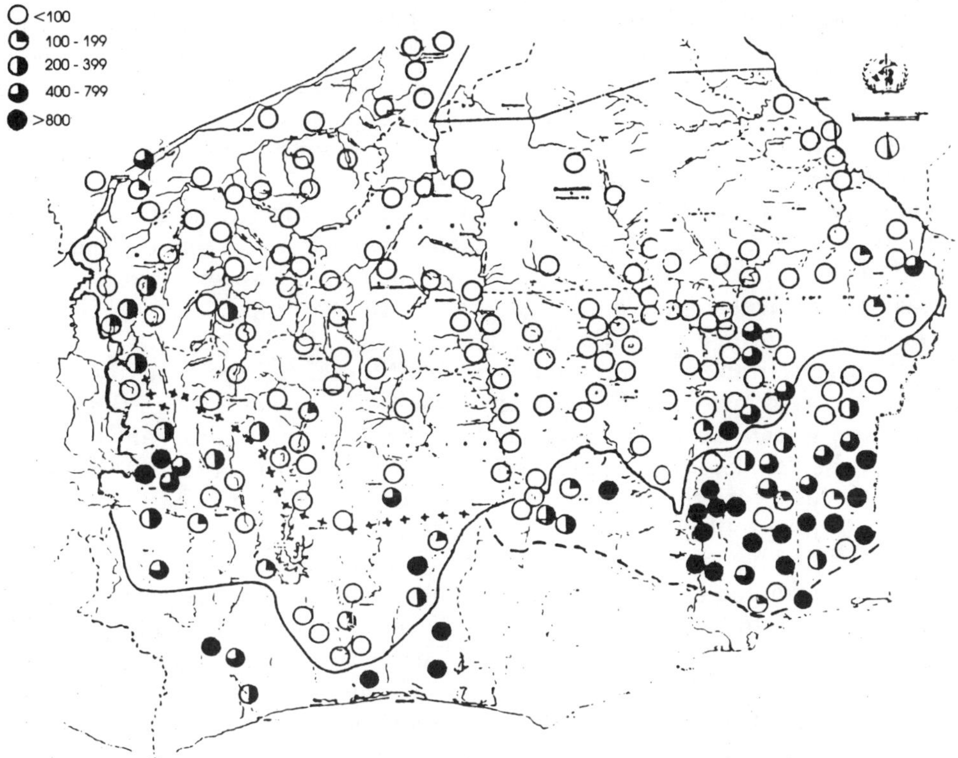

Source: USAID (1986)

Epidemiological Results

The OCP's epidemiological research supports the entomological results. The incidence of onchocerciasis, defined as the percentage of new cases per year, has dropped dramatically. Of a sample of 6,000 children born after the OCP began operations, only 16 were infected, compared to an estimated 300 that would have carried the parasite before operations began (WHO 1985, p. 46). Furthermore, all but one of those 16 cases were found in the reinvasion zones. (Children were examined because it is difficult to tell whether adults with onchocerciasis contracted the parasite before or after the OCP began larviciding.) Thus, it appears that except for those regions reinvaded by blackflies, the OCP has effectively prevented people who did not have onchocerciasis from contracting it.

Another encouraging result is that the interruption in parasite transmission has improved the status of many people who already carried the parasite. In the central zones under OCP control (where no reinvasion has occurred), the average number of microfilaria found in an individual declined by 70 percent in the first eight years of larviciding, and the average number found in the anterior chamber of the eye declined by 80 percent (USAID 1986, p. 14).

These reductions in parasite loads were revealed by very encouraging ophthalmological examinations. A longitudinal survey of 20 villages in the OCP zone showed that in 1982-83:

> subjects free from ocular onchocerciasis before the start of operations were still negative in 96% of the cases...carriers of low microfilarial loads were cured in 70% of the cases, the condition was unchanged in 16%, and it had worsened in only 13%...carriers with heavy loads showed diminution of their loads in 68% of cases. In 30% some worsening was noted, but not such as to threaten eventual blindness (WHO 1985, p. 48).

Thus, not only has the OCP succeeded in preventing new cases of onchocerciasis, it has also managed to reverse the fates of many people who carried the parasite before the OCP began. The World Bank estimates that the OCP prevented 27,000 cases of blindness in its first eight years of operation in Burkina Faso, which constitutes about half the program area (USAID 1986, p. 13).

The two most important problems the OCP has faced are blackfly resistance to larvicides and reinvasion of the program area by flies from outside the area (mostly from further west). Resistance was anticipated, and the program's staff began working on the development of alternative larvicides at the outset of the program. It now has five fully tested and approved larvicides of different chemical composition, so the resistance problem appears solved (Walsh 1986). This has not come without cost, however. The newer larvicides are significantly more expensive than temephos. This helped to drive costs over budget for the first time in many years in 1986 as resistance to temephos necessitated heavier use of alternative larvicides.

Reinvasion has proved more problematic. After control efforts in the central part of West Africa had begun, researchers discovered that blackflies were borne along by the trade winds, and could thus travel very long distances. To prevent the entry of flies from outside the program area, the OCP and its sponsors decided to expand the program area to the west and south to include virtually all the possible upwind breeding sites for blackflies. This has, of course, increased the program's costs, but it has also increased the number of people who will be protected from onchocerciasis. Most importantly, the expansion of the program's area appears to have solved the reinvasion problem in the older program area.

Socioeconomic Results

The elimination of onchocerciasis as a public health problem is likely to have many important socioeconomic effects, though most of these are as yet undocumented. Researchers have, however, investigated the most important economic impact that the OCP is likely to have: substantial amounts of land can now be inhabited without fear of contracting onchocerciasis.[3]

---

3. Estimates of the amount of land made available that can actually be cultivated vary widely. The OCP's Economic Review Mission originally estimated that after making reductions for soil impurities and lack of water, firewood, or infrastructure, 50,610 km^2 of productive agricultural land were available in the original OCP area. However, this figure was revised to 134,000-154,000 km^2 after criticism of the draft report. The mission also estimated that 48,440 km^2 of usable land were available in the southern and western extension regions.

The quality of this land has also been the subject of debate. Originally, the land's location—almost entirely in river valleys—led to hopes that it would be of high quality. But more recent

A study of land use in Burkina Faso before the OCP and in 1983 (Hervouet et al. 1984) shows that prior to OCP operations, roughly 17 percent of the river basins studied were completely uninhabited. During the first ten years of the OCP, about 16 percent (2,844 km^2) of this previously unused land had been settled (see table 2.1).

The speed with which people have settled on newly available land has varied from region to region and culture to culture. The proportion of available land under cultivation has increased dramatically in the area north of the 11th parallel, where population densities are higher and land degradation more severe (see table 2.2). Research also reveals that certain ethnic groups (for example, the Bissa and Nankana) are more inclined to move into the new land than others (Hervouet et al. 1984, p. 6).

Table 2.1 Dynamics of Land Occupation in Several Basins of Burkina Faso *(km^2)*

Basin	Subbasin	Total area	Unused area	Newly settled
Volta	Black Volta	85,000	6,680	n.a.
	White Volta	41,550	8,500	1,500
	Nouaho	4,050	1,850	n.a.
	Red Volta	11,500	3,340	900
	Sissili	6,820	2,080	n.a.
Pendjari		29,100	13,150	n.a.
Comoe-Leraba		17,000	4,880	400
Niger	Banifing	4,000	n.a.	n.a.
	Other tributaries	35,000	n.a.	n.a.
Bougouriba		n.a.	800	44

n.a. = not available

Note: These areas are only some of the OCP area, and are confined to Burkina Faso.

Source: Hervouet et al. (1984), tables 1 and 9

A fraction of the gains in cultivation can be accounted for by the expansion toward the rivers of populations already residing in the areas where the blackfly population is controlled. But most of the gain is due to migration of people from other areas, especially from the crowded Mossi plateau region. Some of this migration has been officially sanctioned and planned, but most of it has been spontaneous—the migrants have no incentive other than the differential quality and availability of land in the newly available regions. Thus, while officials initially debated whether

---

and careful analysis is less optimistic. While the quality of the "new lands" does appear to be higher than that of land currently in use, this is largely because the unused lands have not suffered the environmental degradation of lands in the currently populated regions. The inherent quality of the new land, based on analysis of soil types, appears to be roughly equivalent to land already in use in the OCP area.

or not the land newly freed by the OCP was needed (and therefore of much economic value), an increasing number of migrants believe that the land is useful and more valuable than the land they were previously working.

Table 2.2 Gains in Land Cultivation in Some Newly Available Areas of Burkina Faso

Basin	Percentage of land cultivated 1975	1983	Location
White Volta	9.2	29.0	North of 11° North
Red Volta	8.1	28.0	"
Black Volta	3.0	15.7	"
Tributaries of Black Volta	4.1	24.7	"
Bougouriba	9.9	13.1	South of 11° North
Comoe-Leraba	5.2	15.9	"

Source: Hervouet et al. (1984), table 3

The government of Burkina Faso is the only government in the OCP area to make a concerted effort at planning the development of the newly available lands. For this purpose, the government created the Volta Valleys Authority in 1974. The Volta Valleys Authority has funded the creation of new villages in the OCP area, complete with basic infrastructure and services (roads, wells, clinics, and schools) and land management plans to prevent the soil degradation common in other areas of the country. Yet, because of budget restrictions[4] and a fairly slow planning process, spontaneous settlement of the new land has swamped the authority's planned efforts. For example, Hervouet et al. (1984) report that only 18 percent of the land resettled in the Black and Red Volta regions was accounted for by the authority, and only 29 percent of that in the Bougouriba valley.[5]

4. The Volta Valleys Authority has been criticized for being excessively costly. The 1978 Economic Review Mission reports that prior to 1978, all the authority's settlements had cost in excess of US$10,000 per family settled. However, many spontaneous migrants not associated with the authority's settlements take advantage of the roads, wells, and even clinics provided. Thus, the costs per person should take this larger population into account.

5. The large amount of spontaneous migration has caused the most important development problem facing governments in the wake of onchocerciasis control: migrants who move onto freed lands are not sure that they will be allowed to remain—the property rights to the land are vague. As a result, spontaneous migrants do not care for the land, and environmental degradation in the form of rapid soil erosion and depletion of wood supplies is a serious problem. Governments, perhaps in concert with traditional authorities, must establish a clear set of land use rights on the new lands to prevent, or at least diminish, this degradation.

Costs

The results to date support the contention that the OCP is well on its way to achieving its goal of eliminating onchocerciasis as a significant public health problem. The epidemiological and ophthalmological results are excellent, and the increased use of previously unoccupied lands indicates that the local population recognizes the reduced risk of onchocerciasis.

However, another aspect of the program must be considered—its cost. How do the benefits compare with the costs? As noted, standard cost-benefit analysis of health projects is difficult because the benefits—in this case, reduced incidence of blindness and other complications (such as fatigue) caused by carrying the parasite—are difficult to measure in monetary terms. Nevertheless, attempts have been made at cost-benefit analyses of the OCP, and we will discuss those results shortly.

First, however, note that the OCP has had a remarkable record of staying on or under its budget, as illustrated by table 2.3.

Table 2.3 Budgets and Expenditures, OCP, 1974-86
(nominal US$ thousands)

Year	Proposed budget	Approved budget	Expenditure
1974	2,886	2,886	2,735
1975	6,064	6,064	6,011
1976	10,276	10,726	10,413
1977	13,137	13,133	10,175
1978	13,812	13,812	12,125
1979	12,648	13,895	12,648
1980	15,432	15,432	16,507
1981	16,124	16,646	16,646
1982	18,757	16,654	16,646
1983	22,542	22,542	16,776
1984	24,202	24,202	19,348
1985	20,867	20,867	20,709
1986	21,212	23,212	25,712

Source: OCP (various)

For the first nine years (1974-82), the OCP's expenditures were 12 percent above the original (1973) budget projections, but the program had added 110,000 km^2 of land to its larviciding area, 14.4 percent more than originally planned, and it had additional research and development expenditures for new pesticides and for a chemotherapy program (WHO 1985, p. 20). The budget performance was even stronger in 1983 and 1984, when the OCP was 25 percent and 20 percent under budget, respectively. Indeed, the budget proposal for 1985 was reduced by 14 percent as the program staff were confident that they could continue to provide the same level of service at a reduced cost.

Cost-Benefit Analysis of the OCP

The OCP bears most of its costs itself. Thus costs are easily measured. The benefits fall into three categories. First, there are humanitarian benefits associated with reducing the blindness and suffering caused by onchocerciasis. These benefits are inherently unmeasurable, and we will not account for them here, despite their importance, especially to donors.

Second, there are economic benefits of freeing up significant amounts of land previously unavailable, particularly in Burkina Faso where population pressures have made land scarce.

Finally, there are labor-related benefits brought about by preventing blindness and the early death that is associated with blindness, and thus maintaining the productivity of a significant fraction of the working population. Even when productivity is not lost through blindness, workers who carry the parasite but are not blind suffer from fatigue.

No one has attempted a complete cost-benefit analysis of the OCP, although the issue of how to do it has sparked considerable discussion. Most authors separate the labor- and land-related benefits and then discuss how to value each. However, because of the difficulty of placing a monetary value on land that is not usually traded on any sort of market basis, no one has attempted to value the land freed by the OCP.

We know of two studies that attempt to evaluate the labor-related benefits of OCP. Prost and Prescott (1984) calculate both the present discounted value of the costs of the OCP (in 1978 dollars) and the discounted years of healthy life added to the population of Burkina Faso using a standard discount rate of 10 percent.[6] They then calculate the cost effectiveness of the OCP, defined as the real (1977) cost of adding a discounted productive year of life for a person in Burkina Faso, as US$150 (Prost and Prescott 1984, p. 800). Finally, they compare this figure to the cost effectiveness of measles vaccination for children in the Côte d'Ivoire and Zambia, US$190 and US$221, respectively. Thus, in terms of the costs of additional years of productive life, the OCP is comparable in value to measles immunization, a widely accepted public health program.[7]

---

6. The authors use only 25 percent of the OCP's total cost in their analysis, arguing that this is roughly Burkina Faso's "fair share" of the program. However, because flies can reinvade a region, it is important to control the entire OCP area (the original reason for a multinational effort). Thus, Burkina Faso would not have experienced the reduction in blindness it has if there had been control only in that country. It seems more sensible, then, to do the analysis of the entire program area using all its costs.

7. While these figures may seem quite high, especially in light of the fact that health expenditures in the program area are usually only a few dollars per person, it is important to recognize that only about 10 percent of the population would contract onchocerciasis if there were no control program, and only 1 percent would go blind. This implies that even though expenditures per person for OCP are fairly low, about US$1 per year, the expenditures per case prevented are much higher, as shown in Prost and Prescott's paper. The same would be true, of course, for measles vaccine or any other preventive health measure aimed at diseases that would not affect the entire population if left uncontrolled.

The 1978 Economic Review Mission evaluated the labor-related benefits of the OCP using a more traditional approach. The mission compared the present value of the projected costs of the OCP with the present value of the productivity gains from onchocerciasis control, most of which are due to reduced incidence of blindness. Their major finding was that the present value of the OCP costs usually outweigh its labor-related benefits, sometimes by a large amount, though with longer time horizons (50 years rather than 25) and lower discount rates (3 to 9 percent), this result was reversed.

In general, the mission's *ex ante* cost estimates were far higher than actual costs *ex post*—a tribute to the OCP's operational efficiency—but their estimates of the program's benefits also appear overstated. In annex 2.2 we recalculate net present values of the OCP's costs and benefits, as well as internal rates of return, with generally more encouraging results. Including both the labor- and land-related benefits of the OCP, we find internal rates of return between -6 and 69 percent for a 25-year horizon and between 9 and 69 percent for a 50-year horizon. Such a wide range (even holding many parameters constant) is common for health projects in developing countries because of the great uncertainty about many key parameters' true values. Yet overall, our conclusions are much more sanguine than the Economic Review Mission's. At worst, the OCP cannot be viewed as an economic disaster. At best, it has a fine rate of return.

One further point must be stressed when assigning a dollar value to the labor of workers saved from blindness by the OCP: by valuing a year of life saved at the very low marginal product of poor workers in the OCP area (US$57 to US$107 in 1978 dollars), we automatically force the estimated benefits of the OCP to appear small. Clearly, if the OCP were saving the lives of people earning several times this income, it would appear to be spectacularly successful in a similar cost-benefit analysis. Using income figures to judge the value of a life saved inherently biases a project evaluation against the poor. Yet, in debates about social welfare, experts often argue that we should attach more weight to the benefits of public programs that accrue to the poor than to the wealthy. In fact, this is one of the features that makes the OCP especially attractive: its beneficiaries are largely the rural poor.

Accounting for the OCP's Success

The execution of the OCP has been remarkably efficient and it is this aspect of the program that we focus on here. In particular, we identify several factors that are generally applicable to future projects in a variety of fields.

Nevertheless, some of the factors peculiar to the OCP project deserve mention since they help provide an overall picture of its success. We have already mentioned two of them: the cumulative nature of the disease and the well-defined area in which blackfly larvae mature, both of which make control easier. Another aspect of the disease likely to contribute to the project's success is that the parasite remains sexually active for only about 12 years. This means that after the OCP has completely interrupted the transmission of the disease, it only needs to control the blackfly population for 12 or 13 years, after which the parasite will be eliminated and the blackfly population can be allowed to reappear.[8]

---

8. Again, comparison with attempts to control malaria is useful. Human malaria carriers remain infectious throughout their lives, meaning that to successfully interrupt the transmission of malaria, a program would have to control the mosquito population for 70 or 80 years. Given

Finally, the control strategy does not require the local population to significantly change its customs, living arrangements, or agricultural practices. People need only be willing to allow the OCP staff to test them occasionally for presence of the parasite. This means that the local population has no costs to bear—the project does not impose on them. Consequently, the local population has no reason to resist (and perhaps thwart) the project.

Clear Objectives, Effective Monitoring, and Accountability

Several people have noted that the highly focused nature of the OCP helped it succeed. Right from the start its goal was clear: the elimination of onchocerciasis as a health problem. Equally clear at the beginning was the strategy—interruption of the transmission cycle by killing the blackfly vector—and the principal method of operation—larviciding. Whereas many projects waste time and resources attempting to define their direction and purpose, the OCP's clear goals, strategy, and method of operations allowed it to get off to a quick start and to yield some early results that, among other things, boosted morale and raised the confidence of staff and donors alike.

The OCP has maintained this focus. For example, the one unit of the program that did not have a clearly defined goal at the outset was the socioeconomic development unit, which was assigned the rather vague responsibility of "promoting development" on lands freed by the control of the *O. volvulus* parasite. The OCP as a whole shied away from this assignment, and budgeted it accordingly. Then, after facing up to the diffuse nature of this goal, the focus of the socioeconomic unit was narrowed to *evaluation* of the socioeconomic effects (on migration, land tenure, settlement patterns, and so on) of the OCP. All project planning was left to individual governments.

A common threat to the focus of projects is that after governments, donors, and even project staff observe that the project is being implemented successfully, they tend to add further ancillary responsibilities, confident that if the project is doing one job well, it ought to do others well. This not only dilutes the project's focus, but also overstretches its resources and staff, thereby reducing the project's effectiveness. The OCP is aware of this problem and has avoided it. The program carefully guards its central purpose, and ensures that all tasks contribute to its goals. This is aided by the fact that, even though the OCP's technical operations are complex and sophisticated, the organization's purpose is quite simple, almost unidimensional.[9] In the words of one World Bank observer, "OCP is supposed to kill flies. Period."

Clear goals against which performance may be compared, are not, of course, sufficient. To actually make the comparisons, the program must be adequately monitored. As it happens, entomological monitoring has played a critical role in the project. The OCP evaluates and adjusts its aerial larviciding operations by carefully monitoring biting rates throughout the program area. Indeed, 28 percent of the budget for the third phase of operations (1986-91) is devoted to entomological surveillance (Joint Program Committee 1985a, p. 34). The information derived,

---

the ability of insect populations to develop resistance to insecticides, this would be very difficult to achieve.

9. The analogy with private businesses is difficult to pass over. No matter how complex a firm's operations might be, its efficiency is aided by the fact that its ultimate goal is also unidimensional—to make profits.

which is critical in determining where changes in larvicide application are needed, coincidentally provides the data needed to judge whether or not the OCP as a whole is successfully killing flies. The results obtained by monitoring are broken down by region and sector for accurate tracking of the program's effectiveness. An epidemiological unit then checks that reductions in biting rates are leading to reductions in parasite loads (though this connection is now well established). Finally, an independent Expert Advisory Committee regularly reviews the data produced by the OCP's monitoring system to check progress and advise on operations.

The OCP's keen focus has increased the program's accountability, a factor that we feel is very important. Because everyone understands exactly what the project is supposed to accomplish and how, there is very little ambiguity in determining whether or not the OCP is "delivering the goods." This makes it easy for donors, outside evaluators, and the OCP staff itself to hold the project accountable for its results.

This ease of accountability makes possible one of the features of the OCP that has allowed it to perform so well—its autonomy. While the WHO is the executing agency for the OCP, the program has extrabudgetary status and has been given a great deal of latitude in its operations. This has allowed the OCP to be structured so that decisions go through relatively few clearing points (points where decisions are reviewed and accepted or rejected by donors, participating countries, or WHO) outside the program. This has made the decision-making process at the OCP relatively responsive and unbureaucratic.

Of course, donors or participating countries are unlikely to turn a program loose with tens of millions of dollars and a great deal of autonomy unless they can ensure some way of judging whether or not it was accomplishing what they expected it to. After all, allowing the OCP staff to make their own decisions does not guarantee that they will make good ones. However, if they have latitude and are held accountable for their decisions, the likelihood of good judgments increases. The assurance that donors and participants need is essentially provided by frequent and timely *ex post* evaluation of the results of decisions because comparing them to the goals is relatively easy. This, in turn, allows *ex ante* decisions to be made more quickly.

To summarize, the OCP uses a management style that, while certainly not unique, is unusual. Employees throughout the organization are given precise goals to achieve and are allowed a considerable amount of flexibility in choosing exactly how to pursue them. Allowing employees so much responsibility is somewhat risky, since it implies that the program's overall performance depends on many individuals making good decisions day in and day out. But as employees' performance is regularly (and publicly) monitored, the OCP can identify those people who are making good decisions and those who are not, and the program has been careful to weed out the latter quickly. This approach to project management has helped to make the OCP flexible, responsive, and efficient.

Long-Term Perspective and Forward Planning

Another feature of the OCP that has contributed to its success is that from the outset of the program, both donors and the program staff understood that the OCP had to be a long-term project. At that time (1974), experts thought that the *O. volvulus* parasite could live in humans for as long as 18 years. Thus, they thought that vector control operations would be needed for at least that many years to ensure that onchocerciasis would not reappear after operations ceased. Recognizing this, the donor countries committed themselves (implicitly) to 20 years of support for the program when they signed the Onchocerciasis Fund Agreement.

The long-term commitment has been beneficial in several ways. First, experience often leads to increased efficiency—learning-by-doing—and this appears to be true at the OCP. The staff were given time to orient themselves, experiment with different larviciding schedules and techniques, and become adept at managing and coordinating the task of killing flies. This has paid off in increased operational efficiency.

Second, the implied long-term commitment of donors to the OCP establishes a good incentive for employees. Jobs at the OCP pay well, and the promise of relatively long-term employment at a good wage motivates employees to perform well.[10] Of course, the high accountability of the OCP staff is also important in this connection.

Third, the long-term commitment seems to have allowed, or perhaps even caused, the OCP staff to be extremely forward-looking. The staff have solved many problems quickly because they anticipated them well in advance. Rather than working from year to year and grant to grant, the OCP has maintained a long-run perspective on its work. For example, at the beginning of the program, scientists thought that the blackfly larvae were likely to develop resistance to temephos, the original larvicide used by the OCP. Consequently, they started research into alternative larvicides that were both effective against blackfly larvae and ecologically safe before a problem arose.[11] Thus, when a resistance problem did develop in 1979, the OCP was quickly able to switch to alternative larvicides. What is more, experimentation with the formulation of the most promising alternative, B.t.H-14, has at least halved the cost and greatly reduced the difficulty of applying that larvicide (USAID 1986, p. A-9). While the available larvicides have proven sufficient to date, research to find even more effective and ecologically acceptable larvicides to respond to future resistance problems continues.[12]

A further example of the program's forward-looking nature is in progress today. The OCP is now only at its mid-point, yet the issue on everyone's mind is how the OCP will devolve, that is, shut itself down and pass on the responsibility for onchocerciasis control to the national governments in the program area. The staff are experimenting with different plans years ahead of time. Everyone recognizes that the OCP is a control program, not an eradication program. A constant possibility will be reintroduction of the disease from areas outside West Africa, and some mechanism to detect and control outbreaks will need to be in place.

The staff are also aware that the carefully coordinated aerial larviciding currently practiced probably cannot be carried out without an international operation such as the OCP. At the same time, widespread larviciding on the scale

---

10. This type of argument underlies the efficiency wage hypothesis. For a review, see Stiglitz and Weiss (1985).

11. An independent ecological group reviews and approves all proposed pesticides used by the OCP. The group appears to have real power insofar as it has rejected several proposed pesticides. Further, the USAID (1986) reports that "...no major (ecological) imbalance of concern has yet been noted and that, in spite of insecticide application, the invertebrate and fish fauna appear to be relatively unaffected" (p. A-10).

12. The high quality of the OCP's research facilities and staff has resulted in a significant amount of support and cooperation from the pesticides industry, which is eager to take advantage of a chance to test its new products. Thus, the USAID (1985) reports that in 1983-84, the OCP laboratories received 29 formulations, 20 of which were sufficiently promising to advance to field tests.

practiced today will not be necessary when the whole OCP area has reached the maintenance phase, in which spraying occurs only in response to entomological evidence of a resurgence of infective flies.

The OCP is already experimenting with three different approaches to devolution. One idea is to turn maintenance activities over to host governments, with only a small OCP staff remaining in place as a central point for information processing on fly and parasite activity. This approach will soon be tested in Burkina Faso, which is entirely in the maintenance phase, and also in the Western Extension countries.

A second approach is even more decentralized. In the Dogon region of Mali, the OCP conducted an experiment in which monitoring and some larviciding responsibilities were turned over to local residents (larviciding was done by hand). In a region of 250,000 people, only one OCP staff member was used to train the local population. The results were quite promising, however, because the experiment was done in a particularly dry year and because the region has very few breeding sites, it was a particularly easy area for local people to take responsibility for the larviciding. Nevertheless, the experiment suggests that at least in areas where small-scale larviciding is sufficient to maintain blackfly control, control operations might successfully be devolved to decentralized, self-reliant operations.

Finally, since the late 1970s, the OCP has funded research to explore the possibility of a drug to kill the parasite in humans, thus interrupting its life cycle in humans rather than in the vector. One microfilaricide, ivermectin, is now undergoing advanced testing in humans, with very promising results. A macrofilaricide, CG 6140, is also performing well in the early stages of human testing. Depending on cost, and on whether researchers can develop a simple diagnostic test for the existence of the parasite in humans, the drugs may be widely distributed in areas at risk or directed more narrowly to individuals who test positive for the parasite.

At this point, we cannot say which of these approaches will prove most effective. The point is simply to show that the OCP has recognized that the issue of its devolution is important, and is actively considering how best to approach it well ahead of time. This sort of forward-looking behavior is certain to improve the chances for successful devolution, whatever approach is taken. We might also note that if the OCP does bring about its own termination successfully, it would be a strong testament to the integrity and commitment of the OCP staff. Bureaucratic institutions tend to be self-perpetuating, and an exception to this rule would be remarkable.

Maintaining International Cooperation

One of the OCP's notable achievements is that it has maintained the cooperation of several countries (not all of which are on the best terms with one another) and of several donors, apparently keeping everyone happy. Such a high degree of international coordination and cooperation is unusual and important to understand.

To begin with, the OCP provides a service that everyone values. The affected population appreciates the control effort and therefore cooperates with field staff. Further, the health problem that onchocerciasis posed was sufficiently serious that host governments recognized its importance and were eager for a solution. Finally, donors often place a high value on health projects and can provide funds that complement local government allocations (which often neglect health care due to budget constraints). Thus, the project was neither imposed on anyone who did not want it nor given to anyone who was indifferent to its outcome.

Second, the OCP staff has actively maintained communications with both donors and participating countries, who receive regular reports on operations and budgets. The OCP staff also conduct briefings and consultations on strategy and operational matters. This communication serves two purposes: it establishes a dialogue among the OCP, donors, and participants so that the program staff can discover problems or complaints and address them quickly, before they have time to fester; and it gives everyone involved a sense that they have a real stake in the project. In a word, the OCP has enfranchised both donors and participating countries so that they want to cooperate because they want the OCP to succeed.

Finally, the OCP's actual success has helped: success breeds success. Because so many people recognize the project's effectiveness, efficiency, and integrity and consider it important, the program, its employees, and its operations have attained a remarkable amount of prestige. Thus, OCP field staff freely cross borders without harassment, customs officials expedite the delivery of necessary imports, and so on.

Financial Management and Cost Consciousness

As noted earlier, the OCP has generally been on or under budget, especially in recent years. To some extent, this represents accuracy in forecasting expenses, but it also represents unusual care in preparing budgets and extraordinary cost consciousness.

Part of this is built into the OCP's structure. The central administration reviews budgets and expenditures every month, and staff must defend anomalies. In the words of the program director, budgets are tight-fisted and expenditures closely controlled. For example, sector chiefs have a discretionary spending limit of only about US$80 per month. The program also contracts out highly specialized activities, in particular, the operation of the aircraft used for larviciding, to save on both capital costs and the costs of acquiring the necessary expertise. In addition, all contracts, including purchases, are done on a strictly competitive basis, which prevents contract padding and ensures that the OCP obtains materials at minimum cost. The USAID (1986, p. D-15) notes that there have been no complaints from the private sector about inequity in the awarding of OCP contracts.

Two monitoring devices are especially important for the OCP's budgeting and cost efficiency: members of some donors' staffs work at the OCP and therefore observe financial operations directly; and the program's budgets and expenditures are made available in public documents on a monthly basis. Thus, all the cards are on the table, and anyone who cares to review the program can do so regularly.

Thus, we observe a high degree of accountability in budgeting, just as in operations, which has served the OCP well. But efforts at cost control have often gone beyond meeting budgets. Even sectors or units that are within their budgets take cost cutting seriously. For example, at the beginning of the program, the OCP purchased several Land Rovers for its headquarters in Ouagadougou. However, when a study revealed that the vehicles were used largely on good quality roads or on city streets, the OCP chose not to request replacement of the Land Rovers at the end of their lives, but purchased much cheaper (and less prestigious) Renault 4s, saving roughly US$5,000 per vehicle.[13]

13. In all, by 1986 the OCP had sold 69 Land Rovers. As a result of this sort of diligence, the budget has become a nonissue with donors and external auditors. The auditors' report for 1984,

Conclusion

The OCP's success demonstrates that a large, multinational, technically sophisticated project can work in a developing country context if it is effectively managed. Even though the program's operations are complicated, the target of those operations is simple: to kill flies. This target gives the program a simple yardstick to determine whether or not it is doing what it is supposed to do, which greatly simplifies the management of the program. Thus, one lesson to draw from the OCP, is that defining project objectives that are simple, clear, and measurable establishes incentives that encourage efficient execution of the project.

The program's long-term nature has encouraged the OCP staff to plan ahead and has permitted a significant amount of learning-by-doing, both of which have increased the OCP's effectiveness. This is another example of how the project's structure has provided an incentive for efficient performance.

However, good incentives alone are insufficient to ensure a project's success. The project's staff must respond to the incentives, and donors and host governments must allow them flexibility in how they respond. As we have seen, this is the case with the OCP. The remarkable nature of the OCP's achievements, both in terms of technical efficiency and cost effectiveness, demonstrate how much an enthusiastic, honest, and hard-working staff can accomplish when placed in the right environment.

---

for example, was reviewed in five lines in the minutes of the 1985 Joint Program Committee meeting. Those minutes also include notes such as: "Attention was drawn to the very low level of administrative costs..." and "JPC congratulated the Director of OCP on the efficient and economical management of the Programme."

Annex 2.1 Donors to the Onchocerciasis Control Program, 1974-85

Donor	Percentage of total donated
African Development Bank	1.51
Belgium	3.15
Canada	5.43
Côte d'Ivoire	1.43
France	6.20
Germany, Federal Republic	6.27
Iraq	0.03
Italy	1.19
Japan	8.08
Kuwait	6.56
Netherlands	10.60
Norway	2.21
OPEC Special Fund	1.19
Sabah Al-Salem Foundation	0.12
Saudi Arabia	7.76
Switzerland	4.65
UNDP	2.01
United Kingdom	5.67
United States	13.71
WHO	1.19
World Bank	11.04

Source: USAID, 1986

Annex 2.2 Cost-Benefit Analysis of the OCP

This annex discusses our attempt to calculate the internal rate of return to the OCP. It is important to recognize this as a very imprecise exercise, both because the data are not good and because it is inherently difficult to define the benefits of health-related projects. Nevertheless, we feel that the exercise is worthwhile for two reasons. First, it is obvious that one does a cost-benefit analysis, however subjective, before entering into any project. If the original cost projections for the OCP had been ten times larger, it is likely that the project would have been abandoned due to excess costs. Second, even if the analysis is imprecise, the simple fact of doing it forces one to think more clearly about the evaluation of all the project's costs and benefits. This often helps to make a subjective assessment somewhat less so.

Nevertheless, a cost-benefit analysis of the OCP must be uncertain: how can one put a dollar value on blindness prevention? We have chosen a standard approach—to use the value of productive labor time saved—though this is rather cold. There are obviously humanitarian benefits associated with preventing blindness that exceed the value of labor time saved by the project, but these are extremely difficult to quantify. Technical analyses usually ignore them even though they may be important in an overall assessment of a project's value.

The only previous attempt to calculate the costs and benefits of the OCP was by the 1978 Economic Review Mission (ERM). We begin with a discussion of the mission's methods and results to help put our approach in perspective. The ERM begins by dividing the total benefits of the OCP into labor- and land-related benefits. While it attempts to estimate the amount of land made available by the OCP, it does not put a value on this land, citing the difficulty of doing so when no real market for land exists.[1] The ERM did, however, try to value the labor-related benefits. These were subdivided into the benefits of reduced blindness, reduced debility, reduced disability, and a reduced "nuisance effect" due to the absence of blackflies. It calculated the net present value of these benefits according to the following formula:

$$NPV = \sum_{t-1}^{n} [(P.P_r.P_a)(l+g)^t][V.(l+r)^t](P_1 L_1 + P_2 L_2 + P_3 L_3 + P_4 L_4)/(1+d)^t$$

where

- NPV = net present value of the labor-related benefits of OCP
- t = current year; t = 1 to n
- n = last year of analysis
- P = population in the OCP area
- g = population growth rate
- P_r = proportion of the population at risk of contracting onchocerciasis
- P_a = proportion of the at risk population active in the workforce
- V = value of the marginal product of labor
- r = growth rate of the marginal product of labor

1. In most of the OCP area, traditional authorities control land rights, and they are not transferable in the Western sense. Some "sales" of land occur, though viewing these sales as rentals is probably more accurate, since the local authority usually grants the right to work the land for an indefinite period of time in exchange for a cash payment. Even these transactions are rare, and we know of no systematic data on such transactions. On top of these complications, land sales are illegal in several OCP countries.

P_1 = proportion of the at risk population disabled by onchocerciasis
P_2 = proportion of the at risk population debilitated by onchocerciasis
P_3 = proportion of the at risk population blinded by onchocerciasis
P_4 = proportion of the at risk population suffering a nuisance effect
L_1 = percentage loss of output per worker due to disability
L_2 = percentage loss of output per worker due to debility
L_3 = percentage loss of output per worker due to blindness
L_4 = percentage loss of output per worker due to nuisance
d = discount rate

The ERM used the estimates given by the PAG report for the population living in the original OCP area and the percentages of that population that were at risk (10 percent) and blind (1 percent). It assumed that the proportion of the population active in the workforce was 70 percent as given in ORSTOM (1975). The rate of population growth was assumed to be 2.5 percent.

The mission used estimates of per capita income from the PAG report to approximate the value of the marginal product of labor. Thus per capita income was assumed at US$40-75 in constant 1978 U.S. dollars.[2] Productivity was assumed to grow 3 percent per year.

The mission assumed the productivity impact of blindness to be a 100 percent loss of output, that of disability and debility to be 2.5 to 5.0 percent each, and that of the nuisance effect to be 0.5 to 1.0 percent. Apart from 10 percent of the at risk population being blinded, the report does not specify the values it used for P_1, P_2, and P_4.[3]

The mission used a range of discount rates from 3 to 15 percent, and two time horizons: 25 years and 50 years. The justification for the latter is that the effects of a health program like the OCP are long-lived and tend to accumulate with time, so that a longer horizon is appropriate for its evaluation.

Depending on the set of parameters used, the ERM reports a range of net present values from US$20.5 million to US$93.6 million in constant 1978 U.S. dollars using a 25-year horizon. Using a 50-year horizon, estimates of the net benefits ranged from US$100.5 million to US$1,137.6 million.

The ERM also estimated the net present value of the costs of the OCP to compare them to the benefits. Here, it assumed that the program cost US$25 million per year in constant 1978 dollars. As it happens, this estimate is very high. As table 2.3 of the text shows, the nominal cost of the program did not reach US$25 million until 1986, and the real (in 1978 U.S. dollars) cost has never approached that. Table A2.1 shows the ERM's estimates of the net present values of the OCP's costs and benefits at several discount rates and over 25- and 50-year horizons, and also a re-estimate of the cost using actual cost figures up to 1986, and a conservative assumption of costs of US$20 million (in 1978 dollars) for 1987 to the end of the program.

Thus, using the ERM's original cost estimates, the present value of the labor-related benefits approaches the present value of costs only when using a 50-year horizon, a modest discount rate (10 percent), and the highest marginal product of labor estimate. In light of these results, the ERM pointed out that if the OCP were to

2. As the ERM report notes, these figures seem rather low and may reflect the fact that much of people's production in the area is not marketed and may therefore not have been measured as part of their income.
3. This oversight prevented us from reproducing the ERM's results.

have a reasonable rate of return, the marginal product of the land freed by the OCP had to be between US$6.6-20.8 million (for a 10 percent rate of return), or US$1.20-3.78 per hectare per year. This is a significant, though not extraordinary, amount.

Table A2.1 1978 ERM Estimates of the Net Present Value of Costs and Labor-Related Benefits of the OCP
(1978 US$ millions)

	Costs		Benefits	
Discount rate *(percent)*	ERM	Updated	Blindness	Total
25-year horizon				
10	227	115	26.7 - 50.1	38.4 - 93.6
15	162	74	14.0 - 26.3	20.5 - 50.2
50-year horizon				
10	209[a]	131	n.a.	198.8[b]
15	177	78	n.a.	100.5[b]

n.a. = not available.

a. Costs for the 50-year horizon were assumed to be US$25 million for the first 15 years and US$12.5 million thereafter.

b. These figures use the highest of the ERM's estimates of per capita income.

Source: 1978 Economic Review Mission, appendix II, and authors' calculations

Using our updated cost estimates, however, the results are more optimistic. Using the 50-year horizon, the ERM's estimates of the labor-related benefits are substantially larger than program costs, even at a 15 percent discount rate, indicating that the rate of return to the OCP would be respectable even in the absence of any land-related benefits. However, we have two reasons to believe that the ERM's estimates of the program's labor-related benefits are unjustifiably high as well. First, the assumption that labor productivity will grow at 3 percent per year seems very optimistic given the relatively poor performance of the rural sectors of most OCP countries. More important than this, however, is that even though 1 percent of the total OCP area population were blind at the beginning of the program, it will not be true that 1 percent of the population will be saved from blindness immediately. In the first year of control, the number of workers "saved" is only the number that would have gone blind due to onchocerciasis that year alone. In the second year, it is the number saved in the first two years, and so on until, after several years, no one living is blind due to onchocerciasis. This fact will significantly delay the full labor-related benefits of the OCP and, because of discounting, will reduce the net present value of the benefits considerably.[4] In light of these problems, we

4. In addition to these two points, the calculation of the value of lost labor is questionable. First, the ERM uses total income figures to estimate the value of the marginal product of labor, but

recalculated the net present value of benefits associated with eliminating onchocerciasis-induced blindness.[5] Our results are presented in table A 2.2.

Table A2.2 Revised Calculations of the Costs and Labor-Related Benefits of the OCP
(1978 US$ millions)

Discount rate *(percent)*	Costs	Benefits *(blindness only)* v = 57, r = 0.01	v = 57, r = 0.03	v = 107, r = 0.01	v = 107, r = 0.03
25-year horizon					
5	198	49	70	92	131
10	115	22	30	41	57
15	74	11	15	20	28
50-year horizon					
5	291	167	321	313	606
10	131	42	74	81	138
15	78	15	24	29	44

v = income per worker
r = rate of growth of productivity

We believe the results in the boxed column are the most reasonable. We agree with the ERM that one should use a long time horizon for a health project like the OCP whose benefits appear late in the project, and are likely to be long-lived.

total income reflects the value of all factors of production, not just labor, so the marginal product of labor should be lower than total income. (In the case of the subsistence agriculture practiced in most of the OCP area, land is likely to be the only other significant factor of production.) This oversight is unlikely to be terribly important, however, since so much land is freed by the OCP that it is straightforward to assume that all workers saved from blindness get new land without significantly reducing the number of hectares made available by the OCP. In this case the per capita income figure is a reasonable approximation of the value of the marginal products of labor and land together.

However, children are not severely affected by onchocerciasis since it requires many years of infection to develop the more serious symptoms. As a result, almost all people afflicted are able-bodied workers. This implies that the loss is not income per capita, but income per worker. Using the ERM's estimate that 70 percent of the population works, this implies that the per capita income figure should be increased by 1/0.7. (In any case, the ERM should not have deflated per capita income figures by 0.7, since the fact that their data are per capita and not per worker already accounts for the reduction that would be appropriate if the disease were spread evenly across the population.)

5. Since the ERM report does not provide data on the proportion of the population disabled and debilitated, we did not calculate the gains from reducing these two problems. In any case, the net present values of disability, debility, and nuisance gains are rarely more than 20 percent of the total labor-related benefits in the ERM's calculations.

Because the per capita income estimates of the PAG report are so low, using the highest value in their range makes sense; also, assuming that productivity will grow at 1 percent rather than 3 percent per year seems more consistent with recent experience in the OCP area. Under these assumptions, considering the benefits of reduced blindness alone, the internal rate of return to the OCP will be between 5 percent and 10 percent.

In general, the present value of the 25-year benefit streams is very low, largely because it takes a fair amount of time for the OCP to prevent a large number of cases of blindness. For the 50-year horizon, the only case in which the benefits of blindness reduction do not outweigh costs at a 5 percent discount rate is when the lowest estimate of income per worker and the 1 percent growth rate are used. At 10 percent, benefits outweigh costs only under the most optimistic assumptions on income and productivity growth, and at 15 percent, costs always outweigh benefits.

Our estimates of the labor-related benefits differ from the ERM's in several ways. First, we have used the proportion of the total population that works (70 percent) to inflate the PAG's estimates of income per capita to income per worker, which gives us a range of US$57-107 per worker per year (all figures are in 1978 dollars).[6] We have also assumed that productivity increases by 1 percent per year rather than the ERM's 3 percent assumption, and we have limited our analysis to the gains from preventing blindness since we have no reliable information on the productivity losses due to disability, debility, or the nuisance effect.

Most important, though, is our explicit incorporation of the fact that the number of people saved from blindness by the OCP is not immediately 1 percent of the population, but only the new cases that would have occurred in the absence of the OCP. To calculate the latter figure, we have used Prost and Prescott's (1984) estimates of the number of cases prevented yearly by the OCP in Burkina Faso, divided that by the population of the OCP area in Burkina Faso, and multiplied this ratio by the population of the entire OCP area.[7] This gives us an estimate of the number of new cases prevented in each year of the program. The total number of cases prevented at time t is the sum of this number up to time t. But the total number of cases prevented cannot exceed 1 percent of the population in the original area, since that appears to be the steady-state proportion of the population that suffered from

---

6. By using the total income of workers rather than the marginal product of labor, we are implicitly assuming that enough land is available to give each person saved from blindness an average amount of land to work. The OCP has freed more than enough land to satisfy this assumption. When we calculate the land-related benefits, we will subtract the number of hectares necessary to satisfy this assumption so as not to double count those hectares.

7. After an initial start-up period of seven years in which few cases are prevented, Prost and Prescott find that the number of cases prevented each year is 0.042 percent of the entire population under study. This number is accumulated until it reaches 1 percent of the population (about 40 years after the initiation of blackfly control). The exact gain function is given by:

year 1 = 0	year 5 = 0.00024 population
year 2 = 0	year 6 = 0.00033 population
year 3 = 0.00008 population	year 7 = 0.00040 population
year 4 = 0.00016 population	year 8 to n = 0.00042 population

We have used the Joint Program Comittee's (1985b) figures of a population of roughly 17 million in the entire OCP area in 1984, less the Senegambia extension. For the Senegambia extension, we have used the figure of 5.39 million people in 1980, reported in Project Senegambie (1981). We continue to assume that population will grow at 2.5 percent per year in the program area.

onchocerciasis prior to the OCP. (For the Senegambia extension in the far western part of West Africa, we used the upper limit of 0.63 percent, since the evaluation report for that extension indicates that this is the correct figure for that region.)

Thus, our formula for calculating the benefits of eliminating blindness caused by onchocerciasis is given by the following:

$$\text{NPV blindness} = \sum_{t=1}^{n} V.(1+r)^t(P_t^{sg} + P_t^{old}) / (l+d)^t \text{ where } P_t^{i} = \sum_{j=1}^{t} q_j \, pop_j \quad i = \text{old, Sg}$$

where

- v = value of output per worker, assumed to be US$57-107
- r = rate of productivity growth
- P_t = total number saved from blindness by the OCP up to time t in either the Senegambia extension (sg) or the rest of the OCP area (old)
- q = gain function coefficient (see footnote 8)
- pop = population of OCP region (either the old area or the Senegambia extension)
- d = discount rate

We have also tried to value the land freed by the OCP. The results of this exercise are somewhat unreliable because neither the exact amount of land freed nor its value are known. The ERM reported that 134,000-154,000 km^2 of arable land in the original OCP area could be used if onchocerciasis were controlled, but this range was controversial, and the original draft of the report gave a much lower figure of 50,610 km^2. For our purposes, we have used 50,610-134,000 km^2 for the old area, and have added to this the ERM's estimate of 48,440 km^2 of new arable land in the southern and western extensions.

As for the value of this land, the easiest approach would be to find a market price for average land in the OCP area and apply that to the area freed. Unfortunately, as we have noted, land sales are rare and it is not clear that they involve a permanent transfer of property rights in the Western sense.[8]

As an alternative, we have estimated our rates of return based on a calculation of the increases in incomes of families that migrate to the newly available lands. The only information available comes from an Autorité des Vallées Volta study (Traoré 1983) of incomes and cultivation practices in spontaneously settled new lands around Autorité des Vallées Volta villages. That study reports that villagers' incomes are considerably higher on these new lands than average incomes in the OCP area in general in Burkina Faso—about US$360 per worker (or CFA 500,000) per year seems to be the upper limit of incomes in these areas. This is an extraordinary difference, and is probably due to family farms being larger on the new land than the national average (the study does not control for plot size). Unfortunately, we do not have a means of controlling for this difference, but we have chosen to use much more modest figures in our calculations, US$10 to US$30 per worker. These are quite conservative in relation to the Autorité des Vallées Volta's numbers, but the rate of return they imply is still respectable (see table A2.4).

8. We have unconfirmed reports that land in the northern area of the Côte d'Ivoire is "sold" for about CFA 5,000 per hectare, but it is not clear whether full ownership rights are transferred in such transactions. Using this figure and an exchange rate of CFA 350 = US$1 yields a present value of US$95.9 million (1978 dollars).

Obviously, if we used the income differential suggested by the Autorité des Vallées Volta, the rate of return would be tremendous.

We complete the calculation using figures provided by the Autorité des Vallées Volta that suggest that an average family in the newly settled area uses nine hectares of land and has four active workers. This allows us to calculate the number of workers that could be accommodated on the new lands if they were completely filled. Multiplying this by our range of income differentials gives us an estimated benefit stream from the freed lands.

Of course, not all the freed land will be settled immediately, thus we need to calculate a gain function for settlement as well. To do this, we have relied on the figures provided by Hervouet et al. (1984), which indicate that 16.2 percent of the freed area they studied was settled in the first ten years of onchocerciasis control. While assuming this growth to be exponential is logical (as the first settlers are successfully established, larger inflows might follow), we have simply assumed in-migration proceeds at 1.62 percent of the land available per year—a very conservative assumption.

Our formula for the net present value of the new lands is given by

$$\text{NPV land} = \sum_{t=1}^{n} [\text{new}_t\,(4/9) - (P_t^{sg} + P_t^{old})] \,.\, \text{dif}/(1+d)^t \text{ where } \text{new}_t = \sum_{j=1}^{t} .01620 \,.\, \text{tot}$$

where

dif = income differential between work on old and new lands, assumed to be either US$10 or US$30 per worker

tot = total amount of land freed by the OCP (excluding the Senegambia extension) assumed to be either 99,000 or 182,000 km^2

If our figures for the number of hectares needed per worker and the income differentials are accurate, this calculation obviously gives an estimate of the lower boundary of the value of the freed land, since it accounts only for the difference in incomes on new versus old land. The total value of the new land should actually be equal to this difference plus the value of the old land. So if the old land is worth anything at all, our estimate should be low.

Table A2.3 presents our results for the net present value of the new lands made available by the OCP

According to our calculations, only under the most conservative set of assumptions will the net present value of the benefits of new lands available be less than the present value of the OCP's costs. The assumptions we believe to be the most realistic are for 99,000 km^2 of new land and a US$30 per worker income differential. These show that, using a 25-year horizon, the land-related benefits alone would yield a 5 percent rate of return, while under a 50-year horizon, the return would be somewhat over 10 percent . Thus, our analysis confirms the suggestions of other investigators that the land-related benefits outweigh the labor gains.

Our last set of calculations involves the internal rate of return to the OCP, including both the labor- and land-related benefits as we have already calculated them. The results of this exercise are shown in tables A2.4 and A2.5. As the tables indicate, the rate of return is unacceptable only under extremely unfavorable assumptions. Indeed, if a 50-year horizon is used, allowing the full effect of both reduced blindness and increased settlement to occur, the lowest rate of return is a fair 9 percent, and it is not unreasonable to suppose that the true rate of return is somewhat higher.

Table A.2.3 Present Values of Land-Related Benefits of the OCP
(1978 US$ millions)

	25 years				50 years			
Income differential (1978 US$)	10	10	30	30	10	10	30	30
New land (km^2 000)	99	182	99	182	99	182	99	182
Discount rate *(percent)*								
5	99	188	297	564	190	379	570	1,137
10	52	98	156	294	79	182	237	546
15	30	57	90	171	34	64	102	192
20	19	37	57	111	20	39	60	117

Table A2.4 Internal Rates of Return to the OCP, 25-Year Horizon

v (1978 US$)	=	57	57	57	57	57	57	57	57
r	=	0.01	0.01	0.01	0.01	0.03	0.03	0.03	0.03
km^2 (000)	=	99	99	182	182	99	99	182	182
diff (1978 US$)	=	10	30	10	30	10	30	10	30
rate of return		-6%	31%	12%	65%[a]	0%	32%	14%	66%[a]
v (1978 US$)	=	107	107	107	107	107	107	107	107
r	=	0.01	0.01	0.01	0.01	0.03	0.03	0.03	0.03
km^2 (000)	=	99	99	182	182	99	99	182	182
diff (1978 US$)	=	10	30	10	30	10	30	10	30
rate of return		4%	35%	16%	69%[a]	9%	36%	19%	69%[a]

Once again, the two columns we believe are the most likely to be accurate are boxed. Because of the uncertainty about the amount of land made available by the OCP, these two estimates are the safest, since they use the lowest estimate of new arable land. As noted earlier, the assumption of US$107 per worker seems the most realistic assumption on income (though it may be low), and a 1 percent growth rate of productivity seems more plausible than the 3 percent the ERM used. That leaves only the difference in income between old and new land, which is very difficult to determine. We think that both US$10 and US$30 are conservative figures, but even if the lower figure is used, the rate of return at 50 years is respectable. At the higher figure, the rate is quite good.

Table A2.5 Internal Rates of Return to the OCP, 50-Year Horizon

v (1978 US$)	=	57	57	57	57	57	57	57	57
r	=	0.01	0.01	0.01	0.01	0.03	0.03	0.03	0.03
km^2 (000)	=	99	99	182	182	99	99	182	182
diff (1978 US$)	=	10	30	10	30	10	30	10	30
rate of return		9%	31%	16%	65%[a]	11%	33%	17%	66%[a]
v (1978 US$)	=	107	107	107	107	107	107	107	107
r	=	0.01	0.01	0.01	0.01	0.03	0.03	0.03	0.03
km^2 (000)	=	99	99	182	182	99	99	182	182
diff (1978 US$)	=	10	30	10	30	10	30	10	30
rate of return		12%	35%	19%	69%[a]	15%	37%	21%	69%[a]

a. Because the net benefit stream rises and falls about zero twice in the cases where km^2=182,000 and diff=30, there is no unique solution for these rates. We were able to put a lower boundary on each by reducing the values of the first two or three observations on net benefits below the negative values in the third or fourth year. These are the figures shown here.

References

Berg, Eliot. 1984. *Some Rural Development and Health Sector Implications of Oncho Control.* Washington, D.C.: World Bank (processed).

Hervouet, J.P., J.C. Clanet, F. Paris, and H. Some. 1984. *Peuplement des Vallées Protégées de l'Onchocercose apres Dix Ans de Lutte Anti-Vectorielle au Burkina Faso.* OCP/GVA/84.5 Ouagadougou: OCP.

Joint Program Committee. 1984. *Report to the World Health Organization.* JPC/5. Ouagadougou: OCP.

Joint Program Committee. 1985a. *Plan of Operations for the Third Financial Phase.* JPC/6.6. Ouagadougou: OCP.

Joint Program Committee. 1985b, *Preliminary Report of the Evaluation of the Socioeconomic Impact of the Onchocerciasis Control Programme.* JPC6.3. Ouagadougou: OCP.

OCP. 1978. *Economic Review Mission.* Ouagadougou: OCP.

OCP. Various. Reports to the Joint Program Committee.

ORSTOM. 1975. *Les Migrations de Travail Mossi.* Ouagadougou: ORSTOM.

Projet Senegambie. 1981. *Lutte Contre l'Onchocercose en Guinée, Guinée-Bissau, Mali, Sénégal, et Sierra Leone.* VBC/81.2. Geneva: OCP.

Prost, A., and N. Prescott. 1984. "Cost-Effectiveness of Blindness Prevention by the Onchocerciasis Control Programme in Upper Volta." *Bulletin of the World Health Organization.* 62(5).

Stiglitz, Joseph, and Andrew Weiss. 1985. *Wage Rigidity, Implicit Contracts, Unemployment, and Economic Efficiency.* Discussion Paper No. 67. London: Centre for Economic Policy Research.

Traoré, J.D. 1983. *Développement économique des zones libérées de l'onchocercose.* Autorité des Vallées Volta. Unpublished paper.

USAID. 1986. *Impact Review of the Onchocerciasis Control Program.* Washington, D.C: USAID.

Walsh, John. 1986. "River Blindness: A Gamble Pays Off." *Science.* 232 (May).

WHO. 1985. *10 Years of Onchocerciasis Control: Review of the Work of the Onchocerciasis Control Program in the Volta River Basin Area from 1974 to 1984*, OCP/GVA/85.1B. Geneva: WHO.

3

Malawi: Lessons from the Gravity-Fed Piped Water System

Catharine B. Hill, Department of Economics, Williams College
Katundu M. Mtawali, Ministry of Agriculture, Malawi*

The Government of Malawi is trying to reduce the incidence of disease and the amount of time spent fetching water by providing its population with clean water. This has involved drilling boreholes and constructing gravity-fed water projects and protected shallow wells.

This chapter reviews and analyzes the developments in the gravity-fed water supply system, regarded as one of the best organized piped water projects in Africa. The system's success suggests lessons for all kinds of development projects, not just rural water systems. The Government of Malawi is applying some of these lessons to other projects, but other countries can also profit from Malawi's experiences.

Under the gravity-fed water supply program, 47 piped water systems serving approximately one million people have been completed in Malawi over two decades. A further eight projects are currently under construction. These systems work for heavily populated areas with perennial mountain streams. The source of the water is, in most cases, above the line of habitation, and thereby avoids human contamination. Water is taken from the source and piped by gravity to surrounding villages.

The project is notable because of the amount of "self-help" or community involvement. Self-help contributions have not only kept the government's costs down, but have at the same time contributed to the project's success in important ways. Community participation in the rural piped water projects starts in the earliest stages. In the initial projects, the government was the principal motivating force. Now, however, new schemes are started only at the request of local communities (through the district development committees).[1] The community is not only involved in planning, but also supplies large amounts of self-help labor during both the construction and maintenance phases of the project.

The government's participation in the project has complemented the communities' contributions, greatly contributing to the project's success. The government is involved at several levels. It undertakes feasibility studies and

---

* *Mr. Mtawali works for the Ministry of Agriculture, Government of Malawi. He worked on this project on his own time and not while employed by the government.*

We would like to thank John Briscoe and Craig Hafner for comments on an earlier draft. We would also like to thank Messrs. Mainala, Kufundu, and Mandowa of the Department of Water Supply and Dr. Kandoole of the University of Malawi..

1. Malawi is divided into 24 districts. Each district elects a district development committee, which supervises local development projects, both self-help and government financed. The committees participate in planning as well as implementation.

estimates what materials are required and their costs. It then supplies the pipes, finding funding from a variety of sources, and supervises construction to help ensure adequate quality. The government is also involved during the maintenance phase by paying for monitoring assistants who help communities maintain their systems. The government also helps communities establish the committees that manage the communities' contributions.

Although its role is a more recent development, the Department of Health is also involved from the beginning, being present at the initial local community meeting. It supplies user education on how to increase the health benefits of the water system, and is involved with latrine and washing slab construction.

That the projects have proved successful is demonstrated in part by their reliability. Water is delivered from each tap approximately 90 percent of the time. In addition, the quality of the water is good, comparing very favorably with other water sources.

The project's benefits, although very hard to quantify, include the following:

- It reduces health problems.
- It reduces the time spent each day fetching water, as the average distance to water for the population served has decreased substantially.
- It builds human capital at the community and government levels, which can then contribute to the success of other projects.
- It has contributed to the development of some private sector enterprises.

People in Malawi feel the project has been successful for several reasons.

- The community must request the project (and therefore wants it) and is actively involved in planning, building, and maintaining it. Ownership and repair by the community that directly benefits from the system seem to contribute to its reliability. At the same time, the government has played an important support role.

- The technology is simple and local communities can maintain it. They point out that when a borehole maintained by the government breaks, six months may pass before it is repaired.

- The project started small and developed slowly over some 20 years. This has allowed it to evolve over time. The government has changed aspects of the program as it has discovered better ways to handle them.

- The project has been very flexible, allowing local communities to change aspects to suit their particular needs.

How transferable are the lessons of this project to other rural development projects in Malawi, other countries in Africa, and elsewhere? Obviously, a gravity-fed water system is not appropriate for all countries. It has been successful in Malawi in part because clean water sources exist in part of the country all year round in areas above the line of habitation. In addition, high population density reduces the costs per person of the pipes. Nonetheless, the lessons of the project can be generalized to many different types of development projects, not just piped water systems. Having the community that benefits from a project responsible for it in some way helps make it a success. The community may have information and ideas that can increase the project's benefits. It also lets the government know that the project is valued by the community it is meant to benefit. Simple technology allows those who benefit from a project to help maintain it, as well as to construct it in some cases. Assuming the simple technology is cheaper than more sophisticated alternatives, it is also more likely to be appropriate for capital-scarce developing countries. Starting small and growing slowly over time, plus flexibility of design, allows for learning and helps to avoid costly mistakes. These are lessons that apply to many different types of development projects.

Introduction and Development of the Gravity-Fed Water System

During the 1960s, Malawi became concerned about the water supply in the rural areas. Borehole construction was started in semi-arid areas and people were encouraged to boil water taken from traditional water sources. Initially slow, the rate of borehole construction increased after independence as an improved water supply was a major part of many donor-financed projects.

The Chingale Pilot Project

In 1968, the first gravity-fed piped water system was started in the Chingale area of the Zomba district in southern Malawi, almost as an accident. At that time, 16 villages in the Chingale area were part of a project undertaken by the Ministry of Community Development and Social Welfare. The project's objectives were to increase literacy, to promote income generating activities for women, and to support the self-help construction of schools and health facilities (Glennie 1983, p. 11).

During discussions with the project committee (made up of members of the community) the ministry's engineer realized that the water supply was a major problem for the villages. During the wet season people used shallow, unprotected wells. In the dry season, the women had to walk several miles to find water. When the engineer asked the committee to show him a perennial water source, he was shown a stream flowing off a nearby mountain. He concluded that piping the water to the villages by gravity was possible (Glennie 1983, p. 14). The government, through the ministry, agreed to provide pipes and materials, which would be financed by the U.S. ambassador's self-help fund. The local community would provide labor for digging the trenches (Warner et. al. 1986, p.4). The villagers dug the trenches, laid the pipes, filled the trenches, and installed the public standpipes (Glennie 1983, p. 14; Msukwa 1983, pp. 1-2). The community's contributions, mostly labor, were supplied on a self-help basis.

The Chingale pilot project cost MK6,000 (US$7,200 in 1969 dollars), which primarily reflects the cost of materials. The project used 25 km of pipes, and could supply 3,000 people with up to 25 liters of water each per day. The project was later extended to an additional 2,000 people. This first project was small and was completed relatively quickly (Glennie 1983, p. 14; Msukwa 1983, p. 12; Warner et al. 1986, p. 4).

The Chambe Project

With the success of the Chingale project, the Ministry of Community Development and Social Welfare decided to extend the project, starting with the Chambe area in the Mulanje district, also in southern Malawi. A mountainous area, Mulanje has several perennial streams, therefore the supply source was not a problem. To get the community interested, the ministry took Chambe's leaders to the first project in Chingale, where the local water supply committee took them round the project. These leaders then went back to their own community, convinced of the possibilities and benefits of the proposed project. They explained the role the community was expected to play in the implementation of the project to the villagers and convinced them that their contributions would be worthwhile (Msukwa 1983, p. 12).

This project was much larger than the Chingale project, as the ministry's feasibility study showed that the available water supply could serve up to 30,000 people in 60 villages. The ministry assigned an engineer and support staff to the area, local committees were formed, and as in the Chingale project, local people dug the trenches. Under the direction of the ministry's staff, the community also constructed the intake and sedimentation tanks. The project was completed in 1970 and distributed water to 30,000 people through 180 taps. The total cost of the project was MK64,000 (US$76,800 in 1970 dollars) (Glennie 1983, pp. 15-16).

The government learned some important lessons during the Chambe project. As the project was larger, construction took much longer. Part way through construction, the community began to doubt that it would ever be completed and at one point trench digging stopped. It was completed eventually, but ministry staff felt that starting with a smaller project would have been more appropriate (Msukwa 1983, p. 12). Thus the government started its later large projects by completing a small pilot project first. Such pilot projects demonstrate to the community that piped water—the final goal—is feasible. Community participation is therefore more easily sustained for a longer time.

The Growth of a Nationwide Program

With the success of the two initial projects, requests to the Ministry of Community Development and Social Welfare for similar projects increased significantly. Rather than the ministry approaching communities, communities started approaching the ministry.

Following these initial projects, the ministry undertook two large projects near the Chambe project. During these projects, the procedures and techniques became more standardized and the general technical standards were improved. These developments were in response to problems that had arisen in the initial projects and were one of the benefits of proceeding slowly (Glennie 1983, pp. 19-20).

Next, in response to growing demand, the ministry undertook several small projects in the north and central regions and in new areas in the south. At this point, the government decided on a policy of controlled growth as it realized that because of the limited number of trained people with the necessary experience, meeting the demand would be impossible. It also decided that too rapid development could result in unsuccessful projects and that a slower pace would pay off in the longer run (Glennie 1983, pp. 22-24).

The gravity-fed water supply project has now extended to most areas of the country. Table 3.1 shows the regional distribution in 1987.

Table 3.1 Distribution of Gravity-Fed Water Supply Projects by Region, 1987

Region	No. of projects completed
Northern region	15
Central region	10
Southern region	22
Total	**47**

Source: Government of Malawi 1987

The number of projects in the central region reflects its flat topography and not a lack of demand. Completed projects serve a population of over a million people through approximately 6,700 taps. In addition to the 47 completed projects, 8 new projects are currently under construction. These projects are expected to serve about 229,000 people at an estimated material cost of MK3.4 million (US$1.5 million in 1987 dollars) (annex 1).

The Technology Used

Participation by local communities has been an important aspect of Malawi's piped water program. This participation has been possible and effective, particularly during the construction and maintenance phases, partly because the technology used in the scheme is simple.

The delivery system can be broken down into seven steps, as described below and illustrated in figure 3.1, although any one system may not require all seven. For example, recent research in Malawi shows that some systems may not need a screening tank because the sedimentation tank can carry out the same work (Glennie 1983, Warner et al. 1983, 1986).

1. ***Intake***. The intake draws water from a natural pool in a river. The pool is normally situated in the mountains in an uninhabited area. A caretaker clears flood debris that could block the intake.
2. ***Screening Tank.*** The screening tank, also cleaned by the caretaker, removes debris that has passed through the intake pipes. During the rainy season, the tank may need daily cleaning.
3. ***Sedimentation Tank.*** The sedimentation tank allows fine matter to settle while also providing emergency water storage.
4. ***Storage Tanks.*** The supply system has two storage tank facilities: primary and secondary tanks. The primary storage tank follows the sedimentation tank. The secondary tanks, sometimes referred to as "area storage tanks," are located below the sedimentation and primary tanks.
5. ***Main Pipeline.*** The main pipelines link the primary and secondary storage tanks. In some cases, areas may be served directly by pipes from the main lines. In earlier projects, the main pipelines were made of asbestos cement. However, the Department of Water Supply decided to switch to polyvinyl chloride (PVC) pipes because asbestos pipes are affected by the acidity of water and tend to develop hairline cracks over time. PVC pipes are also relatively light, easy to transport and handle, and produced domestically. This change from asbestos cement to PVC pipe is an example of how the government learned over time and adapted the project as a result of new information.
6. ***Branch Lines.*** These connect the secondary tanks with the villages and are also made of PVC. Many branch lines have their own branch storage tanks.
7. ***Village Taps.*** The tap site has a standpipe made from galvanized steel with a brass tap, an apron, a drain, and a soak-away. In earlier projects, aprons were constructed with bricks, but they are now made of more durable cement. The drain connects the apron and the soak-away, which is circular and filled with large stones. Dirt is piled around the soak-away, the apron, and the drain to reduce silting problems.

The simplicity of the technology has contributed to the project's success. It has kept the cost of materials low and has allowed the communities that benefit from the project to help construct and maintain the system.

Figure 3.1 Schematic Presentation of the Gravity-Fed Water System

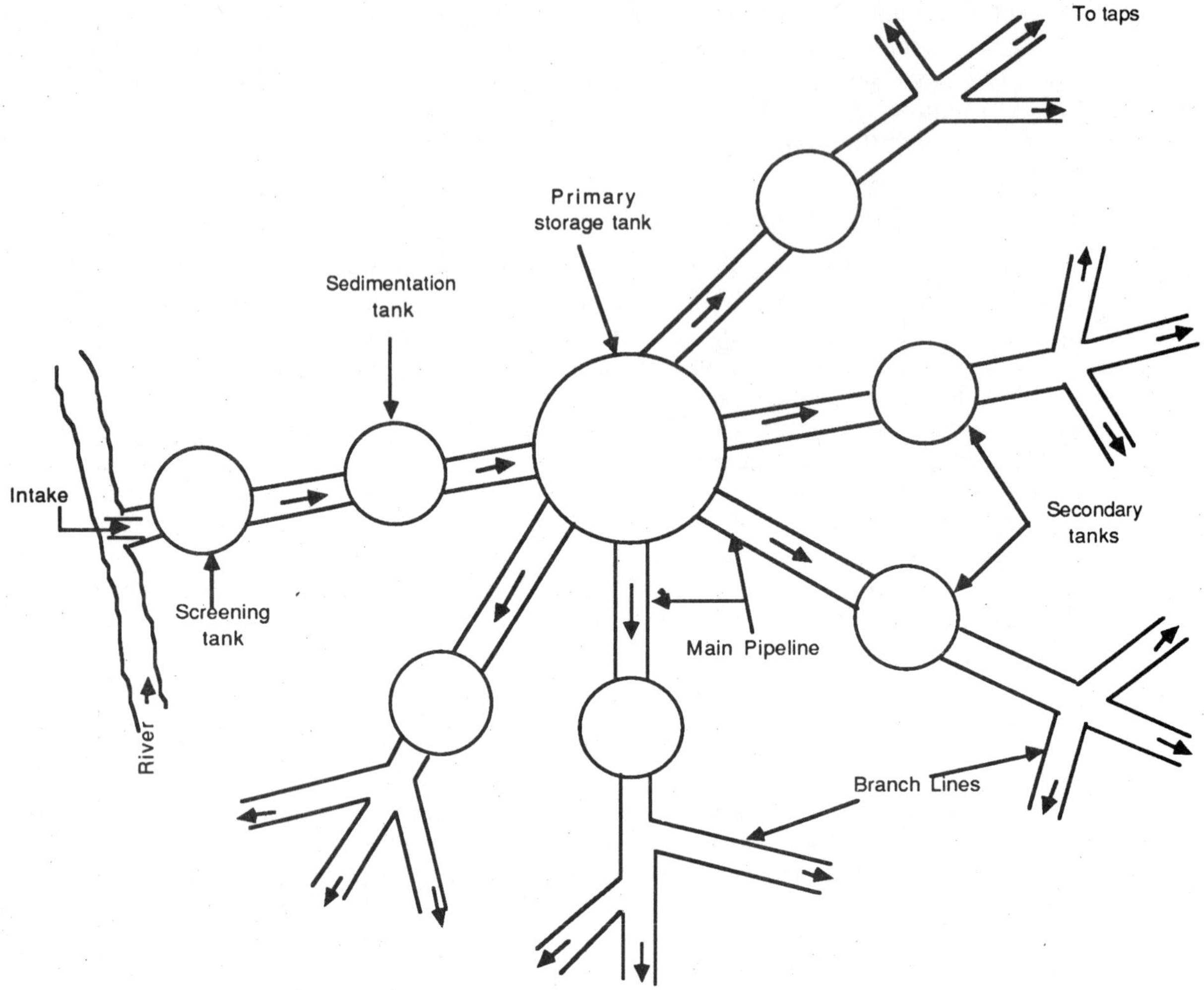

Source: Department of Water Supply

The Roles of the Government and of the Local Communities

The government and local communities have worked well together on the rural piped water scheme, which has contributed significantly to the project's success. Successful cooperation between the communities and the government results in part from the government's openness to community input, as well as the communities' desire for the project to succeed. As with other aspects of the project, the relationship between the government and the communities has evolved over time.

The Role of the Government

As mentioned earlier, the Ministry of Community Development and Social Welfare initiated the gravity-fed piped water scheme, and was also responsible for the wells program. The Geological Survey Department of the Ministry of Agriculture and Natural Resources was in charge of boreholes. In 1979, the government transferred responsibility for all three programs to the Department of Lands, Valuation, and Water within the Office of the President and Cabinet (Msukwa and Kandoole 1981, p. 1). This brought the piped water program, the ground water projects, and urban water supply programs together, allowing better coordination (Warner et al. 1986, p. 4). Eventually, the government decided to place all water development activities together in their own department and in 1984 created the Department of Water Supply within the Ministry of Works and Supplies. The piped water projects fall within the department's Rural Water Section.

Initially, the government was the major initiator of the piped water projects. Today, projects are started at the request of local leaders through the District Development Committees (Msukwa 1983, p. 3). However, the government still plays an important role in complementing communities' inputs. It performs functions that the local communities could not do themselves, such as undertaking feasibility studies, supervising construction, and finding funding for the material costs. In addition, the government supports the contributions of the local communities, for example, by helping to establish the local committees that manage communities' inputs to the project.

After receiving a request, the government's first contribution to the project, through the Department of Water Supply, is to undertake feasibility studies. The department not only examines the project's technical feasibility, but also tries to assess the community's enthusiasm for the project. This is important because if the community does not value the project, it would resist making any contributions in the form of self-help labor.

The department then prepares a project document, which discusses the system's costs and benefits, and an implementation schedule, and presents them to potential donors. Because of its long record of success, the piped water project in Malawi has had no trouble finding donors.[2] Donors have included Oxfam, USAID, Christian Services Committee of the Churches of Malawi, UNICEF, the Danish International Development Agency, and CIDA. In August 1980, USAID provided a major US$6 million grant to undertake a five-year expansion of the piped water system. The grant was to pay for inputs, field staff salaries, and a complementary health education and sanitation project (Warner et al. 1986, p. 4).

During construction, the Department of Water Supply provides such inputs as cement, concrete slabs, and the pipes. The government also supervises construction so as to help guarantee quality. Staff of the Rural Water Section help direct the local self-help labor and any hired skilled workers who do such things as build tanks, which the local labor cannot do. During the maintenance stage , the department's role, except in very special circumstances, is an advisory one through its supervisors and monitoring assistants. The local community does most of the actual maintenance of the water system. Before 1980, the communities were completely responsible for maintenance, with the government supplying some materials, including tools, pipes, and fittings. However, an evaluation of the system by the Christian Services Committee of the Churches of Malawi revealed that this was not working well, partly because of a lack of spare parts. As a result, when something broke, the system was out of action for up to several weeks. In response, in 1980 the government started employing monitoring assistants and created repair teams. Each monitoring assistant is responsible for about 200 taps, oversees the systems, and advises repair teams. Repair teams consist of one person, appointed by

2. The rate of donor finance absorption is constrained by limited technical capacity within the Department of Water Supply and available local resources.

the village headman, from each village served by the same branch line. Monitoring assistants report to supervisors, who are also located in the rural areas (Msukwa and Kandoole 1981, p. 34; Warner et al. 1986, pp. 30-33). The Rural Water Section is also responsible for promoting the local community committees that organize the self-help inputs. Before the project starts, the section's staff explain to community members what is expected of them. It then helps the community set up the committees needed to construct and maintain the system. Major maintenance is also the responsibility of the Rural Water Section, although communities supply any needed labor on a self-help basis (Warner et al. 1986, pp. 33, 41).

A major development of the piped water project has been the introduction by the Environmental Health Division of the Ministry of Health, with USAID funding, of a complementary project, the Health Education and Sanitation Promotion Project (Warner et al. 1986, p. 33). Through this complementary project, field agents—health assistants and health surveillance assistants—from the Ministry of Health work with local village health committees. Activities have included construction of refuse pits, protected water storage, instruction in proper dish drying, oral rehydration (Young and Briscoe 1986a, p.41), and construction of washing slabs and pit latrines in selected villages that have piped water: by July 1986, 103 washing slabs had been constructed. The Ministry of Health provided cement and supervision paid for by donor finance, while villages supplied labor and locally available materials (Warner et al. 1986 p. 37). The combination of health education and piped water should yield large benefits. This institutional change is another example of how the program has developed over time. In the late 1970s, the government recognized that the piped water systems were not producing the maximum possible health benefits all by themselves. Now the health education and sanitation promotion and water programs complement each other and should increase health benefits.

The Role of the Local Communities

Local community labor has been an important input in the piped water projects in Malawi. Each project is a result of a community's own initiative and work. The government reinforces the community's involvement by giving the community substantial responsibility during the planning, construction, and maintenance phases of the water system. Volunteer local labor has not only kept down the government's costs, but it has contributed to the project's success in many ways.

During the planning phase, the staff of the Rural Water Section explain to the communities what their responsibilities will be. The communities set up committees to deal with these responsibilities with guidance and support from the section staff (Warner et al. 1986, p. 33).

During the construction stage, the local community is responsible for digging the pipeline trenches and the foundations for tanks and tap aprons, helping to lay the pipeline, breaking stones, and loading and unloading materials. In addition to labor, the community provides sand, stones, and some digging tools (Warner et al. 1986, p. 78).

During the construction phase, a main water committee (or project committee), mainline (or section) committee, a branch committee, and village committees are responsible for the community's self-help contributions (figure 3.2). The main water committee, which consists of community leaders, distributes work between villages during the construction phase. The mainline and branch committees are responsible for the daily work on the main and branch lines. Village committees organize the village self-help labor on their village's work days and try to ensure a good turnout. The village committees also choose the sites for all the standpipes in their villages (Warner et al. 1986, p. 45-50).

Once construction is completed, the above committees are replaced with maintenance committees (figure 3.2). A main water committee, repair teams, and tap committees monitor and maintain the system on a self-help basis. Their functions include periodically inspecting taps, aprons, pipes, intakes, tanks, and sluice valves; repairing or replacing parts; and cleaning tanks. The main committee supervises repair teams, tap committees, and caretakers, raises small sums of money for a given repair if necessary, and reports any repair work that cannot be done by the local repair teams to staff of the Rural Water Section (Warner et al. 1986, p. 50).

Repair teams are responsible for routine maintenance of the system, such as repairing pipes and aprons and replacing taps. The repair teams receive some basic training in pipe repair from the Department of Water Supply (Warner et al. 1986, p. 40), and as already discussed, receive help from the monitoring assistants when needed.

Caretakers are responsible for cleaning the main intake to the system. Often they are paid by the community (Young and Briscoe 1986a, p.42).

Figure 3.2 Construction and Maintenance Committees

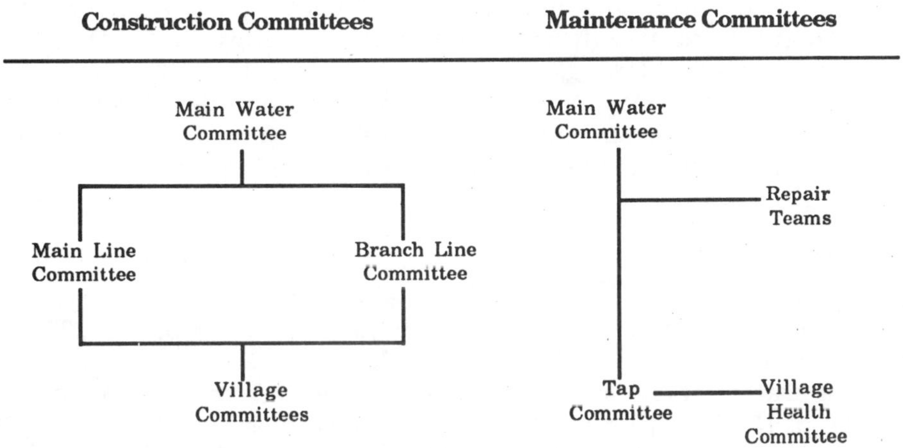

Source: Warner et al. (1986), p. 48.

Each tap committee is responsible for the maintenance of a single tap. The committee cleans the tap site and soak-away pit, raises funds for replacement of a worn out tap or repair of the apron (Warner et al. 1986, p. 51), and reports any problems to the repair teams. Although the committee is responsible for cleaning the tap site, anyone who happens to be at the tap when it needs cleaning generally does so. A study by Msukwa and Kandoole (1981) showed that women are more often on tap committees than on any other committee, and account for over 50 percent of tap committee membership. This is consistent with women's traditional role as managers of water.

Village health committees were formed in Malawi before the initiation of the health education and sanitation promotion project, in response to cholera outbreaks (Warner et al. 1986, p. 39). They were initially organized by the Ministry of Health to promote improved health practices. More recently, through the health and sanitation promotion project, village health committees have become more involved in water supply and sanitation issues (Warner et al. 1986, p.51). The village health and tap committees are considered important for improving health and sanitation in communities with piped water systems (Young and Briscoe 1986a, p. 40). There is at least one tap committee member on the health committee.

On the whole, the committee structure is a success. With communities' support during construction and maintenance, the projects get built and reliably supply water to the communities involved.

Water Reliability, Quantity Consumed, Quality, and Costs

The piped water systems reliably supply water of a quality and at a cost that compare favorably to alternatives.

Reliability of Piped Water Systems

The rural piped water program is extremely reliable—water is available approximately 90 percent of the time, with the exception of a few major pipeline breaks. Pipe breakages can generally be repaired quickly—about 90 percent of breaks are fixed in two days or less (Warner et al. 1986, p.71). The program is so reliable largely because of the monitoring and maintenance programs, which work well in part because of the rural communities' commitment to the water system. This commitment in turn presumably reflects the communities' belief that the benefits of the water system outweigh any costs to themselves. The system's relatively simple technology also plays a role as it allows communities to undertake most repairs, with some help from the government. In addition, government supervision of the initial construction helps reduce future maintenance problems.

Quantity of Water Consumed

Before 1982, the piped water projects were designed to supply 27 liters per capita per day. In 1983, however, the rate was increased to 36 liters per capita per day. These rates refer to an area's design population, which is the area's expected population based on its agricultural potential and population growth over the next 20 years (Warner et al. 1986, p. 13). Metering studies and survey studies have been used to determine how much water people actually use. These reveal that the actual average consumption rate has generally been less than the design rate. If a meter is used, it may either be placed at the outlets of main storage tanks to measure overall delivery or at individual taps to measure village deliveries. Metering has only been used since 1981, and on a very limited scale.

The first meter investigations, conducted in the Mulanje West Project from January 1981 to June 1982, found that water use averaged 10.3 liters per capita per day. A 1982 study of the entire Mulanje West Project showed that the average rate of water use was 18.6 liters per capita per day. A 1984 study of the Lifani project established water use at 20 liters per capita per day (Van Shaik 1983; Warner et al. 1986, p. 67).

Researchers also carried out water consumption surveys in Zomba East (Msukwa and Kandoole 1981), Zomba West (Linskog and Linskog 1985), and Champira North (Easton 1985; Young and Joseph 1986). Their measurement of water consumption was limited to water taken home, that is, excluding water used at the tap. The surveys revealed a consumption rate ranging from 10 liters per capita per day in parts of Zomba West to 20 liters per capita per day in Champira.

These studies of actual water consumption suggest that water use is below the design capacity, and that the water system can meet people's demand adequately. In addition, the system has room for some increase in demand and for further population growth in most areas (Young and Briscoe 1986a, p.6). Increase in demand will result not only from population growth, but from future development.

The low water consumption levels are, however, giving rise to concern. Consumption below the design capacity may be reducing the system's health benefits. Health benefits come not only from better quality water, but from increased water use for personal hygiene purposes, for example, increased use of water for washing can reduce the incidence of some diseases. The government would like to encourage more water use that contributes to health benefits, but at the same time not encourage wasteful water practices. Through user education, the government hopes to increase the use of water in ways that benefit local communities. One of the goals of the USAID-funded health education and sanitation promotion project is to increase water use for hygiene purposes, for instance, by constructing more washing slabs, and increasing hygiene education (Warner et al. 1983, p. 76).

Studies of the piped water projects in Malawi suggest that distance from the tap is important in explaining tap water use. Households living near taps tend to collect more water from taps per day than households who live further away from taps. Msukwa and Kandoole (1981) found that households further away from a tap tended to draw more water from other sources and largely restricted their use of tap water to activities like drinking and cooking.

Government policy is for households to be at most 500 meters from a tap. Warner et al. (1986) found that 90 percent of households are located within 200 to 300 meters of a tap site. Also, Msukwa and Kandoole (1981) in their study of Zomba East found that about 75 percent of people in their sample walked for less than five minutes to the closest tap, while about 95 percent walked for less than ten minutes.

Water use from taps depends not only on how close households are to the taps, but also on how close they are relative to alternative water supplies. It has therefore recently been suggested that more taps be located more closely together in areas where alternative water sources are easily available as a way to increase tap water use. This is seen as a way of getting villagers to abandon traditional water sources and use primarily the better quality piped water (Warner et al. 1986, pp. 75 and 103).

To conserve water, as well as for equity reasons, the government imposed a rule in 1976 against house connections that has been strictly enforced (Warner et al. 1983, p. 85; Young and Briscoe 1986a, p. 84). It is not clear whether proposals to increase the number of taps in water rich areas as a way of increasing water use will ever go so far as to imply house connections. The government would have to consider the cost and equity effects of such a change in policy carefully.

Quality

The water system is designed to work without treatment, except for intake screening and simple sedimentation. Additional treatment is considered too costly and unnecessary if the intake sites are chosen correctly, although some treatment (slow sand filtration) has been used more recently to make the gravity-fed water system feasible for more areas. The project has tried to improve the quantity and quality of water supplied to rural areas "without resorting to inappropriate urban standards or the often unrealistic standards for rural areas found in the development literature (Warner et al. 1983, pp. 74-75). This emphasis has contributed to the system's success for several reasons. To begin with, experience has demonstrated that water systems that only improve water quality are not reliable (USAID 1982, p. 25). Reliability in turn seems to depend on perceived benefits. Communities will try to keep water systems functioning when benefits exceed costs. Rural users do not seem overly concerned about quality, as measured by bacterial content, for instance. If the project had emphasized radically improved water quality, thereby raising users' costs, the project might have been less successful.

The quality of the water supplied by the piped water system has not been tested routinely, however, testing increased with the 1980 USAID project, which gave money to the Central Water Laboratory to test water quality. The USAID has concluded that water quality is better than that of water from unprotected wells, rivers, and boreholes, both at the source and in the home, and that it is not a health hazard, although it is below the standards for urban areas (Warner et al. 1986, p. 69). The USAID has recommended more water quality monitoring in the future.

Costs

Costs of the rural piped water project include the costs of materials (see annex 1), the value of the self-help labor, and maintenance costs. In 1987, the cost of materials per capita was MK15 (US$6.60). The Ministry of Works and Supplies has estimated that the cost of the labor to dig one meter of pipeline trench is MK0.50 (Warner et al. 1986, p. 26). Thus, for the 47 completed projects, the cost per capita of the self-help labor to dig the 4,556 kilometers of trenches equals MK2.25 (US$1.00). Msukwa, in a 1986 study, estimated the self-help per capita maintenance costs at MK0.16 (US$0.07) per year. The USAID estimates that the total annual maintenance cost equals MK0.30 per capita (Warner et al. 1986, p. x).

As mentioned earlier, starting in August 1980, USAID has financed continued expansion of the piped water program in Malawi, as well as complementary health education, sanitation, and research programs. The USAID estimates that the average cost per capita to be eventually served is MK18, of which 20 percent is self-help labor. The direct capital costs are MK17.3 per capita using 1986 population figures (Warner et al. 1986, pp. x and 13). Note that these figures are close to the average cost of completed projects.[3]

The average cost of constructing a borehole nationwide is currently MK7,000 to MK8,000 per borehole. They serve on average 250 people at a per capita cost of from MK28 to MK32 (US$12.40 to US$14.20). It costs approximately MK350 per year to maintain a borehole, or MK1.4 per capita. Shallow wells cost on average MK2,000 to MK3,000 and serve 125 people, at an average cost per capita of MK16 to MK24 (US$7.10 to US$10.60) (see table 3.2).

The per capita construction and maintenance costs of gravity-fed piped water systems are favorable compared to the costs of boreholes and shallow wells. This is consistent with the government's current policy of not drilling boreholes where gravity-fed water systems are feasible.

3. Direct capital costs excluded salaries and overhead paid by the government, self-help labor inputs, and land costs. This corresponds, to the best that we could determine, to the materials costs reported in annex 1.

Table 3.2 Construction and Annual Maintenance Costs Per Capita of Alternative Water Systems
(MK)

Water Source	Construction	Maintenance
Gravity-fed piped water	17.25	0.16-0.30
Boreholes	28-32	1.4
Shallow wells	16-24	n.a.

n.a. = not available

In addition, all the people served by a borehole must go to one location to collect water. With piped water, taps can be distributed at various points, making the system more convenient. Often long lines wait at boreholes, which results in time being wasted that could otherwise be productively used (Msukwa and Kandoole 1981, p. 79). Also, water from boreholes can be saline, and occasionally greasy. In Chilumba, where piped water has been introduced to complement water from boreholes, people have switched to using tap water for drinking, even though this sometimes entails walking further (Mtawali, personal observation).

Another problem with boreholes is their maintenance, resulting in long disruptions to the water supply. Msukwa and Kandoole (1981) report that repairing a broken borehole took an average of eight months. Currently, about 55 percent of boreholes are functioning at any point in time (the figures quoted ranged from 40 to 70 percent), while the piped water system delivers water about 90 percent of the time. This makes the cost of piped water even more favorable than that of borehole water. The reasons for long delays in repair of boreholes include lack of adequate government resources and of spare parts. The situation is made worse because unlike that used for the piped water scheme, the technology used in borehole construction does not allow the local community to maintain the system. Many repairs require the services of a professional.

Currently, when a community requests a water project from the government, the request is usually for a gravity-fed water system rather than a borehole, despite the fact that the piped system involves their labor, while borehole construction often does not (Msukwa 1983, p. 13).

Boreholes and shallow wells are built where piped water is not an option, primarily the central region of Malawi. Currently 47 percent of Malawi's population has access to an improved water supply in the form of piped water, boreholes, and protected wells. Approximately 23 percent of the population has access to piped water. Estimates indicate that in the long run, it will only be feasible to supply 30 to 35 percent of the population with gravity-fed piped water (USAID 1977, p. 3), although the government hopes that gravity-fed piped water systems will be feasible in more areas if some simple water treatment techniques can be developed. In this case, the system could be extended to areas that currently do not have acceptable water sources. USAID has stressed the importance of identifying the remaining potential for piped water projects.

In recognition of the success of the piped water projects, the government has tried since the early 1980s to introduce some of its successful aspects into other water projects. For example, in integrated water projects, which include rehabilitating existing boreholes and constructing new boreholes and shallow wells, introduced in 1981-82 in regions where piped water is not an option, the government has used community participation modeled on the piped water projects. The community chooses the sites for the boreholes and wells, clears the sites, and supplies the water needed for drilling and watchmen to guard the construction equipmcnt. Committees clean and maintain the apron. The community also receives some simple training on pump maintenance. The hope is that these water projects will be more successful if the community can be involved, as in the gravity-fed projects.

Project Benefits

The major benefits of the rural piped water system, although difficult to quantify, have been improved health, reduced time spent fetching water, increased output and employment in the private sector, and increased human capital at the local and government level.

Health Benefits

A main objective of the piped water project, along with improved sanitation, is to reduce disease. Diseases associated with contaminated water supplies include cholera, schistosomiasis, typhoid, dysentery, and hepatitis. Almost 50 percent of diagnosed illnesses in Malawi are related to water and sanitation (USAID 1977, p. 2). The Department of Health started user education only about five years ago. The evidence suggests that the health benefits of the gravity-fed water systems increase substantially when combined with user health education. When a clean water supply is combined with better excreta disposal practices, the health benefits are substantial. When combined with better food hygiene practices, they are even larger. Improved quality of drinking and cooking water can reduce the number of cases of diseases such as cholera, diarrhea, and typhoid. Improved hygiene with cleaner water can reduce the incidence of diseases such as shigellosis and trachoma. Reduced contacts with contaminated surface water can decrease the likelihood of contracting diseases such as schistosomiasis (Warner et al. 1986, p. 81).

The data suggest that many of these health benefits are being realized. A detailed assessment of the effects of the water supply and health education package on diarrheal diseases in rural Malawi has been undertaken (Young and Briscoe 1987). This shows that young children in families with "adequate environmental sanitation" (both improved water supply and a sanitary latrine) have 20 percent less diarrhea than young children in families without at least one of these improvements. Note that the health benefits of a clean water supply, however, depend on what health education and sanitation programs complement the supply of water. A clean water supply is useful, but insufficient to improve health by itself.

The health benefits of a water supply project are hard to measure. A USAID report suggests that if people in a village thought that a project provided health benefits, then it probably did (USAID 1983, P. 13). USAID staff talked with health and tap committees and with women in rural areas served by taps and health committees. They concluded that users felt that small children were having less diarrhea since the introduction of the water system and formation of health committees (diarrhea is one of the leading causes of death in children under five in Malawi) (Warner et al. 1983, pp. 89-90). In Msukwa and Kandoole's study (1981, p. 46), teachers interviewed claimed that the incidence of water related diseases among pupils had declined. Hearsay evidence indicates that a cholera outbreak in Mulanje in 1973 was less severe in areas that had piped water.

Some evidence also exists that the incidence of trachoma, a major cause of blindness in Malawi, can be affected by piped water. Trachoma cases increase with the distance of a village to a water source (Warner et al. 1986, p. 84). Researchers hypothesize that greater distance reduces face washing, which in turn increases the incidence of the disease. Increased access to piped water along with more washing should thus reduce the incidence of trachoma.

The health impacts of an improved water supply depend, therefore, on what other environmental and educational improvements complement the water supply. The Government of Malawi's policy to combine water supply programs with health education and sanitation programs has been and should continue to be productive.

Evidence exists of another channel through which the piped water project improves health. Under a national expanded program of immunization, children receive polio and DPT vaccines. A WHO study showed that the program suffered from high dropout rates—only 35 percent of the children receive the full immunization series (Shafa 1985). The USAID has shown that full immunization rates are twice as high in areas with piped water and health education and sanitation promotion programs. No areas have the health education and sanitation programs without piped water, so it is not possible to determine their independent effects, however, USAID staff hypothesize that health education and sanitation activities without piped water would be less successful at increasing full immunization. They think that it is the combined effect of freeing some time of women as well as increased health education that has resulted in increased full immunizations (Warner et al. 1986, p. 88). The improved community organizational skills resulting from the water and health programs may also have played a role.

Time Saving

The availability of tap water near the house has certainly reduced the time women spend collecting water. This gives them more time for other activities such as growing food, searching for firewood, and taking care of children. The population served by the system has mentioned time saving as the most important benefit of the project (Warner et al. 1983, p. 92). Msukwa and Kandoole (1981) note that about 98 percent of all water collectors are women and the majority are over the age of 16. Therefore, if time is saved, it is of "economically active women."

Taps are meant to serve populations within 500 meters. The community decides where to locate taps, which contributes to their being placed at convenient spots. Whether the taps end up being more convenient than traditional water sources for any one village depends on the traditional water source and the time of year. Obviously, in drier areas, taps are more apt to improve accessibility to water.

Contributions to the Development of Private Sector Enterprises

The water system has had a positive effect on several private industries in Malawi. First, the project uses PVC pipes produced locally. At the beginning of the USAID project, the Department of Water Supply got price quotations from suppliers in the Federal Republic of Germany, Holland, Zimbabwe, Kenya, and the single producer in Malawi. Pipes from foreign suppliers were more expensive than the local pipes because of the high costs of transportation to Lilongwe—a situation likely to continue (Young and Briscoe 1986a, p. 35). In addition, local contractors construct the tanks and intakes used in the water system. This has contributed to the development of small private sector firms in the rural areas (Warner et al. 1983, p. 92).

In addition, more land may be under cultivation in areas that had previously suffered from limited water supplies, however, this has not been documented. In Msukwa and Kandoole's (1981) study, people served by piped water said that they were not allowed to use piped water for their businesses, but that other traditional water sources that had previously been used by households were now more readily available for such activities as brickmaking, growing vegetables, and raising livestock.

Building Human Capital

In 1985, the Centre for Social Research at the University of Malawi conducted a study commissioned by the USAID of the social and institutional effects of the gravity-fed water program (Warner et al. 1986, p. 80). The study concluded that the program increased communities' leadership and organizational skills, as well as those of Malawi government staff involved with the project. These additions to human capital, at the local and government levels, are additional benefits of the program (Msukwa 1986).

Lessons from the Malawi Piped Water Project

Although exact duplication of Malawi's experience with the piped water project in other countries is impossible, there exist a number of lessons relevant to other development projects.

A major explanation of the success of the piped water project in Malawi is community enthusiasm and participation and the constructive working relationship between the government and local communities. The government involves communities throughout the planning, implementation, and maintenance phases of the project. In many cases, project users are the best ones to make decisions about certain aspects of the project, for example, in the water project, communities decide such things as tap locations. As a result, the project is likely to yield greater benefits.

A community's willingness to become involved in a project suggests that the community believes the project will benefit them. Under these circumstances, a project is both more likely to succeed and to yield net benefits. In addition, if the community values a project, it is more likely to provide inputs in the form of labor and materials.

Another lesson is that a pilot stage can contribute to a project's success. During this phase, a project's strengths and weaknesses can be revealed. For example, during the Phalombe project pilot phase, the government learned that local communities could not carry out some of the necessary tasks. In response, the Department of Water Supply staff now either carries out the tasks or helps the community carry them out. In addition, the pilot phase has contributed to successful community participation. By demonstrating that the system's goals can be realized, community commitment to the project is strengthened (Glennie 1983).

The piped water project has evolved slowly over some 20 years. This has had advantages in that over time, the government has maintained a flexible approach and changed specific aspects of the project in response to problems that arose in earlier projects. The introduction of a pilot phase is one example, as is the decision to switch from asbestos cement to PVC pipes. Another example is the introduction of supervisors and monitoring assistants to help in the maintenance phases of the project when the government learned, over time, that the local communities could not maintain the system entirely on their own.

Once the government realized the potential for gravity-fed water, it could have decided to build rapidly all possible systems in the country. If successful, the benefits of such a strategy would have been that more people would have had access to piped water sooner. However, the problems of such a strategy would have been higher costs and a greater possibility of failure. More rapid development of the water project would have required increased government and field personnel. The government might have been able to find people with the necessary technical training (although it probably would have had to hire mainly expatriates), but not with the commitment or experience of those government employees who had worked on previous projects. Since much of the success has resulted from the interaction of the government and local communities, this would have been a risk. Also, if projects had been built much more rapidly, mistakes avoided in later projects because of lessons learned in earlier projects would probably not have been avoided.

Simple technology can also be an advantage. In this case, it allows the local community that benefits from the project to help build and maintain the system. As a result, the system has proved very reliable.

The water system in Malawi also demonstrates the possible complementarities between development projects. Warner et al. (1986) conclude that "the Malawi Rural Piped Water Programme and its associated HESP (Health, Education, and Sanitation Promotion) component are an excellent example of the overall development success that can be achieved through the proper integration of water supply, hygiene education, and sanitation."

Malawi's piped water projects have been a success, while other water projects in Africa, including Malawi's borehole program, have been much less successful. The lessons from the piped water projects are lessons that apply not only to other water projects, but to other development projects in general. The Malawi government has learned from the water project, and is currently trying to apply some of these lessons to its borehole and integrated water systems programs.

Annex 3.1 Rural Piped Water Projects in Malawi: Completed Projects

Project	District	Region	Population served	Length of piping (km)	Number of taps	Cost of material (MK)	Date completed
Chingale	Zomba	South	5,000	40	60	6,000	1969
Chambe	Mulanje	South	30,000	96	180	64,000	1970
Migowi	Mulanje	South	6,000	24	45	12,000	1971
Chilinga	Mulanje	South	2,000	10	14	4,000	1972
Ng'onga	Rumphi	North	2,000	17	20	6,000	1972
Muhuju	Rumphi	North	1,000	19	21	7,000	1973
Chinkwezulu	Machinga	South	700	2	9	1,000	1974
Ighembe	Karonga	North	4,000	17	36	7,000	1974
Mulanje West	Mulanje	South	90,000	237	460	170,000	1975
Luzi	Mzimba/Rumphi	North	8,000	59	44	24,000	1975
Chinunkha	Chitipa	North	4,000	25	51	12,000	1975
Chilumba	Karonga	North	4,000	17	29	8,000	1975
Chilombwe	Ntcheu	Central	1,200	6	14	2,000	1975
Phalombe	Mulanje	South	140,000	400	660	500,000	1977
Dedza	Dedza	Central	1,400	8	10	5,000	1976
Mchinji	Mchinji	Central	20,000	136	215	52,000	1976
Chagwa	Machinga	South	7,000	80	110	15,000	1976
Kalitsilo	Ntcheu	Central	1,000	6	13	3,000	1977
Lifani	Zomba/Machinga	South	20,000	100	152	72,000	1977
Hewe	Rumphi	North	8,000	42	42	30,000	1977
Nkhamanga	Rumphi	North	12,000	75	120	134,000	1978
Luzulu	Ntcheu	Central	6,000	24	34	20,000	1978
Namitambo	Chiradzulu/Mulanje	South	60,000	290	360	480,000	1979
Sombani	Mulanje	South	40,000	184	300	240,000	1979
Ntonda	Ntcheu	Central	25,000	120	194	120,000	1980
Lingamasa	Mangochi	South	12,000	43	118	50,000	1981
Zomba (Domasi)	Zomba	South	100,000	448	813	711,000	1981
Luwazi	Mzimba	North	8,000	80	54	79,400	1981
Nalipiri	Mulanje	South	9,000	27	55	40,000	1980
Muloza East	Mulanje	South	32,000	150	180	120,000	1980
Luchenya/Muloza	Mulanje	South	46,000	168	270	180,000	1982
Karonga	Karonga	North	30,000	195	250	290,300	1983
Kawinga	Machinga	South	70,000	571	450	926,600	1983
Nthalire	Chitipa	North	3,000	21	46	66,500	1983

Project	District	Region	Population served	Length of piping (km)	Number of taps	Cost of material (MK)	Date completed
Liwonde	Machinga	South	23,000	110	130	198,000	1983
Kasinje	Ntcheu	Central	14,000	32	95	60,000	1983
Nanyangu	Ntcheu	Central	20,000	53	131	150,000	1983
Iponga	Ka Ronga	North	5,600	24	35	40,000	1983
Muloza South	Mulanje	South	8,000	22	45	40,000	1983
Dombole	Ntcheu	Central	22,000	107	140	286,700	1984
Champira North	Mzimba	North	24,000	167	154	236,000	1984
Mwansambo/Kasakula	Nkhotakota/Nchisi	Central	25,000	60	145	157,300	1984
Misuku	Chitipa	North	3,700	17	70	40,900	1984
Sumulu	Machinga	South	23,500	80	100	261,000	1984
Livingstonia	Rumphi	North	3,000	15	21	9,600	1984
Mirala	Machinga	South	13,000	56	81	108,000	1985
Kakwawa	Zomba	South	16,000	68	101	93,000	1985
Total			1,009,100	4,556	6,685	6,148,900	

Annex 3.2 Projects Under Construction, 1987

Project	District	Region	Population to be served	Length of piping (km)	Number of taps	Cost (MK)
Chitipa extension projects	Chitipa	North	46,000	323	300	303,400
Mwanza	Chikwawa	South	40,000	218	400	1,079,400
Chimaliro South	Mzimba	North	32,000	221	200	512,400
Zomba West	Zomba	South	60,000	340	353	690,800
Msaka	Mzimba	North	3,000	37	35	58,200
Lifutazi	Nkhata bay	North	6,000	40	43	33,800
Mwansambo/ Mwadzama	Nkhota-kota	Central	18,000	50	100	60,800
Mulanje South West	Mulanje	South	24,000	117	140	708,000
Total			229,000	1,346	1,571	3,444,800

References

Briscoe, J., and D. de Ferranti. 1988. *Water for Rural Communities, Helping People Help Themselves.* Washington, D.C.: World Bank.

Easton, A. 1985. *Water Collection and Use Survey of Champhira North Piped Water Project.* Lilongwe, Malawi: Water Department, Ministry of Works and Supplies.

Ettema, W. 1983. *The Rural Piped Water Evaluation Programme: Some Baseline Data and Recommendations.* Zomba, Malawi: Centre for Social Research, University of Malawi.

Glennie, Colin. 1983. *Village Water Supply in the Decade: Lessons from Field Experience.* John Wiley.

Government of Malawi. 1987. *Completed Rural Piped Water Projects in Malawi.* Lilongwe, Malawi: Ministry of Works and Supply (processed).

Linskog, P.A., and R.U.M. Linskog. 1985. *Household Water Supply–A User's or a Supplier's Problem.* Progress Report No. 5. Sweden: Linköping University.

Msukwa, L.A.H. 1983. *Participation of Rural Water Supply–The Malawi Experience.* Paper presented at the 9th Water and Waste Engineering for Developing Countries Conference, Harare, Zimbabwe. April.

Msukwa, L.A.H. 1986. *Institutional Building for the Maintenance of Rural Piped Water Schemes.* Zomba, Malawi: Centre for Social Research, University of Malawi. May.

Msukwa, L.A.H. 1986. *Management of Rural Piped Water Schemes: The Case of Malawi.* Paper Presented for the Economic Commission for Africa Workshop on The Role of Women in Water and Sanitation Development. Salima, Malawi. January.

Msukwa, L.A.H., and I. Chirwa. 1980. *An Evaluation Report of Christian Service Committee Funded Water Programmes.* Blantyre, Malawi: Christian Service Committee of the Churches of Malawi.

Msukwa, L.A.H., and B.F. Kandoole. 1981. *Water by the People: An Evaluation of the Rural Water Supply Programme in Zomba District.* Zomba, Malawi: Centre for Social Research, University of Malawi. December.

Shafa, E.O. 1985. *Evaluation of National Immunization Coverage:* Malawi. Geneva: WHO. August.

USAID. 1977. *Malawi: Rural Water Supply Project Sessions Guidelines.* USAID WASH handout to accompany 1977 film on Malawi's gravity-fed rural water project. Lilongwe: Ministry of Information, Government of Malawi.

USAID. 1982. *Community Water Supply in Developing Countries: Lessons from Experience.* USAID Program Evaluation Report No. 7. USAID. Evaluation Publications. September.

Van Schaik, H.H. 1983. *Report on Flow Measurements in Nalipili Rural Water Supply*. Lilongwe: Department of Lands, Valuation, and Water, Malawi Government.

Warner, D.B., R.B. Isely, C. Hafner, and J. Briscoe. 1983. *Malawi: Rural Water Supply Program:* A Mid-Term Evaluation of the USAID-Financed Project. WASH Field Report No. 105. December.

Warner, D.B., J. Briscoe, C. Hafner, and Bert Zellmer. 1986. *Malawi Self-Help Rural Water Supply Program: Final Evaluation.* WASH Field Report No. 186. July.

Young, B., and J. Briscoe. 1986a. *Water and Health in Rural Malawi.* Prepared for the USAID mission to Malawi. February.

Young, B., and J. Briscoe. 1986b. *Health Impact Evaluation of the Malawi Rural Piped Water Supply: A Case-Control Study of Diarrhea.* Chapel Hill, N.C.: University of North Carolina.

Young, B., and J. Briscoe. 1987. "A Case Control Study of the Effect of Environmental Sanitation on Diarrhea Morbidity in Malawi." *Journal of Epidemiology and Community Health. Vol. 42, pp. 83-88.*

Young, B., and J. Joseph. 1986. *Water Use Survey of Champhira North Rural Piped Water Project.* Chapel Hill, N.C.: University of North Carolina.

4

Kenya: A Case Study of the Production and Export of Horticultural Commodities

Morton Owen Schapiro, Department of Economics, Williams College
Stephen Wainaina, Central Bureau of Statistics, Kenya

Horticulture is the branch of agriculture that deals with the growing of fruits, vegetables, and flowers. Horticultural commodities are grown in many parts of Africa and throughout the developing world. Kenya's experience with horticulture is, however, unique because with the government's support and help, this sector has expanded rapidly during the past 20 years to become a dynamic source of exports.

While horticultural commodities have been grown in Kenya since the 1950s, the government only began to allocate resources for research and export promotion programs in the late 1960s. The resulting growth of this sector has been extraordinary. Production increased from 1,476 metric tons of fresh horticultural exports worth KSh 3.1 million in 1968 to 36,211 metric tons worth KSh 630.4 million in 1986 (see notes to table 4.1 for exchange rate information). Today, horticultural commodities are the third largest source of foreign exchange among agricultural exports and account for over 3 percent of the value of all exports; a dramatic increase from 0.3 percent in 1968.

The goal of this study is to examine the roles played by the government and the private sector, and to identify other factors that contributed to this success story.

Background

The presence of a dynamic private sector that has earned substantial profits by selling a wide range of horticultural products in diverse markets has been a major contributor to the expansion of horticultural production and export. With the notable exception of floriculture (flower production), where economies of scale in production, transport, and marketing are critical, the vast majority of production comes from small-scale producers.

The government based its program on a recognition of the continued benefits of private ownership, and has intentionally limited its role mainly to that of a guide. This does not, however, imply that the government has been hesitant to supply key inputs or perform certain tasks, such as maintaining quality control. On the contrary, the government contributed substantially in these areas, along with various research and marketing efforts and the provision of infrastructure.

The government's program has included production plans and targets and, through its various branches, it has participated directly in horticultural development. Yet the government has clearly sought to limit its role to areas where the private market is lacking, thereby reinforcing private incentives rather than undermining them. But, before examining the evolution of the government's program, a quick look at the state of Kenya's economy at the time when serious interest in horticultural development first surfaced is important.

In the 1960s, the country was highly dependent on two principal export crops, coffee, and to a lesser extent, tea, with horticultural exports making a negligible contribution to export earnings (see table 4.1). Even as late as 1970, horticultural exports accounted for only 0.5 percent of all export earnings. In addition to the problem of dependence on a few crops, the country was faced with a rapidly growing population (with an annual rate of population growth around 3.3 percent during the 1960s and even higher in the 1970s), excessive rural-urban migration, and regional inequities.

The objectives of the horticultural development plan (set out in various documents since 1969, see, for example, Ministry of Agriculture 1981) were to ameliorate several of these problems. Specifically, the government hoped that the sector's growth would

- increase the productive use of land without depleting land resources;
- create employment;
- generate income, especially for small-scale landholders;
- generate foreign exchange earnings;
- increase domestic food production, thereby raising nutritional levels and saving those foreign exchange reserves spent on food imports.

These goals were realistic given the nature of horticultural production. Horticulture makes intensive use of land, often using marginal land, while employing a relatively large share of the labor force, particularly during the harvest season. Substantial markets usually exist for its output, both domestic, especially when urban development has been considerable, and foreign. In addition, strong indications suggest that small-scale production can be quite profitable, especially when compared with small-scale production of coffee and tea. The latter point was critical in Kenya since the scarcity of productive farmland was becoming increasingly apparent at the same time that the government was beginning to recognize the need for diversification.

With these goals in mind, we can trace the expansion of Kenya's horticultural sector. First, note that this sector comprises an extremely wide range of products. It includes fruits ranging from temperate to tropical, many vegetables, and an increasing variety of flower crops. Major exports by air now include french beans, bobby beans, avocados, courgettes, chilies, Asian vegetables (such as okra, eggplants, peppers, bitter melons, and squash), mangoes, pineapples, passion fruit, melons, strawberries, and cut flowers (see table 4.2). The latter group includes carnations, roses, and orchids. Furthermore, some produce—such as bananas, apples, and grapes—has been grown to replace imports, and domestic processing, notably pineapple canning, has become an important part of the horticultural sector.

The government realized early on that there were a number of obstacles to successful expansion of the horticultural sector. For one, it anticipated considerable irrigation expenditures, which have indeed been necessary at times, although for small-scale producers, rainfed methods usually suffice. Other problems include a lack of trained personnel, the need for some extension services, certain infrastructure limitations, and, very importantly, a shortage of air cargo space. Kenya has also had to match or overcome a good deal of external competition, namely, Pakistan and India for Asian vegetables, Israel for avocados and other products, Europe for floriculture, the Côte d'Ivoire for pineapples and flowers,

Morocco for flowers, Zambia and Ethiopia for melons, and South Africa for avocados and other products.

Table 4.1 Commodity Composition of Kenyan Exports, 1962-86

Year	Value of coffee exports (KSh millions)	Percentage of total exports	Value of tea exports (KSh millions)	Percentage of total exports	Value of fresh horticultural exports (KSh millions)	Percentage of total exports
1962	211.1	27.9	103.8	13.7	...	...
1963	220.3	25.1	113.3	12.9	...	...
1964	307.9	32.7	121.1	12.9	...	...
1965	281.9	29.9	121.7	12.9	...	...
1966	375.6	32.3	174.3	15.0	...	...
1967	313.4	29.3	147.9	13.8	...	...
1968	256.2	22.2	200.8	17.4	3.1	0.3
1969	336.7	26.6	225.4	17.8	5.1	0.4
1970	445.2	31.1	254.1	17.7	6.5	0.5
1971	390.6	26.8	237.5	16.2	10.9	0.7
1972	495.3	27.3	328.3	18.1	17.1	0.9
1973	715.5	29.2	339.3	13.8	29.6	1.2
1974	767.7	23.6	387.5	11.9	33.9	1.0
1975	704.5	20.9	458.6	13.6	83.3	2.5
1976	1,867.0	29.3	635.2	10.0	102.3	1.9
1977	4,086.7	42.5	1,435.6	14.9	128.7	1.3
1978	2,493.4	33.7	1,263.7	17.1	159.8	2.2
1979	2,211.4	28.7	1,256.9	16.3	194.7	2.5
1980	2,162.6	22.2	1,160.1	11.9	227.1	2.3
1981	2,187.4	21.3	1,222.1	11.9	251.6	2.4
1982	2,891.3	26.5	1,551.7	14.2	272.7	2.5
1983	3,201.7	25.3	2,468.5	19.5	350.6	2.8
1984	4,072.4	27.0	3,789.6	25.1	415.9	2.8
1985	4,612.5	29.4	3,833.1	24.4	469.2	3.0
1986	7,769.7	40.6	3,455.8	18.0	630.4	3.3

... = negligible

Notes: The current exchange rate is approximately KSh 16 = US$1. During 1968-80, it fluctuated between KSh 6.9 = US$1 to KSh 8.3 = US$1. Values in all tables are computed at free on board (fob). Fresh horticultural exports include all horticultural production other than canned products.

Source: Horticultural Crops Development Authority (various), *Statistical Abstract* (various issues), *Economic Survey* (various issues)

Given these various concerns, what led the government to decide that horticultural production had the potential to become an important and viable part of the economy? A number of good reasons led them to this conclusion. A major advantage was the Kenyan climate, which makes it possible to grow tropical, semitropical, and temperate fruits and vegetables, for which there is a large demand during the European winter, within a relatively small area. Also important is Nairobi's central location and its use by many world airlines. Furthermore, towns are well distributed and are often expanding as a result of high population growth rates, thereby helping to maintain substantial internal demand. Finally, the well-developed tourist industry, favored by the exceptional climate, beaches, and game parks, creates a consistent domestic demand for high quality horticultural produce.[1]

Table 4.2 Composition of Exports of Fresh Horticultural Produce,1983 and 1986

	1983				1986			
Product	Volume (metric tons)	Percent-age	Value (KSh millions)	Percent-age	Volume (metric tons)	Percent-age	Value (KSh millions)	Percent-age
Cut flowers	5,209	18.1	145.85	41.6	8,265	22.8	247.95	39.3
French beans	6,447	22.3	70.92	20.2	9,097	25.1	154.65	24.5
Mangoes	1,446	5.0	17.35	5.0	2,941	8.1	50.00	7.9
Okra	1,873	6.5	16.86	4.8	1,738	4.8	21.90	3.5
Chilies	1,895	6.6	15.16	4.3	2,087	5.8	26.30	4.2
Bitter melons	1,010	3.5	10.10	2.9	1,279	3.5	17.39	2.8
Eggplants	2,152	7.5	9.68	2.8	1,692	4.7	12.69	2.0
Courgettes	1,164	4.0	8.15	2.3	231	0.7	1.98	0.3
Avocados	1,073	3.7	7.35	2.1	2,151	5.9	17.21	2.7
Pineapples	1,093	3.8	5.19	1.5	863	2.4	5.18	0.8
Passion fruit	425	1.5	4.25	1.2	646	1.8	11.23	1.5
Squash	499	1.7	3.99	1.1	868	2.4	9.29	1.5
Bobby beans	400	1.4	3.20	0.9	478	1.3	5.06	0.8
Melons	156	0.5	1.56	0.5	...	...	...	...
Strawberries	...	...	...	...	275	0.8	11.01	1.8
All Others	4,008	13.9	30.96	8.8	3,600	9.9	38.53	6.1
Total	28,850	100.0	350.57	100.0	36,211	100.0	630.37	100.0

... = negligible
Source: Horticultural Crops Development Authority (1984, 1987)

1. This statement is at least partially at odds with the often stated belief (see, for example, Carroll 1985) that the take-off in the horticultural sector was boosted by the tourism slump in the mid-1970s, when small investors needed another area to put their money. However, even before the growth spurt in the horticultural sector, the government had demonstrated its willingness to devote considerable effort to developing this area of the economy, and some expansion in horticultural production is likely to have occurred regardless of the state of the tourist industry.

Proof of these various advantages was found in the success of those private firms that were early leaders in the horticultural sector. Although horticultural exports were at very low levels during the late 1960s (table 4.1), the period in which the government first became actively involved, there was an important demonstration effect at work as the experiences of these entrepreneurs encouraged the government. Thus, the government optimistically set out to promote the horticultural sector and to increase its export orientation.

The expansion of the sector could not have taken place without the contribution of three groups of participants: local individuals, foreign enterprises, and the government. From the earliest stage of Kenya's horticultural development, individuals commonly established their contacts before going into the horticultural export business. Growers need a reliable marketing plan because horticultural produce is highly perishable, much more so than traditional exports. For example, for flowers the goal is to have them in European shops within 48 hours of being picked in Kenya. This may explain why many of the early large-scale enterprises were joint ventures between local investors and foreign companies that already had interests in other parts of the world, thereby helping solve the problems of market penetration and the establishment of delivery networks.

Some new investors were encouraged by African Asians who had become United Kingdom residents. Members of this large group of immigrants were actively seeking new trading opportunities and naturally turned to their contacts in Kenya. The combination of already established enterprises and new, enthusiastic investors provided the necessary stimulus for this sector—a sector that has traditionally been dominated by relatively small-scale (under two hectares) private enterprises for production of crops other than pineapples and cut flowers. While large farms are able to use their own export networks, most small farmers rely on export agents who collect the produce from the farmers and arrange for its transport and sale abroad.

The government's role began with legislation that established the Horticultural Crops Development Authority (HCDA) in 1967. The HCDA did not become fully functional until 1969, when it began to carry out some of the tasks with which it had been charged. Around the same time, the government appointed a working group on horticulture that consisted of government representatives, producers, processors, and other people concerned with the industry. The objective was to assess the potential growth of the market, to develop strategies, and to find ways to promote the rapid development of horticulture as an industry.

The working group identified problems in several areas and made a series of recommendations. Some of their main points concerned research, training, inputs, marketing, statistical information, and the role of the HCDA.

- **Research**. The group noted the lack of basic funds, personnel, and ways to disseminate results. They recommended enlargement of existing horticultural centers and establishment of others.
- **Training**. The group recommended an intensification in horticultural training, which at this point was concentrated at the National Horticultural Research Station (NHRS) and its substations. The group suggested four kinds of training: specialist (postgraduate or technical), diploma and certificate, junior field staff, and the actual farmers. For farmers, the group saw demonstration schemes as critical.
- **Inputs**. The working group highlighted the role of inputs, especially for small-scale farmers, who lacked suitable seed varieties and credit to purchase other inputs. It therefore recommended that supervised credit schemes and extension services be made available.

• **Marketing**. Large wholesale markets needed expansion, while grading stations were needed to handle grading standards for exports. Also necessary was a revision of the previous export grading system, which was not sophisticated enough for the demands of dozens of new export products.

• **Statistical information.** More extensive and reliable statistical information was clearly needed, and the group recommended that the HCDA play a major role in data collection.

• **The HCDA's role**. While the HCDA, the Ministry of Agriculture (Crop Division), and the NHRS were all involved in the sector, the HCDA was given the leadership role. The stated functions of the HCDA were very broad and included control and supervision of the purchase and sale of planting material, inspection of growing and harvesting, and the authority to appoint agents to oversee the implementation and performance of any function that they decided was relevant. With government approval, the HCDA would also regulate and control the cultivation, picking, transportation, and marketing of horticultural crops, tax growers to finance its operations, fix prices, and take any other actions that it determined were conducive to the growth of the industry.

Clearly, the government decided to give the HCDA extraordinary powers to facilitate the rapid expansion of horticultural production. The authority has used some of these powers extensively, while to its credit, it has not used others. First, the HCDA developed a set of procedures to regulate exports. It licensed all exporters of horticultural produce, participated in the allocation of air cargo space, and has been involved in the standardization of containers. Second, in the early 1970s, the HCDA established packing stations for smallholders in different areas. Third, it helped produce and market specific crops, including macadamia nuts and onions, and involved itself in new crop trials. Fourth, it developed a market information system along with the International Trade Center, and has helped the Ministry of Agriculture meet the industry's extension and research needs. To support all these activities, the HCDA has raised funds through taxes levied on fresh horticultural exports. This has the highly favorable feature of having those who benefit most from the HCDA's services contribute directly to its operating costs. The HCDA has, however, left prices largely in the hands of the private market, thereby allowing market incentives to flourish.

The Ministry of Agriculture has also been directly involved in the growth of the horticultural sector. Its crop division has initiated various studies and developed several major projects within the industry. It has also coordinated and participated in a number of projects funded by outside institutions such as the FAO. In addition, the ministry has provided the manpower and funds for research while acting as the link between donors and institutions involved in horticultural research. Finally, as the ministry that implements government policy within the industry, it carried out the Horticultural Development Program, an in-depth study of the horticultural sector (see, for example, Ministry of Agriculture 1978), and drew up plans for the sector's development (Ministry of Agriculture 1971).

Costs and Benefits

Government expenditures within the horticultural industry have been made through the HCDA and the Ministry of Agriculture. Direct government assistance has been rather small, although the government has spent a good deal on improving the infrastructure, which has helped horticultural exports. For example, between 1968 and 1975, the important early period when the volume of fresh horticultural exports increased almost ten-fold (table 4.3), the HCDA received a total of KSh 536,700 from the government. This was supplemented by money from external sources, for example, a loan of KSh 633,000 from the International Coffee Organization. The operations of the three packaging stations established in 1970 provided the rest of the funding.

Table 4.3 Exports of Fresh Horticultural Produce, 1968-86

Year	Volume (metric tons)	Value (KSh millions)	Annual change in value (percent)
1968	1,476	3.13	–
1969	2,519	5.14	64.2
1970	3,224	6.48	26.1
1971	5,123	10.87	67.7
1972	7,856	17.11	57.4
1973	10,158	29.57	72.8
1974	11,335	33.85	14.5
1975	13,115	83.27	146.0
1976	14,719	102.34	22.9
1977	18,844	128.72	25.8
1978	21,007	159.76	24.1
1979	21,377	194.72	21.9
1980	22,266	227.06	16.6
1981	23,352	251.61	10.8
1982	24,597	272.68	8.4
1983	28,850	350.57	28.6
1984	31,298	415.86	18.6
1985	30,002	469.23	12.8
1986	36,211	630.37	34.3

Source: HCDA (various), *Economic Survey* (various issues), *Statistical Abstract* (various issues)

The private sector, both foreign and domestic, has been the main supplier of finance. While reliable data on the sources of investment funds are not available, we know something about the major budget items. Marketing costs have been held down by the link to external markets offered by foreign interests, but other costs include those associated with irrigation, seeds, fertilizers, pesticides, and other inputs. In floriculture, for example, Sheehan (1975), an FAO consultant, estimated that a minimum of KSh 50,000 per acre (fixed costs plus working capital) is necessary before the grower can expect a profit. In the case of crops that are processed (such as pineapple, mangoes, and passion fruit), the investment involved is substantially higher. Processors had to import machinery and have to maintain their factories. For these crops, much of the investment provided by foreign firms is in processing plants.

Fortunately, better data on government expenditures exist. During mid-1973 to mid-1978, out of a total budget of KSh 3,540 million, the Ministry of Agriculture allocated about KSh 840 million to horticultural production (Government of Kenya 1973). Of this amount, about 13 percent was to be spent on research, 12 percent on farm management, and 10 percent on training, with the remaining 65 percent to go to the crop production division. About 35 percent of the funds came from foreign sources. The fact that the amount allocated for the five-year period was almost one quarter of the ministry's budget demonstrates the government's commitment to expanding the horticultural sector.

Moreover, the government was also spending money through its other ministries on investments that would help the agricultural sector. These investments included expanding the road network, constructing a new airport at Nairobi, and expanding the training institutions. Thus, direct public investment in the horticultural sector represented only a small proportion of the government's total contribution.

There have also been a number of externally financed projects relating to horticulture that provided both funds and personnel. The long list of countries who have contributed bilateral assistance includes Canada, Denmark, the Federal Republic of Germany, Finland, Israel, Italy, Japan, the Netherlands, Norway, Sweden, Switzerland, and the United Kingdom. The projects have been wide ranging and include horticultural research and production, agricultural training, crop research, irrigation, water development, cooperative societies, and other assistance. (For a summary of the findings of a number of research projects see UNDP/FAO 1984.)

The central institution for the implementation of horticultural research activities is the National Horticultural Research Station, which occupies 1,350 acres at Thika, of which 200 are used for research and development activities. The Horticultural Training Center is located at the station, which also operates substations at different agroecological zones and is linked with farmer training centers throughout the country. Training personnel for research and extension services has been an important priority of the research station since the 1970s. By 1983, the station had 21 professionals, 18 technical officers, and 27 assistants. The station also conducts courses for district agricultural officers, horticultural crop officers, and managers of government nurseries run by the Department of Prisons. In addition to its research and training activities, the station distributes about 20,000 fruit plants every year.

The government contributes to the sector in a number of other ways. It is involved in the distribution of seeds through the Kenya Green Growers Union and its network of agents and through the cooperative movement. The government also runs farmer training centers in the horticultural production zones that, like the Horticultural Training Center, are equipped with various teaching aids, demonstration plots, and equipment relevant to horticulture. District horticultural specialists have used the farmer training centers to train extension workers and horticultural farmers. Fortunately, most horticultural production relies on relatively simple technology so that massive extension and demonstration programs have not been needed. Further, the quick response of farmers reacting to changes in market incentives has, in some cases (as in Asian vegetables), produced a situation where producers have led the extension services rather than the reverse.

The government plays a small but essential role in marketing. In the case of exports, many producers or their agents deliver their produce directly to the airport to be sent to their representatives abroad. However, the HCDA also collects produce from many farmers through its stations and then does the marketing. For some commodities (such as onions), the HCDA has agents both to sell in the local market and to export. In the case of flowers, almost all the produce is for export and, since they are highly perishable, deliveries are made with prior arrangements to accelerate the distribution process.

Fruits and vegetables that are not exported are usually sold in wholesale markets, especially in the urban areas. The Nairobi market, for example, handles over 80,000 metric tons of fresh produce annually, while the Mombasa wholesale market handles over 45,000 metric tons. Smaller towns have centrally located markets that handle the produce, with producers often doing the selling.

The government's role in marketing consists mainly of quality control and the dissemination of information. As noted earlier, the HCDA, helped by the International Trade Center, has an information network to advise exporters on market trends in importing countries. This information is crucial for small exporters with no other source of regular market information, although exporters with established contacts in other countries get up-to-date information on prices, demand, and competitors.

Another task of the HCDA is to oversee the allocation of cargo capacity. This important function is done by the Central Control Agency, which meets weekly during the main export season. Represented are carriers, cargo agents, charter operators, and the Ministry of Transport and Communications.

The HCDA is also responsible for preshipment inspection at the airport, both to maintain quality standards and to ensure that regulations are followed. This monitoring function is extremely important given the probability that some producers will try to sell substandard products, thereby affecting the reputation of Kenyan produce.

What have been the benefits associated with these various costs? It is natural to begin with one of the more successful parts of the horticultural sector—floriculture. Cut flower exports have expanded rapidly since 1972, and HCDA data show that they currently account for about 40 percent of the industry's export earnings. Amazingly, Kenya, a country with almost no flower exports as recently as 15 years ago (table 4.4), is currently the fourth largest exporter of flowers in the world. It is not surprising that large-scale commercial growers have been the leaders in flower production, since flowers require specialized and particularly careful culture, handling, and packaging. These are predominantly foreign-owned concerns, including a number of European growers who moved their operations to warmer climates after the oil price hikes of the early 1970s, which meant they faced larger fuel bills in the winter. Unfortunately, in making air cargo space available for flowers, other exports, such as canned pineapples and mangoes, have been allocated less space. This, presumably, is because cut flowers have the highest value to weight ratio.

The expansion of floriculture, and of horticultural production in general, took place largely because of the response of private producers and exporters to market opportunities, made more attractive by government promotion. The government recognized that the conditions were ripe for a major expansion of the horticultural sector, and then set out to facilitate its growth. The government program reinforced private incentives, and the limited government involvement probably helped these largely private enterprises to prosper. As production and export figures show, the industry took off after 1970 and has continued to expand year after year.

Table 4.4 Cut Flower Exports, 1972-86

Year	Volume (metric tons)	Value (KSh millions)
1972	458	6.6
1973	1,096	14.6
1974	1,299	31.9
1975	2,746	65.0
1976	3,561	72.3
1977	2,757	71.8
1978	3,214	64.4
1979	4,223	71.1
1980	3,499	60.0
1981	4,068	55.0
1982	4,194	69.8
1983	5,232	111.9
1984	6,941	128.6
1985	6,682	132.5
1986	8,164	204.5

Source: Annual Trade Reports (various issues).

Note: These data, based on customs reports, differ somewhat from the HCDA data used in tables 4.1, 4.2, 4.3. HCDA data on cut flower exports for the most recent years are as follows:

1983	5,209	145.9
1984	6,961	174.0
1985	7,474	209.3
1986	8,265	248.0

Furthermore, the range of products has increased, while the composition of exports has changed along with relative market prices. For example, while pineapples, eggplants, french beans, chilies, mangoes, courgettes, avocados, and okra were the main nonflower fresh produce exports (by volume) in 1972, the order in 1983 was french beans, eggplants, chilies, okra, mangoes, courgettes, pineapples, avocados, and bitter melons. Thus, several of the major horticultural exports in 1983, such as okra, had been much less important a decade earlier, while some previously important products, such as pineapples, became less important. Data from 1986 show that french beans now dominate nonflower fresh produce exports, accounting for about one third of the total volume.

The area under horticultural production has also increased. The *Farmers Voice* (1987) estimates that 216,000 hectares, or 4.1 percent of Kenya's arable land, are currently being used in horticultural production. Of this land, 50 percent is planted with fruit trees and plants, 37 percent is used for vegetables, and 13 percent for nuts. As has been observed, a number of large commercial enterprises have been and continue to be active in horticultural production, but the more recent increases in horticultural production have largely been due to increased smallholder output. While exact figures are not known, most horticultural production is grown using small-scale irrigation systems or rainfed methods on small to medium size holdings.

Flower production continues to be centered in the highlands around Nairobi where access to the airport is easy, but some expansion to other areas has occurred. While cultivators are growing more than 50 varieties on plots that range from under 10 acres to well over 100 acres, much of the total production comes from large estates. However, large tracts of land are certainly not mandatory. Experts consider five to ten acres adequate given that flower production, while requiring a lot of inputs, yields high returns. Within the horticultural sector, the minimum viable farm size varies substantially. Crops that need the greatest amount of land are cashew nuts, pineapples, macadamia nuts, and citrus fruits.

How far has the growth of the horticultural sector met the goals outlined earlier? To begin with, it has generated considerable employment. The HCDA estimates that vegetable cultivation requires approximately two man-years per hectare, fruits use about 66 percent of a man-year, and nuts use about 4 percent. Processing firms have created both permanent and temporary jobs. The *Farmers Voice* (1987) reports that Kenya Canners, a large-scale enterprise, employs over 1,900 people in its factory and more than 3,000 on its plantation. Other large enterprises include Sulmac's 2,000-hectare carnation farm at Naivasha (the largest in the world), which employs over 3,000 people (*African Farming and Food Processing* 1986).

Little information on the income generated through horticultural production exists, but the indications suggest a relatively high rate of return at the producer level—not a surprising fact given the significant response of farmers who have reacted to market incentives by entering the horticultural sector. In terms of income per hectare, HCDA data indicate that vegetables and potatoes yield a return of KSh 22,240 per hectare, fruits return KSh 920 per hectare, and nuts return KSh 3,240 per hectare. Sheehan (1975) estimates that in floriculture, a minimum investment of KSh 50,000 per acre yields a minimum return of 20 percent. The HCDA estimates that the total income for horticultural production is about 12 percent of the value of Kenya's total agricultural production.

An important aspect of the expansion in horticultural production is that it has not displaced coffee or tea. The Government of Kenya (1986) even argues that there is still room for increased production in all three areas. Many large-scale commercial enterprises involved in horticulture have operated in semimarginal areas with irrigation systems providing the water, while many small landholders with underutilized land have embarked on horticultural production to supplement their other sources of income. Thus, as the government hoped, this type of farm activity has led to greater utilization of land, along with increased agricultural productivity.

Evaluating whether another goal, improved nutrition, has also been realized is difficult. However, the bulk of horticultural produce continues to be consumed locally. In 1983, 809,000 metric tons of horticultural crops were grown, with 724,000 metric tons—almost 90 percent—consumed domestically (Government of Kenya 1986). Horticultural produce is increasingly becoming part of the Kenyan diet, not only in the major urban areas, but in rural areas as well. This trend should continue as the government expects horticultural production to expand more rapidly than agriculture overall, with a 6.0 percent versus 5.1 percent projected annual growth rate during the remainder of the century (Government of Kenya 1986). The government also expects that local consumption will grow by 5.6 percent per year while exports grow by 8.7 percent. Moreover, the employment and income effects noted above imply an increase in consumption of foodstuffs in general, presumably improving the population's basic nutrition, especially that of small landholders.

In terms of exports, the sector's performance has been remarkable. During 1968-86, the volume of fresh horticulture produce exports rose almost 25-fold. The market for this produce has also diversified, although the United Kingdom continues to be the main destination (table 4.5). In 1983, over 50 percent of exports went to the United

Table 4.5 Amount and Destination of Kenyan Fresh Horticultural Produce, 1983 and 1986
(percent)

Country	1983	1986
United Kingdom	51.5	43.7
Federal Republic of Germany	14.2	13.9
France	11.2	13.1
Netherlands	7.0	12.6
Belgium	4.7	4.7
Switzerland	2.4	2.3
Saudi Arabia	2.4	5.3
Djibouti	1.9	1.1
United Arab Emirates	0.6	0.7
Seychelles	0.6	0.4
United States	0.6	0.4

Note: The percentages are based on volume.
Source: HCDA (1984, 1987)

Kingdom, with the Federal Republic of Germany and France far behind in second and third place, respectively. In 1986, the share for the United Kingdom fell to under 44 percent, while the Netherlands and Saudi Arabia each had a major increase in their share of Kenyan horticultural exports. Exports now go to about 30 countries, with the Middle East becoming an increasingly important market. Shipping fresh produce to this region by sea began in 1985 on a trial basis, and if this becomes a regular practice, the goal of exporting 45,000 metric tons of fresh produce annually by 1992 will be achieved.

Again, floriculture represents the most dynamic part of the horticultural sector. Trade data show that while Kenya exported only 458 metric tons of cut flowers in 1972, this increased to 8,164 metric tons in 1986 as cut flowers became the leading earner among air freighted horticultural exports. The value of cut flowers exported in 1972 was under KSh 7 million, rising to over KSh 204 million in 1986. The Federal Republic of Germany imports over 80 percent of the total, followed by the Netherlands and the United Kingdom. As more countries import Kenyan cut flowers, and as Kenya grows a greater variety of flowers, it is likely to start exporting year round (not mainly during September through May as is currently the case), thus increasing further the volume of annual exports.

Future Prospects

The remarkable growth of the horticultural sector has not occurred without problems, and the pace of continued expansion depends, in large part, on their successful resolution.

One problem concerns the transport of horticultural produce. Air cargo space is in short supply even though the government obligates all airlines stopping in Nairobi to reserve 20 percent of their holds for Kenyan exports and to charge a relatively low freight rate. If Kenya continues to rely on regularly scheduled passenger flights while the supply of horticultural exports continues to grow, air cargo space could become a critical bottleneck. One major worry is that erratic, unforeseen space shortages could leave large amounts of produce to rot in storage. Further, the availability of space may actually fall if the number of south bound flights beyond Nairobi decreases, meaning less returning cargo space for exports bound for Europe. Thus, for continued expansion of the industry, a greater use of cargo charters is called for.

The difficulties in arranging for cargo space are aggravated by the problems inherent in the sea freighting of fresh produce (a common practice for horticultural exports from Israel and South Africa), despite the experiment with exports to the Gulf region. Currently, Kenya has neither regular shipping services nor the facilities needed to transport fruits and vegetables. If the Middle East experiment succeeds, the Kenyan government will no doubt attempt to rectify this situation.

The transportation of horticultural produce is also a problem within Kenya. The road network needs improvement and more refrigerated vehicles are needed.

Another problem relates to the provision of quality inputs, particularly for small-scale producers. Too often farmers use seeds from their own harvests rather than special high quality seeds from nurseries, leading ultimately to lower quality produce. Furthermore, some private nurseries sell fruit plants of inferior quality, which has led to reduced yields. Government efforts to provide inputs have kept problems of this type to a minimum, although some small landholders have been unable to borrow the necessary working capital to purchase inputs as horticulture crops do not qualify for the government's agricultural integrated loan schemes. In addition, horticultural produce exporters are treated differently from some other agricultural exporters in that they are not eligible to receive export compensation from the government. Given these disadvantages, the success of the horticultural sector is even more impressive.

Processing firms have had their own problems and have often operated well below capacity. This results, in part, from unreliable sources of supply.

There have also been serious problems with packaging and handling. High grade handling and packaging of fruits, flowers, and vegetables is essential to ensure that these highly perishable products reach their destinations in acceptable condition. The lack of suitable packaging materials has at times been a major bottleneck. Handling techniques must also be improved to help ensure that Kenya remains competitive in world markets. This is particularly true for flowers, since the recent fall in energy prices could mean more vigorous foreign competition, particularly from greenhouses in Europe and North America. About 25 percent of all produce is currently wasted as a result of poor packing and handling, as well as inadequate storage and preservation facilities (see Njuguna 1985).

In the domestic market, a study of major urban areas—Nairobi, Mombasa, and Kisumu—found that wholesale markets' facilities for handling horticultural produce are completely inadequate (Ministry of Agriculture 1979). Complaints include insufficient storage and preservation facilities and overcrowding. Although some of the study's suggestions have been acted upon, the overall situation remains much the same.

Another problem is the lack of personnel to do research and to provide extension services to the farmers. Despite continuing efforts to train researchers, technicians, and assistants, the supply has not been able to keep pace with the demands created by this rapidly growing industry. The shortages have not been limited to personnel. The National Horticultural Research Station lacks adequate irrigation facilities, greenhouses, and the screening facilities necessary for studying disease control.

The problems have been particularly acute in the case of flowers. Despite the lack of trained floriculture personnel to provide extension services, no floriculture training or research is currently underway in Kenya. Airport inspection is also poor—only 2 percent of all flower exports are inspected. In addition, the airport has limited storage facilities for when planes are delayed (Sulmac recently opened its own cold storage area at the Nairobi airport). Finally, flower growers around Nairobi face severe labor shortages, especially when the harvesting of flowers coincides with coffee picking. The coastal area also has the problem of a lack of water, particularly in times of extended drought.

The HCDA has done a commendable job in addressing many of these problems, but it has clearly been stretched to its limits. Funding and personnel constraints have adversely affected its ability to carry out its production, marketing, and regulatory functions. Modest increases in government support should enable the HCDA to continue to promote the growth of the horticultural sector in a productive and successful manner.

Conclusions and Lessons Learned

The growing of horticultural produce is practiced elsewhere in Africa and throughout the developing world. Almost all countries grow some vegetables and fruits for local consumption, and in many cases have some available for export. What is unusual about Kenya is the successful expansion of this sector to permit large-scale export of a wide variety of fruits, vegetables, and cut flowers.

The number of developing countries enjoying more limited success is growing. The Côte d'Ivoire exports pineapples and cut flowers, and has even surpassed Kenya in its export of flower plants. Ethiopia exports peppers and melons. Zambia also exports melons as well as cut flowers, while Morocco exports courgettes along with several varieties of flowers. In Latin America, Brazil, Colombia, and Guatemala, among others, sell flowers. Can these countries expand their horticultural production? Can other developing countries also produce and export these products? In short, which aspects of the Kenyan experience are transferable?

While Kenya's climate and geography worked in its favor, these advantages are not unique. The level of development of Kenya's infrastructure is also not extraordinary. However, the combination of factors is fortuitous. Political stability and the availability of markets, investors, labor, and air transport service all help to explain the relative success of Kenya's horticultural program. However, it is the way that the program has been made to work that may be the biggest key to its success, and of the greatest interest to other developing countries.

In terms of horticultural production, it is possible that some countries could achieve greater success, but far more could benefit from the lessons learned from the role played by the Kenyan government. After identifying certain needs and examining various possibilities, the government selected the horticultural sector as an important area of concern. Most experts believe that the HCDA, the major government agency responsible for the horticultural sector, played a critical role in the industry's development (*Kenya Farmer* 1985). Its important contributions include providing market information, controlling quality with input supply and preshipment inspections, and advising farmers. The government oversaw the sector's growth as a facilitator and coordinator, but relied on private incentives that it encouraged by various means. In this manner, it stayed on the sidelines while foreign and local concerns led the way.

In sum, government sponsored research, training, monitoring, and other activities facilitated the expansion of the horticultural sector. However, it is what the government did not do—create a large bureaucratic structure and interfere to a significant extent with the market mechanism—that is the most impressive. Without this combination of government assistance and government restraint, it is highly unlikely that the expansion in horticultural exports would have been rapid or as large.

References

African Farming and Food Processing. 1986. November/December.

Carroll, Jane. 1985. "Horticultural Exports." Kenya Profile. *Africa Review.*

Economic Survey. Various issues. Nairobi: Central Bureau of Statistics.

Farmers Voice. 1987. Vol. 3, No. 2. February.

Government of Kenya. 1973. *Development Plan 1974-78, Part II.* Nairobi: Government of Kenya.

Government of Kenya. 1986. *Economic Management for Renewed Growth.* Sessional Paper No. 1. Nairobi: Government of Kenya.

Horticultural Crops Development Authority. Various, 1984, 1987. Nairobi: Horticultural Crops Development Authority.

Kenya Farmer. 1985. No. 48. July.

Ministry of Agriculture. 1971. *Horticultural Development Plan 1972/73-1978.* Nairobi: Government of Kenya.

Ministry of Agriculture. 1978. *First Phase Report on Horticultural Development Study.* Vol. 1, *Main Report and Summary.* Nairobi: Government of Kenya.

Ministry of Agriculture. 1979. *Wholesale Market Feasibility Studies.* Vol. 1, *(Executive Summary), Horticultural Development Studies.* Nairobi: Government of Kenya.

Ministry of Agriculture. 1981. *National Horticultural Policy.* Nairobi: Government of Kenya. December.

Njuguna, S. K. 1985. *Some Observations of Packaging of Fresh Horticultural Produce.* Thika: National Horticultural Research Station.

Sheehan, T. J. 1975. *Floriculture Potential in Kenya.* Nairobi: FAO. January.

Statistical Abstract. Various issues. Nairobi: Central Bureau of Statistics.

UNDP/FAO. 1984. *Horticultural Research and Development: Kenya, Project Findings and Recommendations.* Rome: FAO.

Part II. Macro Studies

5

Mauritius: A Case Study of the Export Processing Zone

Rundheersing Bheenick, Ministry of Economic Planning and Development, Mauritius
Morton Owen Schapiro, Department of Economics, Williams College

In December 1970, the Mauritian parliament passed the Export Processing Zones Act, which provided the legal framework for the formation of an export processing zone (EPZ). This legislation was aimed at luring foreign investors to the island using fiscal concessions and other incentives to establish export processing activities. The goal was to create jobs, to provide opportunities for local capital, and to promote economic development in general.

The EPZ has achieved what other sectors of the economy had been unable to realize in decades despite concentrated efforts and injections of an appreciable amount of investment and other resources. In short, the export processing sector's performance in terms of growth in employment, output, and gross export earnings has been remarkable.

This study describes the Mauritian attempt at export-led industrialization and highlights the conditions needed for the successful implementation and operation of an EPZ. It emphasizes the requirement for an appropriate policy framework within which an EPZ scheme should function and the effort required by government policymakers to understand the intricacies of this approach to industrial development. The aim is to shed light on a number of issues that policymakers must address in designing an EPZ scheme, but equally important, we believe, are the lessons learned from the role that the Mauritian government played in promoting its objectives. These lessons may be transferable even where the particular export promotion program is not.

Background

The Mauritian EPZ originated with the publication in July 1970 of the government's intention to create an export processing zone on the island. At this time, the government gave details of how it would operate the zone and the incentives it would offer to investors, both overseas and local. Six months later, the Mauritian parliament approved the EPZ Act.

Obviously, this simple review does not explain the whole story. It overlooks the factors that obliged the authorities to shift their preference from an import-substitution industrial development option to a radical alternative. It also ignores

The authors would like to thank Mr. A. H. Nakhuda, Principal Economist of the Ministry of Economic Planning and Development, Mauritius, for his valuable help.

the fact that back in 1961, a report to the Government of Mauritius stressed the urgent need for Mauritius to diversify its economy.

In this famous publication (Meade et al. 1961), widely known as the Meade Report, the authors drew attention to the dangers that unchecked population growth posed to Mauritius. In effect, the elimination of malaria in the years immediately following World War II and improvements in public health had altered the balance between births and deaths. Population growth, which had been about 0.5 percent per year before World War II, had risen to about 3 percent per year by the late 1950s. This led the report's authors to observe that:

> This demographic revolution is very sudden and very recent, and as a result of it the rate of increase of the Mauritian population has become one of the highest in the world. Recent calculations suggest that, if fertility rates remain at their present high level and if at the same time the progress of medicine and of public health in Mauritius bring mortality rates down to levels comparable with those in medically advanced communities, the population of the island will rise from its present 600,000 to no less than 3,000,000 by the end of the century (Republished 1968 version of the report, p. 3.)

A population explosion of that magnitude would have large-scale economic and social effects. For example, the working age population (aged 15 years and over) was projected to increase by some 50 percent during 1957-72; a situation that would present Mauritius, then exclusively dependent on sugar to provide employment and output growth, with a bleak prospect. Population control could provide some hope, but while family planning can decrease the size of families in the future given sufficient motivation to restrict fertility, it offers no help for those already born who would soon be seeking employment. The Meade Report recognized the limitations of the sugar industry to generate additional jobs:

> One cannot rely upon the sugar industry to provide any substantial volume of increased employment, and other agriculture is likely to provide employment for only a strictly limited, if appreciable, labour force. It is, therefore, to the institution and expansion of manufactures that one must turn to seek productive employment for substantial numbers. (p. 25)

But even industrial expansion was not without problems. The lack of raw materials, the small size of the domestic market, the lack of financial institutions, and the dearth of technical knowhow in manufacturing all presented a formidable challenge to any large-scale manufacturing venture. The report, in full cognizance of these handicaps (particularly the first two), emphasized the need to increase manufacturing for export, something tried with some success in countries such as Jamaica and Hong Kong. Yet, despite the report, the government did not come to an explicit decision in favor of export-based industrialization.

Meanwhile, the gloomy predictions—intolerable unemployment levels, slow economic growth associated with the country's reliance on sugar for 99 percent of its export receipts, and so on—began to come true. The government reacted by introducing, in 1963, a series of incentives and concessions under the Development Certificate Scheme to encourage import-substitution industries. The domestic environment had greatly improved by 1963 as a result of a record sugar crop and higher prices, and was therefore conducive to new investment. Thus, it was no surprise that the private sector responded positively to the concessions offered by the government.

The Development Certificate Scheme achieved a measure of success in transforming the traditionally cautious Mauritian business community into one that took greater risks, and a number of new manufacturing units emerged on the country's industrial scene. These basically catered to the local market by producing products ranging from packaging materials to chemical fertilizers. The private sector owned and operated almost all the manufacturing industries (the two exceptions being the now defunct sack factory and a livestock feed factory, where direct public investment was involved).

A major stimulus to the Development Certificate Scheme came from the Development Bank of Mauritius. Formerly an agricultural bank, it was converted in 1964 into a development finance institution for the agricultural, industrial, and tourism sectors. Between 1964 and 1970, the bank sanctioned 111 loans and 8 equity investments with a total value of Rs. 32 million (approximately US$5.75 million) for medium- and large-scale industrial projects. The bank emerged as the principal institutional source of term finance and became a significant motivating force behind the establishment of new manufacturing units.

By the late 1960s, however, opportunities for import substitution began to dry up, with the more profitable activities already exploited. The small size of the Mauritian market prevented the realization of the economic benefits generally associated with economies of scale, especially since most Development Certificate firms were unable to compete in export markets due to the high rate of effective protection that had rendered most of them inefficient. Further, value added was low in many cases owing to the lack of local raw materials, while the employment impact was far less than the government had hoped. It was clear that the import substitution strategy held little promise for solving an unemployment problem that had begun to reach alarming proportions (table 5.1). While a government sponsored "relief work" program provided employment for over 30,000 workers in 1976, the resulting fiscal drain along with a limited increase in output made this little more than a stopgap policy.

Table 5.1 Registered Unemployed and Relief Workers, 1965-70

Year	Number of registered unemployed	Number of relief workers	Total	Total as a percentage of working age population
1965	7,795	7,755	15,550	n.a.
1966	12,283	19,137	31,420	n.a.
1967	8,666	31,228	39,894	9.7
1968	8,127	14,777	22,904	5.4
1969	13,274	13,674	26,948	6.2
1970	19,754	16,094	35,848	8.0

n.a. = not available

Note: Relief workers were temporary employees employed by the government on a four-day week basis. The working age population consists of everyone 15 years and over.

Source: Central Statistical Office, Mauritius

By the late 1960s, the political situation in Mauritius had changed as the country achieved independence in March 1968. This followed an intense debate about the advisability of Mauritius gaining full autonomy from the United Kingdom. Dismal economic prospects had raised serious questions about the nation's ability to survive without external aid. In the face of these prospects and of the large-scale outmigration of Mauritians immediately following independence, the new Mauritian government was determined to usher the country into an era of economic prosperity and development.

The new government faced some major challenges. The late 1960s were characterized by relatively slow economic growth: the GDP grew at an annual average of less than 4.5 percent during 1965-69, and fell in two of these years (table 5.2). In addition, unemployment grew substantially as the labor force was increasing at almost twice the rate of population increase, a direct consequence of the high fertility rates of the 1940s and 1950s (table 5.3). Although the country's dependence on sugar to balance its external payments position was less than earlier, it was still considerable: this sector accounted for 16 percent of GDP in 1970 compared to 34 percent in 1959. In short, forecasts of the future continued to be depressing.

Table 5.2 Gross Domestic Product at Current Factor Cost, 1965-70

Year	GDP at current factor cost (Rs. millions)	Percentage change
1965	823	+8.2
1966	805	-2.2
1967	856	+6.3
1968	841	-1.8
1969	903	+7.4
1970	1,017	+12.6

Note: Figures for 1970 are not strictly comparable with those for the preceding years because of a change in the accounting methodology used.
Source: National Accounts of the Central Statistical Office, Mauritius

Table 5.3 Crude Birth and Death Rates, 1946-60

Year	Crude birth rate (births/1,000 of population)	Crude death rate (deaths/1,000 of population)	Rate of natural increase (crude birth rate minus crude death rate)
1946-50 (average)	44.7	20.8	23.9
1951-55 (average)	44.3	14.7	29.6
1956	43.3	11.7	31.6
1957	42.6	12.8	29.8
1958	40.4	11.7	28.7
1959	38.1	10.8	27.3
1960	39.3	11.2	28.1

Source: Central Statistical Office, Mauritius

It was becoming increasingly apparent that the solution was to expand the economic base by widening the role of the manufacturing sector and exploiting the potential of tourism, which had, up to this point, remained untapped. The import-replacement strategy followed from 1963 to 1969 was clearly not a viable option in the long run, although it served the valuable function of creating a new dynamism in the country, enabling Mauritian industrialists to acquire experience and a new industrial culture to take root. The need now was to build on this experience by adopting a completely new approach to industrial planning.

Hong Kong, Jamaica, Puerto Rico, Singapore, and Taiwan, where conditions were similar to those in Mauritius, provided examples of what could be done to overcome the handicaps posed by a small population and a lack of raw materials. The government's first step, therefore, was to send a team to study industrial development in these and other nations where manufacturing was export oriented and where free zones were in operation. Based on the team's report, the government announced its intention in July 1970 to create an export processing zone on the island. The Export Processing Zones Act followed in December of the same year as Mauritius embarked on an entirely new form of manufacturing activity—the processing of imported raw materials into finished goods for export—and selected an industrial development option that it would pursue in the years to come.

Establishment of the Export Processing Zone

The particulars of the new scheme were subject to debate, especially its timing. There were two schools of thought on this issue (Arouff 1973). One favored creating the necessary infrastructure before proceeding with what appeared to be a revolutionary move. The other argued that the creation of new jobs was urgent and that the country could not afford any delay. The latter group stressed that the existing infrastructure was already adequate and preferred offering foreign investors benefits that would compensate for any infrastructural weaknesses. The island already had an adequate road network, electricity supply and water availability were good, telecommunications facilities were adequate, and factory space in Plaine Lauzun (close to the capital, Port Louis) was waiting to be occupied. Furthermore, labor was plentiful, fairly literate, and easily adaptable, and wage rates were highly competitive compared to those in most other countries. Hence, it is not surprising that the export promotion scheme proceeded without delay.

The idea was simple: to provide a package of fiscal concessions and other benefits that would lure overseas manufacturing firms with established markets to locate the labor-intensive part of their activities in Mauritius. The incentive package would include a tax holiday, the option to repatriate profits, and duty exemptions on imports of machinery, equipment, and raw materials. (The precise package of incentives is described in the annex.)

At this point, many economists would likely shudder at the thought of special treatment afforded to EPZ firms. Would this not create major price distortions resulting in a gross misallocation of resources? The view of the Mauritian government was that these distortions were necessary, at least in the short run. Without fiscal incentives of the type described above, the export promotion plan would undoubtedly fail. As described later, the government eventually sought to rectify the problems associated with discriminatory tax treatment. At the same time, however, the import substitution factories also had special treatment in the form of high effective rates of protection. Thus, the distortions implicit in the creation of the EPZ have to be compared with the existing distortions that were an important part of the other industrial sectors. The consensus was that the benefits from preferential treatment of EPZ firms would have a greater payoff in foreign exchange earnings, employment, and so on.

The government decided that the EPZ was not to be a geographically restricted free zone. A limited zone would have called for additional investment in factory buildings that would have postponed the implementation of the scheme to a much later date. Instead, EPZs were defined in the most general terms as any area of land on which an eligible factory had been, is being, or is likely to be built. These "bonded factories" were to enjoy all the advantages normally granted to enterprises in a geographically limited zone, while offering potential investors the choice of locating their plants in places best suited to the nature of their industrial activities (from the points of view of climate and the availability of labor, water, electricity, and transport).

The EPZ Act clearly delineated the legal framework within which export units were to operate. It laid down rules governing the activities of bonded factories, prescribed conditions for the issue of an Export Enterprise Certificate, defined export products, and indicated the duty relief to which export enterprises were entitled. A good deal of effort went into distinguishing among EPZ factories, those with Development Certificates, and other enterprises, such as those involved in sugar production and processing. The benefits accruing to EPZ firms were not to be generalized to other firms since these concessions were made for a specific reason: to attract foreign capital. Hence, providing a long-term tax holiday for, say, a sugar manufacturer, would not serve any useful purpose and would deny the government-needed tax revenues. Of course, as mentioned above, discriminatory tax treatment threatens to lead to a misallocation of resources; a problem that did arise and that the government eventually dealt with.

The next step in the drive to stimulate foreign investment in eligible industrial ventures was to put in place the requisite administrative machinery and to introduce suitable institutional reforms, including creating new organizations to support the industrial development strategy and to ensure that viable investment proposals took the least possible time to translate into factories and goods-producing plants.

The government found, however, that providing the institutional and administrative support for the scheme was a formidable challenge. The task warranted a reorganization of the government, in particular, of the Ministry of Commerce and Industry, the agency responsible for the industrial reform. Suitable mechanisms to meet the funding requirements of the export sector and to provide insurance to protect exporters against defaults by importers were equally critical. Moreover, action was needed to penetrate new markets, find profitable niches, and to make Mauritian products known to overseas buyers. In brief, a host of measures were called for to support the export-led industrialization. The existing machinery was designed to meet the requirements of an inward oriented trade policy where international competition mattered little, and could be tackled by bringing about desired changes and refinements in the domestic trade and tariff regime. It was totally unsuited to deal with the stiff competition that characterizes export trade.

Institutional strengthening and reform began with the restructuring of the Ministry of Commerce and Industry. Expert services were secured under bilateral and multilateral technical assistance programs to make up for skill shortages within the agency and to bolster its staff strength. In addition, new cells were created to reinforce the ministry's capacity for project evaluation, monitoring, investment promotion, and export marketing.

Investment capital was already available from the Development Bank of Mauritius, while commercial banks were active in the provision of working capital within the limits authorized by the Bank of Mauritius for foreign-controlled companies registered in the country. Commercial banks were also involved in the provision of term loans, either on their own, or jointly with the Development Bank of Mauritius when the size of the loan entailed consortium lending. A fortuitous coincidence during the first half of the 1970s was the record sugar crop—718,000 tons in 1973—and a remarkable surge in sugar prices from 1970 to 1974 of over 20-fold. Investment funds became plentiful and the balance of payments situation improved considerably. Thus, EPZ enterprises were able to benefit from a generous allocation of foreign exchange for the importation of raw materials, machinery, and equipment.

Attracting foreign investment was obviously crucial to the success of the EPZ scheme. It required introducing Mauritius to overseas industrialists and apprising them of the benefits contained in the package of incentives and other concessions. The government set out to do this by mounting a coordinated promotional campaign comprising (a) the dissemination of information on the Mauritian EPZ and the incentive package through brochures, articles in newspapers and trade magazines, displays at trade and industrial fairs, and talks by officials working in Mauritian overseas missions; (b) the organization of seminars for business people, industrialists, and potential investors; (c) direct approaches to individual organizations; and (d) the organization of visits to Mauritius by selected entrepreneurs and representatives of private investment organizations.

At the same time, the Mauritian authorities appointed foreign consulting firms, paid for with funds provided by overseas aid programs, to carry out investment promotion work. However, with a few exceptions, the consultants' performance was below expectations, probably, in part, because payment for services was not linked to the amount of investment brought to the country. Eventually, the government decided to dispense with the services of private consultants and to assume total responsibility for promotion abroad.

Mauritian authorities then intensified their efforts to expand existing markets and to open up new outlets. Although as a signatory to the Yaoundé and, subsequently, Lomé conventions, Mauritius enjoys duty free access for its manufactures to the EEC countries, the government was fully conscious of the risk associated with heavy dependence on a few markets. It therefore undertook an all out effort to explore new market niches in North America and the Middle East. A Foreign Trade Division was created within the Ministry of Commerce and Industry responsible for locating new markets and monitoring export trends to ensure that a too rapid expansion of exports would not engender demands from importing countries for import restrictions or lead them to impose quotas.

With the passage of time and as the authorities acquired experience with implementing the EPZ scheme, the need for further institutional and policy reform became evident. The international economic environment had been adversely affected by the two oil price hikes and the general recession in the industrialized countries, which were the providers of export markets and investment for the EPZ. Moreover, competition from export processing zones in other developing countries was increasing. On the domestic front, cyclones and floods disrupted water and electricity supplies during the late 1970s. Also, generous wage awards, which had been granted with retroactive effect while production in the manufacturing sector was adversely affected by work stoppages and slowdowns by workers in the port and transport industries, resulted in a sudden, substantial rise in real labor costs.

Finally, the political climate deteriorated with the approach of elections in 1982, and the general air of instability made potential investors reluctant to commit new investment in the EPZ, which had been under some attack by the opposition.

The authorities recognized that they needed a new set of institutions and incentives to maintain the EPZ's viability and inherent attractiveness. Their response to the EPZ's deteriorating performance in the late 1970s and the early 1980s was two-fold: to reorganize and reinforce the existing institutions while also setting up new ones, and to modify the incentive structure.

In terms of institutional reform, the government's first action was to separate the responsibility for industry and commerce by setting up a new Ministry of Industry so that industrial development received the attention it deserved. The government commissioned studies to review the industrial sector, with particular reference to possibilities for further development of investment and export promotion capability within the public domain. These studies pointed to the need for streamlining administrative procedures for processing and approving applications for Export Enterprise Certificates so that investors no longer had to go from one agency to another for various clearances and licenses. The studies also recommended a separate organization to carry out investment and export promotion in a manner that would contribute to export-led industrial development.

In line with these proposals, the authorities set up an Industrial Coordination Unit within the newly created Ministry of Industry, primarily for streamlining application procedures for Development, Export Enterprise, and Export Service certificates.[1] The Industrial Coordination Unit was also to act as a "one-stop-shop" where all facilities would be available to would-be investors. In 1984, the Mauritius Export Development and Investment Authority (MEDIA) Act was passed, establishing MEDIA as "a body corporate" with executive and advisory functions. MEDIA's principal objectives are (a) to promote the export of goods and services from Mauritius; (b) to engage in investment promotion activities designed to promote Mauritius as an attractive base for the establishment of manufacturing industries and services with special emphasis on those that are export oriented; (c) to develop and operate industrial sites and estates; and (d) to plan, implement, and review programs to develop exports and investment in export oriented manufacturing.

By the end of 1986, MEDIA had engaged in both investment and export oriented promotional activities. The government established a MEDIA office in London for investment promotion activities in Europe. The authority fielded several high-level missions for promotional tasks, and organized "Mauritian Weeks" to draw the attention of business interests to the variety and range of industrial products manufactured in Mauritius. MEDIA also became involved in industrial park development to meet the mounting demand for factory space.

With regard to the incentive structure, in July 1980, the government amended the Income Tax Act of 1974 to extend the tax holiday for export enterprises beyond the first ten years of operation. Under the new legislation, from the 11th to the 15th year of operation, 50 percent of profits would be exempt from tax liability, while from the

1. The Export Service Zones Scheme was set up in 1981 to encourage the establishment of export oriented service enterprises. The benefits available under the scheme are (a) exemption from the payment of income tax on dividends for the first ten years; (b) free repatriation of capital (excluding capital appreciation) and remittance abroad of profits and dividends with the approval of the Bank of Mauritius, and (c) complete exemption from payment of duty on machinery, equipment, spare parts, and goods for re-export.

16th to the 20th year, 25 percent would be tax free. The amendment also provided for the tax exemption of dividends paid out during the first five consecutive years after the enterprise decides to pay dividends to its shareholders, provided that the five consecutive years are within the first ten years of operation of the enterprise.

Gradually, it became clear that even this fiscal reform was inadequate because it provided for benefits that were limited in time. The weakness of the fixed tax holiday period was that after its expiration enterprises faced the full impact of the corporate tax, which often led them to close down and form new companies to carry out the same activities without forgoing the full fiscal benefits of an EPZ unit. This favored those enterprises yielding quick profits, but penalized those that were profitable only in the long term. It also discouraged "production-deepening" activities while encouraging enterprises that concentrated on the latter stages of the production line where value added was smaller. Another result was that firms used fringe benefits and company services to provide free income to management, while reducing taxable profits by showing company services as a cost rather than as a distribution of dividends.

Another problem was that over the years, different tax regimes had evolved to cater to the specific needs of agriculture, industry, and tourism. Until July 1985, the sectors had enjoyed varied corporate tax benefits under separate schemes (Minister of Finance 1985): an EPZ company enjoyed complete tax exemption for the first 10 years and was taxable at half the normal rate during years 11 to 15 and a quarter of the rate during years 16 to 20, while dividends were tax free for any consecutive 5 years during the first 10 years; a company holding an Export Service Certificate paid corporate tax at a rate of 10 percent and enjoyed the same dividend concessions as an EPZ company; under the Hotel Management (Incentives) Scheme,[2] hotel companies got a partial tax holiday for 15 years, with the rate of corporate tax for the first 8 years being 10 percent, rising to 15 percent for the subsequent 7 years; and, finally, a company with a Development Certificate or Agricultural Development Certificate enjoyed a corporate tax holiday for 5 to 8 years with an exemption from payment of income tax on dividends similar to that of an EPZ company.

These tax regimes were framed under varied economic circumstances, with the result that at the same time at least four widely differing tax rates were in effect for various sectors of the economy. Discriminatory tax treatment threatened to distort resource allocation between sectors, in particular, between the Development Certificate and EPZ firms. This provided strong incentives for the government to enact a system of uniform tax treatment across all sectors. It therefore announced the following measures in the 1985/86 budget: (a) all companies holding an Export Enterprise, Export Service, Development, Hotel Management Scheme, or Agricultural Development certificate would henceforth pay corporate tax at the rate of 15 percent during the life of the company—this new system would apply to all new companies, but existing ones would have the option to select either the old or new tax regime; and (b) dividends paid by companies holding any of the certificates would be exempt from income tax for a period of ten years from the beginning of production.

---

2. The Hotel Management (Incentives) Scheme of 1982 was designed to attract, promote, and provide specialized managerial and marketing services in the hotel industry. Under the scheme, a Hotel Management Service Certificate is issued to any company that proposes to provide specialized managerial and marketing services in either a new hotel or in an existing hotel complex to which new rooms are added.

At the same time, the government introduced an additional tax reform to stimulate exports by import-substitution enterprises. A year earlier, the 1984/85 budget had introduced a graduated tax reduction of 2 percent for every 10 percent of turnover exported, with a maximum tax reduction of 10 percent. In the 1985/86 budget, the authorities removed the 10 percent ceiling. Therefore, a company exporting 100 percent of its turnover would get a 20 percent tax rebate and would pay tax at the nominal rate of 15 percent. Exporters of traditional products (sugar, tea, and molasses) were excluded from this measure.

In addition, in a move designed to mobilize resources from small savers for investment in the industrial, tourist, and nonsugar agricultural sectors, the government raised the investment tax credit from 20 percent of the amount paid in cash to 30 percent. The value of the credit is spread over three consecutive years.

To eliminate the risk of double taxation, a potential disincentive for investment in Mauritius, the authorities negotiated double taxation agreements with those countries that have been the traditional sources of investment funds. Mauritius has signed agreements with France, the United Kingdom, the Federal Republic of Germany, and India.

More recently, fiscal incentives have been introduced for private individuals for the construction of factory buildings with at least 1,000 square meters. The Industrial Buildings Investment Scheme is aimed at raising the island's overall factory capacity and encouraging private initiative in an industrial building sector that has been dominated by public sector institutions, especially the Development Bank of Mauritius, and, in recent years, MEDIA.

Export activity is a hazardous business with an ever present chance of default. To provide a cushion against the risks, the authorities established an Export Credit Guarantee Scheme and an Export Credit Insurance Scheme. The Export Credit Guarantee Scheme is intended to provide collateral support to commercial banks to stimulate liberal and flexible export credit. The scheme covers banks against losses on preshipment and postshipment advances to exporters arising from the failure of the exporter to repay the guaranteed advances through protracted default or insolvency. The Export Credit Insurance Scheme is also designed to protect exporters against losses, in this case as a result of commercial risks, namely, the insolvency of the buyer, the buyer's protracted default to pay, and the buyer's failure to accept goods, and country (or political) risks. Country risks include the imposition of restrictions on remittances by the government in the buyer's country or any government action that blocks or delays the transfer of payments, including war, revolution, or civil disturbances in the buyer's country plus the sudden imposition of import licensing restrictions. The Development Bank of Mauritius operates both insurance schemes.

The government has also introduced fiscal measures and other incentives to help the EPZ. A prime example is a cautious wage policy that ensured that wages were set at levels that would not radically raise unit labor costs. This has played a critical role in holding down production costs and, consequently, the price of EPZ products offered for sale overseas. The Mauritian authorities, however, were well aware that wages were not the only factor influencing the competitiveness of the EPZ.

Monetary policy, in particular exchange and interest rate policies, influences the real cost of borrowing and, ultimately, the price of export goods, and this affects the price advantage or competitive edge of Mauritian products compared to the manufactures of its rivals. The need to maintain the EPZ's competitiveness was a central factor in the currency devaluations of October 1979 and September 1981.

Relative price developments and the appreciation of the Special Drawing Rights against most currencies other than the U.S. dollar, however, reversed some of the gain in competitiveness achieved by the second devaluation. Therefore, in February 1983, the government delinked the Mauritian rupee from the Special Drawing Rights and linked it instead to a basket of currencies that are more representative of the country's trade patterns.

The change in the basket and the implementation of a flexible exchange rate policy gradually restored the real effective exchange rate to its September 1981 level, thereby improving the competitiveness of Mauritian exports internationally. Simultaneously, the government liberalized lending and deposit rates, initially with respect to nonpriority sectors (which excluded agriculture, tourism, and industry). Finally, it lifted all ceilings on interest rates and bank credit to introduce greater competition in the credit market.

Effects of the EPZ on the Mauritian Economy

The institutional and policy reforms just described created an environment in which the EPZ could grow and prosper. The government expected the reform measures and its attempts to provide an adequate infrastructure along with an institutional framework within which private entrepreneurs could flourish to improve most macroeconomic indicators. In fact, every major indicator points to the success of the EPZ.

Perhaps the most basic measure of the EPZ's success is the number of enterprises established. After being officially launched by the EPZ Act of December 1970, nine units were set up within one year of the scheme's initiation. Despite setbacks during 1977-82, the Mauritian EPZ has grown well beyond expectations.

As table 5.4 indicates, the growth of the EPZ shows three distinct phases. In the first phase, beginning in 1971, the sector expanded rapidly because of the buoyant economic conditions accompanying the record sugar crop. With the economy liquid and capital funds plentiful, investors took advantage of the incentives available under the EPZ proposition, the result being an impressive number of new units added each year until 1977.

The second phase, 1977-82, was marked by a deceleration in EPZ expansion. The momentum created in the earlier phase was lost. In general the number of units operating continued to increase but at a much slower pace. During this time, nearly one-third of the existing firms shut down, with the highest number of closures in any one year being 15 in 1978. The EPZ had borne the brunt of the recession in the industrialized countries and of their increasingly protectionist policies. Plus, on the domestic front, the expansionary fiscal policy the government pursued in the wake of the boom conditions of the mid-1970s raised wages faster than productivity, leading to higher unit labor costs and pricing some EPZ products out of world markets.

In the third phase, beginning in 1983, the situation was reversed under the impact of the stabilization and structural adjustment programs that the authorities initiated in 1979 with the help of the IMF and the World Bank. Economic forecasts for the world economy became more optimistic and the demand for EPZ products, particularly knitwear and garments, grew. The government reinforced these positive developments by putting in place appropriate institutional and policy reforms. The combined effect of these events was a sudden surge in new applications for Export Enterprise Certificates, along with an expansion of existing units. By March 1987, the number of enterprises operating in the EPZ increased to 437, nearly a five-fold rise over 1977.

Table 5.4 Growth in the Number of EPZ Units, 1971-87

Year	New units	Closures	Total units operating
1971	6	0	10
1972	12	2	20
1973	13	1	32
1974	25	3	54
1975	12	2	64
1976	20	0	84
1977	7	2	89
1978	12	15	86
1979	16	7	95
1980	10	4	101
1981	19	11	109
1982	18	9	118
1983	45	17	146
1984	55	6	195
1985	101	6	290
1986	139	21	408
1987 (March)	38	9	437

Source: Ministry of Industry

Textile plants, which spearheaded the initial EPZ revolution, continued to dominate the sector. In 1977, they accounted for about 52 percent of all units in the zone, while by 1987, the figure had risen to almost 72 percent (table 5.5). The authorities are well aware of the risks associated with heavy dependence on one line of activity; after all, it was the country's reliance on a single product (sugar) that had led the government to seek economic diversification in the first place. The authorities also learned from the experience of 1977-82 that concentrating so much on textiles is particularly dangerous.

Geographically, the EPZ has not been confined to a single location, but has spread all over the island (table 5.6). The government's decision not to limit the zone to a clearly delineated geographical area has spared Mauritius many of the problems (transportation constraints, urban congestion, and so on) that often go with a concentration of industry in a single area. However, the decentralization of industries has required extra expenditures on site development and on infrastructure. The amount of additional expenditure can be held down if sites are carefully selected, taking into account their proximity to such facilities as telephone lines, water, and electricity.

Table 5.5 Distribution of EPZ Units by Activity, 1977 and 1987
(number of units)

Activity	1977	March 1987
Textiles	47	314
Spinning/weaving/dyeing	6	18
Knitwear	11	55
Garments	19	236
Gloves	6	5
Synthetic printing and knitting	3	0
Lace and ribbons	2	0
Toys	4	4
Watches	3	5
Food and agriculture	10	10
Plastics	6	10
Electronics	6	0
Jewelry	6	9
Crafts and miscellaneous	9	85
Total	91	437

Source: Ministry of Industry

Table 5.6 Geographical Distribution of EPZ Units, 1977 and 1985
(number of units)

Location	1977	1985
Plaine Lauzun Industrial Estate	27	32
Coromandel Industrial Estate	5	25
Mon Desert Alma Industrial Estate	3	3
St. Antoine Industrial Estate	8	9
Port Louis City and periphery	14	48
Units in urban areas other than Port Louis	21	118
Rural areas	17	77
Total	95	312

Note: Some EPZ firms have multiple units operating at different locations.
Source: Mauritius Chamber of Commerce and Industry

The EPZ has had a major impact on employment generation. A primary motivation behind creation of the EPZ had been its potential for new job opportunities. As the 1971-75 Development Plan put it:

> For the entire Mauritian labour force to be gainfully employed by the end of the decade [i.e. by 1980], the main increase in economic activity must come from manufacturing. Because of the limited size of the domestic market, this will mostly be in manufacturing for the export market. The basis for such a development already exists in a labour force well adapted to acquiring mechanical skills. Both the relative costs and quality of the labour force in Mauritius as compared with those of more highly industrialised countries can be expected to work increasingly to the comparative advantage of Mauritius in the manufacture of comparatively labour intensive products and in labour intensive processes in the production chain. (p. vii)

Employment data for the sector confirms this optimism. Total employment in export enterprises has shown a consistently upward trend since 1971 (table 5.7), although net job creation moderated in the late 1970s following the slow growth in the number of new enterprises. As of March 1987, employment in the EPZ reached an all-time high of 78,007. At that time, the EPZ accounted for 85 percent of total employment in large manufacturing establishments[3] compared to only 57 percent a decade earlier (table 5.8). One-fifth of a total estimated labor force in the neighborhood of 400,000 is employed in the EPZ sector, a major increase from 6 percent a decade earlier.

Knitwear factories provide nearly 44 percent of employment in export firms while garment industries provide an additional 41 percent. Traditionally, knitwear has accounted for a large proportion of new employment, but since 1983, garment firms have been demonstrating unusual dynamism. This is consistent with the dominance of the textile subsector in the EPZ. The implication is clear: the large-scale collapse of these firms would have a disastrous effect on employment. The authorities are conscious of the danger and are actively seeking ways to diversify the EPZ product mix.

Another worrying factor in EPZ employment is the share of jobs going to female labor. Historically, women, mostly teenage girls, have held roughly 80 percent of all jobs in the sector (table 5.9). One reason for this preference for female labor is that their wages average 30 percent less than those of males. Such a development can hardly be described as healthy when many men are unemployed. A positive sign, however, is that the most recent figures point to increasing recruitment of men and boys in almost all branches of manufacturing. By March 1987, males comprised one-third of all EPZ employment.

---

3. Large establishments are defined as (a) agricultural establishments comprising (i) sugar cane plantations where 25 arpents (an arpent is slightly smaller than an acre) or more were harvested; (ii) tea plantations where 5 arpents or more were harvested; (iii) all "flue-cured" tobacco establishments; (iv) other agricultural establishments employing at least 10 persons on the day of the survey; or (b) nonagricultural establishments comprising (i) all central and local government departments; (ii) those employing at least 10 persons on the day of the survey. Note that "outdoor" workers are excluded; these are piece workers who although employed by an establishment are working in their own homes.

Table 5.7 Net Employment Increase in EPZ Firms, 1975-87

Year	Total employment	Net increase	Percentage increase
1975	10,320	1,601	18.4
1976	16,404	6,084	59.0
1977	18,953	2,549	15.5
1978	18,010	-943	-5.0
1979	20,484	2,474	13.7
1980	21,208	724	3.5
1981	22,508	1,300	6.1
1982	22,619	111	0.5
1983	25,495	2,876	12.7
1984	37,532	12,037	47.2
1985	53,951	16,419	43.7
1986	70,704	16,753	31.1
1987	78,007	7,303	10.3

Note: The data are from September for all years except 1987, when they refer to the situation in March.
Source: Bi-Annual Survey of Employment and Earnings, Central Statistical Office

Table 5.8 Employment in Large Manufacturing Establishments, 1974-87

Year	Large establishments	EPZ enterprises	EPZ employment as a percentage of employment in all large establishments
1974	20,813	8,719	41.9
1975	22,517	10,320	45.8
1976	29,348	16,404	55.9
1977	33,241	18,953	57.0
1978	33,077	18,010	54.4
1979	35,589	20,484	57.6
1980	36,360	21,208	58.3
1981	37,178	22,508	60.5
1982	36,884	22,619	61.3
1983	38,310	25,495	66.5
1984	48,613	37,532	77.2
1985	62,949	53,951	85.7
1986	84,370	70,704	83.8
1987	91,795	78,007	85.0

Note: The data are from September for all years except 1987, when they refer to the situation in March.
Source: Bi-Annual Survey of Employment and Earnings, Central Statistical Office

Table 5.9 EPZ Employment by Sex, 1974-87

Year	Total EPZ employment	No. of male employees	Percentage of male employees	No. of female employees	Percentage of female employees
1974	8,719	1,162	13.3	7,557	86.7
1975	10,320	1,801	17.5	8,519	82.5
1976	16,404	3,307	20.2	13,097	79.8
1977	18,953	3,589	18.9	15,364	81.1
1978	18,010	3,105	17.2	14,905	82.8
1979	20,484	3,704	18.1	16,780	81.9
1980	21,208	3,741	17.6	17,467	82.4
1981	22,508	3,939	17.5	18,569	82.5
1982	22,619	4,252	18.8	18,367	81.2
1983	25,495	4,786	18.8	20,709	81.2
1984	37,532	7,923	21.1	29,609	78.9
1985	53,951	14,883	27.6	39,068	72.4
1986	70,704	22,174	31.4	48,530	68.6
1987	78,007	25,868	33.2	52,139	66.8

Note: The data are from September for all years except 1987, when they refer to the situation in March.
Source: Annual Survey of Employment and Earnings, Central Statistical Office

A highly favorable corollary to increased female employment is the reduction in fertility rates during the past 15 years. The total fertility rate (which measures fertility in terms of the number of children born to a woman during her reproductive life, if the current fertility conditions prevail throughout) dropped from 3.19 in 1975 to 1.98 in 1985 (table 5.10). The age-specific fertility rate for women aged 20-24 dropped from 173.6 in 1975 to 119.0 in 1985 (table 5.11). However, the age-specific fertility rate for girls aged 15-19, the preferred target group for recruitment in the EPZ, showed a much more erratic trend, climbing to 63.3 in 1979 before retreating to 36.9 in 1985. A variety of factors probably caused the overall decline in the birth rate, including increases in education and income levels and the greater availability and acceptability of family planning methods, but the EPZ has undoubtedly contributed to some of these changes. In addition, by increasing the opportunity cost of women's time spent in the home, the "price of children" rose with increasing female employment in the EPZ. In sum, the decline in fertility experienced in Mauritius during the past few decades is nothing short of remarkable when compared with similar developing countries. The EPZ, without a doubt, has helped account for this phenomenon.

Table 5.10 Fertility Rates, 1975-85

Year	Crude birth rate	Total fertility rate
1975	24.8	3.19
1976	25.3	3.13
1977	25.5	3.04
1978	26.7	3.09
1979	27.2	3.07
1980	26.6	2.86
1981	24.9	2.68
1982	22.1	2.39
1983	20.6	2.23
1984	19.7	2.10
1985	18.8	1.98

Source: Digest of Demographic Statistics, Central Statistical Office

Table 5.11 Age-Specific Fertility Rates, 1975-85

	Age group							
Year	15-19	20-24	25-29	30-34	35-39	40-44	45-49	15-49
1975	56.6	173.6	176.5	125.6	72.0	30.5	3.0	101.9
1976	60.5	174.8	179.2	116.2	65.6	27.4	2.3	103.3
1977	60.0	168.1	172.7	117.8	64.5	23.2	2.0	101.5
1978	62.2	179.6	175.6	114.2	61.9	21.6	2.3	105.0
1979	63.3	178.9	171.6	113.4	64.2	19.4	2.9	104.7
1980	60.6	172.3	159.4	104.9	58.3	19.5	2.5	98.9
1981	54.4	160.6	146.1	101.7	54.9	16.1	2.4	91.4
1982	48.8	143.5	132.8	86.1	49.5	14.3	1.9	81.8
1983	40.1	132.6	131.0	85.7	40.8	13.5	1.9	76.4
1984	37.0	127.3	123.9	78.5	39.4	12.7	1.3	72.3
1985	36.9	119.0	115.8	73.2	39.0	11.6	1.6	68.3

Source: Digest of Demographic Statistics, Central Statistical Office

The EPZ has also had a favorable effect on wages. While average monthly earnings in the EPZ vary across activities, for the EPZ as a whole, recent data show that monthly earnings have been increasing in both nominal and real terms (table 5.12). Across industries, value added per person varies widely, reflecting the differing capital intensities and skill composition of labor. In 1984, value added per person ranged from Rs. 19,500 for apparel to Rs. 68,200 for jewelry and related articles (table 5.13). While increases in productivity over time are clearly discernible, distinguishing among the different causes is difficult. Possibilities include the accumulated experience of both workers and managers and the various incentive schemes initiated by management, for example, productivity and attendance bonuses and the provision of free transportation and improved working conditions. As for the immediate future, the government's policy of wage restraint, pursued as part of the stabilization program agreed upon with the IMF, is expected to exercise downward pressure on unit labor costs, making the Mauritian EPZ even more competitive.

Table 5.12 Average Monthly Earnings in the EPZ by Industrial Group, 1983-86 *(rupees)*

Industrial Group	1983		1984		1985		1986	
	Nominal	Real	Nominal	Real	Nominal	Real	Nominal	Real
Manufacturing	809	317	927	339	998	341	1,030	346
Textiles	1,150	450	1,235	451	1,423	486	1,404	471
Apparel (except footwear)	748	293	894	327	953	325	990	332
Wood and furniture	919	360	1,131	413	1,142	390	1,200	403
Jewelry and related articles	1,243	487	1,243	454	1,492	510	1,613	541
Other	913	357	920	336	1,089	372	1,205	404
Nonmanufacturing	936	366	1,114	407	1,275	435	1,494	501
Total	810	317	928	339	999	341	1,032	346

Note: Real figures use 1976 as the base year.
Sources: Biannual Survey of Employment and Earnings, Central Statistical Office, and Survey of Employment and Earnings in Large Establishments

The combination of improved labor productivity and declining unit labor costs has greatly enhanced manufacturers' export potential and competitiveness. As a result, the EPZ's export earnings have continued to grow, rising from about 3 percent of all exports in 1971, to more than 15 percent in 1976, 37 percent in 1981, and almost 53 percent in 1986. In 1986, EPZ exports reached an all-time high with receipts of Rs. 4,960 million, far surpassing sugar as the principal export earner (table 5.14). The EPZ has therefore effectively shattered Mauritius' image as a monocrop economy and given it a wider economic base to cushion it from the risk of too heavy a reliance on a single crop for foreign exchange earnings, employment, and output growth.

Table 5.13 Value Added per Worker (at Current Factor Cost) in EPZ Industries by Product, 1980-84
(thousands of rupees)

Industry	1980	1981	1982	1983	1984
Textiles	33.0	46.1	48.8	45.9	44.4
Apparel	11.6	14.1	15.5	17.5	19.5
Wood products and furniture	n.a.	n.a.	n.a.	n.a.	20.6
Jewelry and related articles	34.0	34.9	34.6	44.3	68.2
Other products	19.9	25.0	24.7	30.1	33.8
Total	15.0	18.4	19.8	21.6	23.1

n.a. = not available
Source: Digest of Industrial Statistics, Central Statistical Office

Table 5.14 EPZ Export Earnings, 1981-86

Exports	1981	1982	1983	1984	1985	1986
Total exports, fob value (Rs. millions)	2,929	3,900	4,233	5,086	6,526	9,401
EPZ exports, fob value (Rs. millions)	1,087	1,236	1,307	2,151	3,283	4,960
EPZ exports, as a percentage of total	37.1	31.7	30.9	42.3	50.3	52.8
Sugar exports, fob value (Rs. millions)	1,623	2,427	2,679	2,523	2,867	3,545
Sugar exports as a percentage of total	55.4	62.2	63.3	49.6	43.9	37.7

Source: Digest of Industrial Statistics, Central Statistical Office, and Economic Indicators

Yet, as indicated earlier, the dramatic surge in export receipts came almost exclusively from a relatively small group of enterprises, mostly those producing knitwear and garments. In 1986, this group accounted for over 80 percent of EPZ exports (table 5.15) and, remarkably, Mauritius ranks among the top four exporters of knitwear in the world.

Table 5.15 EPZ Exports by Product, 1981-86
(fob value, Rs. millions)

Product	1981	1982	1983	1984	1985	1986
Canned tuna	55	47	68	99	114	97
Textile yarns, fabrics, made up articles	72	89	66	78	86	101
Apparel	800	877	921	1,585	2,539	4,015
Optical goods	27	29	33	60	82	91
Watches and clocks	21	38	65	84	146	245
Pearls, precious, and semiprecious stones	28	52	49	89	127	174
Jewelry and other articles of precious and semi-precious materials	18	27	31	48	58	82
Toys, games, and sporting goods	16	30	34	50	44	58
Other	50	46	40	58	87	97
Total	1,087	1,236	1,307	2,151	3,283	4,960

Source: Digest of Industrial Statistics, Central Statistical Office, and Economic Indicators

Another worrying feature of the development of the EPZ is the concentration of export markets. EEC countries import nearly 80 percent of Mauritian industrial exports, particularly France (32 percent), the United Kingdom (17 percent), and the Federal Republic of Germany (13 percent). Canada and the United States also take in some EPZ exports, but their combined share was less than 30 percent in 1985 and the bilateral agreements negotiated with these countries effectively rule out any further market expansion. The focus on a few export products and a limited number of markets is an unhealthy development, and efforts to diversify both markets and the narrow product mix continue through a vigorous market penetration and investment promotion campaign under the control of the Mauritius Export Development and Investment Authority.

Another indicator of EPZ performance is net export earnings. The import content of EPZ output in 1986 stood at 77 percent, compared to 65 percent three years earlier. As a result, net earnings in the mid-1980s were a smaller percentage of gross earnings than during the early 1980s (table 5.16). Note, however, that a disproportionately large import content in EPZ output is not unusual across free zones throughout the world, since they make heavy use of externally secured raw materials, components, and capital goods for manufacturing.

Table 5.16 Net Export Earnings of EPZ Firms, 1980-86

Year	EPZ imports (cif value, Rs. millions) Capital goods	Intermediate goods	Total	EPZ exports (fob value, Rs. millions)	Net exports (Rs. millions)	Net exports as percentage of gross exports
1980	66	592	658	895	236	0.26
1981	61	621	682	1,087	405	0.37
1982	35	707	742	1,236	493	0.40
1983	62	785	847	1,307	460	0.35
1984	160	1,491	1,650	2,151	500	0.23
1985	304	2,220	2,524	3,283	759	0.23
1986	491	3,346	3,837	4,960	1,123	0.23

Source: Digest of Industrial Statistics, Central Statistical Office, and Economic Indicators

Net export earnings aside, the EPZ has overtaken sugar in manufacturing value added and brought about a fundamental restructuring of the component mix in the manufacturing sector. In the early 1970s, value added in manufacturing was entirely accounted for by sugar milling and Development Certificate companies. By 1976, the share of the EPZ in manufacturing value added had risen to 17.1 percent and in 1986 it rose to 54.5 percent, well in excess of sugar milling (table 5.17). The share of the EPZ in total GDP at factor cost (constant prices) followed the same upward trend, rising from 2.6 percent in 1976 to 7.5 percent in 1985, with a preliminary estimate of 9.2 percent for 1986 and a forecast value of 11.0 percent for 1987. Value added per worker in the EPZ is generally lower than in the Development Certificate sector owing to the high capital intensity of Development Certificate enterprises. The introduction of skill-intensive industries and the greater experience of workers suggest that this gap will narrow over time.

The growth of the EPZ in its initial phase can be attributed almost entirely to foreign investors, who played a pioneering role in the zone's take-off. However, credit should also go to the local business community, which has invested sizeable resources in what seemed initially to be very risky activities.

A 1982 survey indicates that local participation in equity is on the order of 50 percent; a highly favorable statistic compared with data from free zones in other developing nations (Forget 1983). The pattern of equity holdings varies considerably across enterprises according to the type of activity. Rough estimates suggest that equity holdings by principals in the Far East are concentrated in the knitwear, garment, and textile industries, while equity holdings by principals in advanced industrialized countries are concentrated in other industries (Marsden 1982).

Table 5.17 Value Added of the Manufacturing Sector by Main Industrial Group, 1976 and 1981-86 (at current factor cost)
(Rs. millions)

Industrial group	1976	1981	1982	1983	1984	1985	1986
Sugar milling	228	251	313	265	326	438	490
Tea processing	11	11	12	30	80	n.a.	n.a.
EPZ	108	421	449	548	865	1,333	1,950
Other	284	694	786	835	912	1,093	1,135
Total manufacturing	631	1,377	1,560	1,678	2,183	2,864	3,575
EPZ value added as a percentage of total manufacturing value added	17.1	30.6	28.8	32.7	39.6	46.5	54.5

n.a. = not available
Notes: 1986 data are provisional. "Other" data for 1985 and 1986 include tea.
Source: Digest of Industrial Statistics, Central Statistical Office, and Economic Indicators

Foreign investment in textiles, garments, knitwear, and similar labor-intensive activities is usually motivated by the desire to take advantage of competitive labor costs. Mauritius is no exception. In addition, some Hong Kong garment and knitwear manufacturers have located their plants in Mauritius because of voluntary restraint agreements and other restrictions on suppliers based in the Far East and, more recently, the sense of instability following the Sino-British agreement on Hong Kong's future after 1997. For its part, the government has not taken a definite stand on foreign equity participation in the EPZ, although it has hinted that it prefers to have at least 30 percent local shareholding in any new enterprises set up in the country. The 50 percent equity participation achieved by Mauritians is therefore especially impressive.

Unfortunately, the same cannot be said about internal linkages developed by the EPZ. As with its counterparts in other parts of the world, the Mauritian zone has few linkages with the domestic economy. Forward linkages—the processing of products from the zone within the country—are difficult if not impossible to realize simply because EPZ enterprises are legally required to produce for export only. Neither are backward linkages with local production activities possible on a large scale, as companies in the zone import almost all their supplies of intermediate goods and raw materials. This, of course, results from the special concessions for importing inputs, as well as the affiliation with parent companies overseas and the nature of the manufacturing activities carried out in the zone.

In this situation, integration of the export sector with the local economy is possible primarily through purchases of labor and infrastructural facilities. Notwithstanding these basic constraints, limited backward linkages have evolved through opportunities created for the products of import-substitution firms engaged in producing thread, knitted fabrics, cardboard boxes, plastic bags, packaging materials, and so on. Ancillary industries manufacturing buttons, braid, trimmings, ribbons, zip fasteners, and other items required by the textile sector have also been established. These lists are by no means exhaustive as other activities are being pursued to support the EPZ, including those in the banking, insurance, and other service sectors. One important development likely to promote close integration is the increase in subcontracting on a cut, make, and trim basis. Accurate data on the number of persons working at home in this field are not available, but estimates run into the hundreds.

Moreover, evidence of a positive demonstration effect from the EPZ to other enterprises is increasing. Encouraged by the help available to small businesses under diverse schemes operated by the Development Bank of Mauritius, entrepreneurs have launched small-scale industrial and trading ventures, thereby raising employment levels and manufacturing output. It is likely that some of these units will eventually produce inputs for the EPZ, thus increasing the degree of integration between the zone and the national economy.

Finally, the income generated by the EPZ leads to purchases of other goods and services produced domestically, thereby supporting non-EPZ industries.

Strengths and Weaknesses of the EPZ

The Mauritian EPZ will soon complete its second decade. Factors operating on the supply, demand, and institutional sides are at the root of its outstanding success.

On the supply side, the most critical element was the generous package of fiscal and other incentives offered under the EPZ scheme. The government has continually refined the incentive package in line with the rapidly changing international and domestic economic environment. No doubt tax free dividends were the strongest inducement for local business people to invest, while tax advantages were important in luring foreign entrepreneurs, especially from countries with which Mauritius has signed double taxation agreements. The availability of capital funds and working finance from the Development Bank of Mauritius and local banks, and competitive wages for workers were added attractions for overseas investors.

On the demand side, the single most important factor tempting investors was, and continues to be, free and unlimited access to the EEC market, first under the Yaoundé and subsequently under the Lomé conventions. Mauritius was in a better position than most African, Caribbean, and Pacific nations to capitalize on the advantages conferred by the agreement with the EEC, both because of the relative development of its entrepreneurial class and its educated and easily trainable labor force. Further, cultural relationships with countries such as India and Hong Kong and past colonial ties with France and the United Kingdom worked in Mauritius' favor. Finally, the years 1971-74 and 1983-86 were periods of relative prosperity in the industrialized countries and demand was buoyant, especially for those manufactures that were the mainstays of the Mauritian EPZ.

Institutional factors also played a significant role in the growth of the EPZ. The authorities had already put in place a special mechanism in the form of an interministerial committee—the Industrial Development Committee—to examine and approve applications for Development Certificates. The committee put the substantial experience it had acquired with respect to industrial project proposals under the Development Certificate Scheme to good use in the early processing of export applications. The Development Bank of Mauritius, which operated the industrial estates, also constituted a strong institutional base supporting the EPZ experiment. More recently, reforms aimed at cutting red tape, simplifying procedures for administrative clearances by the Industrial Coordination Unit, and promoting both Mauritius as an offshore processing base and EPZ exports have contributed to the increase in industrial activity in the zone.

The country's liberal, democratic traditions have certainly played a positive role in shaping the growth pattern of the EPZ. These traditions help guarantee against government excess, including any efforts that infringe upon an individual's right to own property. A 1963 Sessional Paper (No. 2) explicitly assures investors that nationalization is not a possibility.

A final positive factor is the presence of a well-developed education and training system that has offered entrepreneurs a literate and highly adaptable labor force. As a result of free education at the primary level, and at the secondary level since 1977, Mauritius has achieved a literacy rate of close to 90 percent. Technical training has been available at the Industrial Trade Training Centre, and a new centre and Lycée Polytechnique were opened in the early 1980s to satisfy the mounting demand for a variety of industrial and other skills. In addition, the University of Mauritius provides degree and diploma courses in various areas of agricultural administration and industrial technology.

Many of these factors will continue to operate in favor of the EPZ. However, remember that in the recent past (1977-82), the EPZ's health was failing. Value added stagnated in real terms, net earnings barely increased, foreign investment slowed substantially, and employment levels increased but slowly. This particular phase in the EPZ's evolution laid bare some fundamental weaknesses.

The EPZ has come to rely on the EEC and North America to provide much needed export growth. These two markets together take in some 90 percent of EPZ exports, consisting mostly of knitwear and garments. The exceptionally high dependence on few markets and limited products took its toll in the late 1970s when exports to Europe were restricted by a series of bilateral agreements with France and the United Kingdom (which accounted for 50 percent of all EPZ sales in the EEC), requiring Mauritius to exercise "voluntary restraints." Recession in the European countries added to this burden. Recent bilateral agreements with the United States and Canada specifying limits on knitwear and garment sales following a rapid rise in exports to these countries, highlight the EPZ's vulnerability to protectionist pressures, which continue to manifest themselves in various forms.

The Mauritius Export Development and Investment Authority's current emphasis on market diversification and on expanding the product mix is a step in the right direction. Participating in trade fairs in Europe and elsewhere, holding "Mauritian Weeks" abroad, organizing textile exhibitions at home, fielding trade missions to potential importing countries, and opening up regional markets should have a positive impact on future export growth.

Concurrently, Mauritius will need to move into a second stage of industrialization based on the production of light engineering goods and "high-tech" products, both to expand possibilities for greater local value added and to prevent the EPZ from becoming an ideal place for "fly-by-night" investors. Most of the knitwear and garment firms in the zone have been attracted by Mauritius' low wages—wages constitute a high proportion of their total production costs. A major upward movement in real unit labor costs would have an immediate adverse effect on the industry's international competitiveness, creating the risk of large-scale plant closures. Again, the experience of the late 1970s is an excellent example. During that period, ten textile firms ceased operations following a significant rise in real wages. A diversified EPZ with more capital- and skill-intensive industries offers the best hope for the zone's long-term viability. Mauritius is not lacking in professional skills at various levels, and their mobilization to create a more diversified industrial structure is vital.

The nature and extent of linkages between industrial activities in the zone and those in the domestic economy are another key issue affecting the ultimate success of the EPZ. As discussed, forward linkages face legal impediments, but backward linkages have not been fully exploited. While the high prices and scarcity of local inputs are probably responsible, the absence of such linkages makes the EPZ appear to be more of a separate entity; an outgrowth of the national economy with few organic links. This, of course, is not a welcome development. The EPZ must be integrated into the domestic economic structure. One way to accomplish this is to encourage subcontracting arrangements between export firms and import-substitution enterprises, including establishing plants producing inputs for the EPZ.

The scope for further backward linkages in the textile subsector, the linchpin of the export industry, certainly exists. What is required is an investigation into the production chain of the textile industry to identify, with due regard to costs and constraints, processes that may be started outside the export zone. Direct and indirect linkages between producers in the EPZ and the domestic service sector also need to be exploited further. Possibilities exist to provide locally some of the maintenance, repair, and testing services that export enterprises currently obtain from overseas. The creation of firms specializing in such services will help develop linkages between domestic and export industries.

Backward and forward linkages aside, there is the problem of distortions introduced in the allocation of resources between industrial activities. This results from the incentive structure for Development Certificate firms, together with the need to direct more resources to manufacturing for export and to motivate non-EPZ enterprises to operate in a competitive environment, which would lead to greater industrial efficiency across the manufacturing sector.

As a result of quotas and tariffs introduced as part of a package of incentives to import-substitution industries, Development Certificate firms have come to enjoy high effective rates of protection. Thus their activities have become increasingly lucrative because of the near monopolistic power that such a system confers upon the beneficiary. Firms producing for the local market have no incentive to move into export manufacturing, where the competition is stiff and the profits highly unpredictable. A natural consequence of the policy of granting significant protection is the diversion of resources from export to import-substitution activities, and from labor-intensive to capital-intensive sectors, implying the creation of fewer jobs.

A study of the effective rate of protection for import-substitution firms found that the amount of capital needed to create a job rises systematically with the effective rate of protection (Centre for Development Technology Inc. 1984). Enterprises with an effective rate of protection of over 300 percent require 80 percent more capital to create one job than those with a negative effective rate of protection. Quota restrictions have since been removed and some duties reduced in an effort to make import-substitution enterprises more efficient. Further cuts in tariffs will reduce high effective rates of protection, create a more competitive environment, and eliminate the distortionary effect of the current system of protection on resource allocation.

Tariff reforms will influence investment in the export sector positively, requiring concomitant policy changes to facilitate dispersion of the increased production in new markets. The Export Credit Guarantee and Export Credit Insurance schemes (introduced in early 1981) are important steps in mitigating the risk exporters face when looking for new outlets for their manufactures. Some fine tuning of each scheme is still required. Additional measures to facilitate overseas sales include modernization of the system of foreign exchange cover and reductions in the unusually large margins on currency transactions. The recent government announcement that it will gradually liberalize the foreign exchange market should have a long-term positive impact on export efforts.

In addition, the government has recently paid greater attention to the availability of venture capital. It recognizes that venture capital will be needed to accelerate product diversification and to encourage entrepreneurs to embark on new activities to reduce the present predominance of textiles in the zone. However, the government has yet to adopt proposals for setting up an Equity Finance Fund to provide seed money to aspiring business people to start new ventures or equity money for the expansion of existing enterprises.

In any case, Mauritius' geographical location will continue to hinder attempts to reach export destinations on time and without cost over-runs. Delays and high costs associated with distance and infrequent shipping services have seriously handicapped the expansion of exports. Improvements in the port infrastructure have substantially curtailed vessel waiting times, but the garment and knitwear industries are still exposed to shipping problems resulting from tight schedules between the receipt of orders and the requested time of delivery. Shipment by air is an ideal solution, but its costs can easily put Mauritian exporters at a disadvantage compared with other low-cost producers. Freight negotiations with airlines can help, along with the expansion of the airport, which is already under way. The problems cited here illustrate the extent to which a country's location can affect the growth prospects of an export industry.

The EPZ, confined as it is to specific industrial parks, generates its own transport problems: traffic congestion, excess demands on public transportation, and so forth. The short-sighted planning that led to the development of two major industrial zones within the immediate vicinity of Port Louis has resulted in substantial urban congestion. The current government initiative to set up regional industrial parks is commendable.

Workers in the EPZ are the principal victims of transport congestion. On occasion, they have also criticized the work conditions set by some foreign employers. Their grievances include low wages, forced overtime, poor supervisor/worker relations, the lack of an effective role for labor unions, and little employment security. However, the Mauritius Export Processing Zone Association warns against generalizing from the complaints of some workers, arguing that poor conditions are the exception rather than the rule. Furthermore, the government has taken steps to improve work conditions. The announcement in the 1986/87 budget of the government's intention to set up an EPZ Labor Welfare Fund, where employers contribute to the provision of social services for EPZ workers, is a step in the right direction.

Lessons and Conclusions

In retrospect, the EPZ has made very good use of Mauritian resources in terms of direct value added, multiplier effects, and the spur provided to industrial initiative and activity in the economy. Mistakes have been made, but they are dwarfed by the successes.

The Mauritian EPZ was not a new idea on the international industrial and economic scene. Free zones have existed elsewhere and some have achieved considerable success. Countries such as Hong Kong and Singapore, constrained by the size of their domestic markets and the scarcity of raw materials for industrial processing, had already opted for production for export, using liberal packages of incentives to lure foreign investors. Thus, the Mauritian authorities had before them several successful free zone models to choose from or, instead, they could have developed one better suited to local economic, political, and social circumstances.

The model developed has many of the elements commonly found in free zones in other countries, but with some idiosyncratic features. For example, the Mauritian approach differed fundamentally in one important respect: the zone's geographical definition. The flexibility inherent in the Mauritian concept of a free zone allows exporters the ability to locate industries in places they consider best from the production point of view. This feature, along with generous fiscal and other concessions, the efforts of local entrepreneurs, and the presence of an able, competitively paid labor force, have been behind the success of the export-led industrialization strategy. Factors operating on the demand side, particularly free access to the EEC and various institutional efforts, have also helped explain the shape of today's EPZ.

A point well worth re-emphasizing is the high level of domestic investment efforts, something not achieved in most other successful export zones. Mauritian nationals control nearly 50 percent of the equity in export enterprises, a remarkably high percentage by international standards.

The major weakness in the Mauritian approach was that the authorities, in their concern to tackle the unemployment problem and to industrialize rapidly, did not pay much attention to the type of manufacturing units that were coming in. The result was the influx of "footloose" textile firms that were attracted by the availability of comparatively low-wage labor and the free access of Mauritian manufactures to the EEC. The result is a zone that has become heavily dependent on a few major markets and on a limited range of export products. Hence, the EPZ is vulnerable to changes in the world economic environment. In addition, this form of industrialization has largely failed to stimulate the transfer of high technology and, therefore, has not actively encouraged the transition of the Mauritian economy into a higher stage of industrial development.

With the exception of these weaknesses, the Mauritian model is sound and offers reasonable prospects of success if implanted in other countries, provided certain basic conditions prevail. These include (a) a relatively well-developed infrastructure; (b) a literate labor force earning competitive wages; (c) a business community that is industrially motivated and prepared to enter into risky export manufacturing activities; (d) political stability; (e) easily accessible international trade routes and relatively inexpensive transport links with external markets; (f) export outlets that are guaranteed or can be established; and (g) reasonably well-established money markets with finance available.

The forgoing list is not necessarily exhaustive. Other prerequisites may have to be added to reflect the particular situation of a country wishing to embark on export-led industrialization. However, the lessons from the Mauritian experience with the EPZ are not limited to countries seeking to follow its example.

The Government of Mauritius identified a series of problems, systematically evaluated potential remedies, set up a program that took advantage of private incentives, and implemented policies that helped it reach the goal of export-led industrialization. Moreover, it continuously monitored the results of its efforts and adjusted its policies as it acquired new information.

A summary of the key methodological lessons follows:

- the government intelligently sought a development strategy in an apolitical manner;
- it stuck to its strategy in the long run rather than reverse course at the first sign of trouble;
- it encouraged market incentives rather than undermined them;
- it showed a good deal of adaptability, meeting each challenge with creative solutions rather than maintaining the *status quo*;
- it adjusted the general export promotion program to suit its own particular needs and characteristics;
- it consciously guarded against the creation of a unwieldy bureaucratic structure.

The government's methodology may be as worthy of emulation as is its specific industrial scheme.

Annex 5.1 The Export Processing Zone Scheme

Export enterprises benefit from the following incentives, advantages, and facilities:

1. Complete exemption from payment of import duty on capital goods (i.e., machinery, equipment, and spare parts).
2. Complete exemption from payment of import and excise duty on raw materials, components, and semifinished goods (except spirits, tobacco, and petroleum products).
3. Corporate income tax holiday for a minimum of 10 years and a maximum of 20 years depending on the merits of each case.
4. Exemption from payment of income tax on dividends for five years.
5. Free repatriation of capital and remittance abroad of profits and dividends to companies with an approved status.
6. Electric power at preferential rates.
7. Loans at preferential rates (from commercial banks) for the importation of raw materials.
8. Provision of reinforced factory buildings for use by industrialists.
9. Loans of up to 50 percent of total building cost for a ten-year period.
10. Favorable labor legislation to help export industries meet their export objectives.
11. Export finance at preferential rates of interest from commercial banks.
12. Exemption from payment of crane and other harbor handling dues chargeable by the government on imported content of export products.
13. Exemption from payment of registration fees on land and buildings purchased by new industrial enterprises.
14. Leases at preferential rates of land in the vicinity of certain housing estates.
15. The issue of permanent residence permits to promoters and shareholders as warranted by the size of their interest.
16. Completion within 24 hours of customs inspection of incoming or outgoing commodities.
17. Priority, wherever possible, in the allocation of investment capital by the Development Bank of Mauritius.
18. The services of the Government Foreign Trade Unit made available to facilitate access to foreign markets and provide market information to exporters.
19. Government contribution to the cost of approved trade missions, trade fairs, and collective advertising.
20. Direct negotiation by the government with shipping lines and airlines for favorable terms of freight.
21. Exemption from income tax on profits earned from foreign investments in Mauritius if these are not transferred but are re-invested in Mauritius.
22. Immediate issue of import licenses for machinery and raw semifinished materials and of export licenses for the finished products.
23. Guarantee against nationalization (Sessional Paper No. 2 of 1963).

24. Equitable settlement of disputes assured by the government's adherence to the Convention on the Settlement of Investment Disputes administered under the auspices of the International Bank for Reconstruction and Development.

Source: Government of Mauritius (1973)

References

Arouff, Benoit. 1973. *The Industrial Development Strategy of Mauritius.* October (processed).

Centre for Development Technology Inc. 1984. *Industrial Policy Review.* August (processed).

Forget, Philippe A. 1983. *Wishing a Future for the EPZ is not Enough.* November (processed).

Government of Mauritius. 1973. *Mauritius—Export Processing Zones.* Port Louis: Ministry of Commerce and Industry. February.

Marsden, J. S. 1982. *A Review of Manufacturing in Mauritius.* (Processed.)

Meade, J. E. et al. 1961. *Report to the Government of Mauritius: The Economic and Social Structure of Mauritius.* Port Louis: Government of Mauritius. Republished in 1968 as *The Economic and Social Structure of Mauritius.* London: Frank Cass.

Minister of Finance. 1985. 1985-86 Budget Speech. June.

6

Ghana: Economic Recovery Program
A Case Study of Stabilization and Structural Adjustment in Sub-Saharan Africa

Stephen D. Younger, Department of Economics, Williams College

During the 1950s, Ghana was one of the more developed countries in Sub-Saharan Africa. Per capita income was high by African standards, the educational system was the best in Africa, and infrastructure and government institutions were relatively well developed. Indeed, Roemer (1984) reports that in current parlance, economists would have considered Ghana a middle-income country.

This is, to say the least, no longer the case. The prosperity of the 1950s continued into the early 1960s, buoyed by high international cocoa prices. But prices soon fell, significantly reducing government tax revenues, which depended heavily on the cocoa export tax. The government did not respond and large fiscal deficits ensued. The deficits were, in turn, monetized, and the resulting excess demand pressure brought both inflation and balance of payments problems.

The government's reaction to these problems was increasingly statist. It imposed price controls in response to the inflation and import controls to "solve" the balance of payments problem. Even though the government made occasional attempts at liberalization, these met with strong political opposition and were always short-lived. For the better part of 15 years, Ghana's economy was increasingly subject to administrative control and the inefficiency and corruption that accompanied it.

The results were disastrous. The economy stagnated in the late 1960s and declined steadily through the 1970s. Not only did per capita incomes fall (by 2.6 percent *per year* from 1970-82), but the institutions that had made Ghana stand out in 1960, especially its schools and efficient civil service, were also ruined. Living standards deteriorated so dramatically that many well-educated Ghanaians left the country for employment elsewhere.

In the early 1980s, three shocks caused Ghana's limping economy to collapse completely: the terms of trade fell, a drought reduced agricultural output, and Nigeria expelled one million Ghanaian workers. In response to this crisis, in April 1983, the government initiated a sweeping stabilization and structural adjustment program. The program is still in effect, and its success at reversing Ghana's economic decline is the topic of this paper.

I am indebted to many people for helpful discussions. At the World Bank, Polly Jones provided much useful information and David Davies commented extensively on an earlier draft. In Ghana, I had productive discussions with Samuel Daisie and Seung Hong Choi. David Lindauer commented on an earlier draft at the Northeast Colleges Development Conference, as did Joseph Abbey at an EDI/HEDCO conference on structural adjustment in Africa. Finally, the project participants at Williams made several useful comments. The responsibility for any errors is mine.

For the most part, the package is an "orthodox" stabilization and liberalization program. It has included a series of exchange rate devaluations and a reduction in the growth of domestic credit, made possible by sufficient fiscal austerity to eliminate the government's need to print money to cover its deficit. The program has also liberalized domestic price controls, eliminating many rents associated with administrative allocation of large numbers of goods, and rationalized the relative prices of many key commodities, especially petroleum and export goods. Government investment has been focused on export-promoting development of infrastructure.

The program was not implemented without problems, but the program's successes have thus far outweighed the failures. Whereas in 1983, the economy (except for the black market) had simply ceased to work, Ghana's economy is now growing, and markets and institutions are functioning. To evaluate the effects of the recovery program on the economy, an understanding of how Ghana's economy deteriorated so badly is important. To accomplish this, a review of Ghana's recent economic history follows.

Macroeconomics

Table 6.1 compares several macroeconomic indicators for Ghana and Sub-Saharan Africa as a whole. Ghana's performance has been worse than average in a region noted for its disappointing economic development. Growth of real GDP was only 2.2 percent per annum in the 1960s; decidedly worse than the 4.0 percent average for all Sub-Saharan Africa. The situation became even worse in the 1970s, with zero growth for 1970-82,[1] including a rapid decline in 1979-82, when growth rates averaged -3.1 percent per year. Combined with a 2.6 percent growth rate of population, this led to a decline in per capita incomes of one-third from 1970-82. Even more striking is the 62 percent decline in the real minimum wage between 1970-82 (annex 6.3, table A3.1).

This decline in overall GDP was accompanied by equally disturbing changes in the types of economic activity. Growth rates in agriculture and industry were even more negative than the growth in GDP during the 1970s, indicating a shift from the productive sectors of the economy into government and trading activity. Indeed, in just two years, 1979-81, the share of retail and wholesale trade in GDP rose from 14 percent to 26 percent (annex 6.3, table A3.2). An extensive system of price controls and administrative licensing meant that the most profitable activities in Ghana had become the pursuit of rents (by traders). The World Bank (1983, p.2)

1. These figures, and all figures in this paper, are measures of officially recorded economic activity only. In a comment on an earlier draft, David Lindauer pointed out that this growth figure may be overly pessimistic since an increasing portion of economic activity in Ghana took place in black markets, and was therefore not included in official output figures. May (1985) attempted to estimate the importance of parallel market activity in Ghana and found that by 1982, it had grown to 32 percent of the GDP. If we accept this figure, it implies an average GDP growth rate of 1.7 percent from 1970-82. But May's figures are almost certainly too high: they imply that the overall economy (official plus parallel markets) grew by 12.1 percent in 1980, shrunk by 9.9 percent in 1981, and grew by 6.1 percent in 1982. All of this is obviously far from the truth. I have "smoothed" May's output series by using the lowest estimate of parallel market activity for the three years, 16 percent of GDP, and this yields an average growth rate of 0.6 percent for 1970-82, a slightly more optimistic performance than the official figures alone indicate, but still very poor.

also found that economic activity had shifted from the monetary to the subsistence sector, indicating a withdrawal from the monetized economy by some people and a collapse of organized markets.

Table 6.1 Ghana's Relative Economic Performance, 1960-82
(percent)

	1960-70		1970-82	
Category	Ghana	Low-income Sub-Saharan Africa	Ghana	Low-income Sub-Saharan Africa
Growth of GDP	2.2	4.0	0.0	1.8
Agriculture	n.a.	n.a.	0.0	1.6
Industry	n.a.	n.a.	-2.4	2.3
Manufacturing	n.a.	n.a.	-4.9	2.3
Services	n.a.	n.a.	1.5	4.3
Growth of per capita food production	0.3	1.0	-2.9	-1.2
Growth of consumption and investment				
Public consumption	7.2	4.8	3.3	5.0
Private consumption	1.7	3.6	-1.3	3.0
Gross domestic investment	-3.1	5.2	-4.9	2.6
Average annual inflation	7.5	2.6	34.9	10.8
Growth in merchandise trade accounts				
Exports	0.1	6.0	-5.3	-2.6
Imports	-1.5	6.2	-4.5	0.0
	1972		1982	
Government budget (percentage of GDP)				
Expenditure	19.5	22.2	10.1	16.6
Current Revenue	15.1	17.0	8.9	10.0

n.a. = not available

Sources: World Bank (1984a), statistical appendices to this paper

Data on domestic savings and investment also suggest that the development process had been reversed in Ghana. Savings as a percentage of GDP had declined from 17 percent in 1960 to a mere 3.9 percent in 1982 (annex 6.3, table A3.3). Some of the blame falls on real interest rates, which averaged -30 percent during the 1970s, but most falls upon dissaving by the government. The government deficit rose from 2.3 percent of GDP in 1970 to 12 percent in 1976 and 1977, only to be forced back down to 7 percent in 1980-82 by an inability to borrow (annex 6.3, table A3.4). Government absorption of most available domestic savings is also reflected in the poor performance of investment. From a respectable 24 percent of GDP in 1960, gross investment had fallen to 12.4 percent in 1970 and only 3.5 percent of GDP in 1982. Thus, it is likely that net investment was negative through much of the decade. Furthermore, Ghana was losing more than physical capital. The rapid deterioration of real wages and living standards caused many of Ghana's better educated workers—teachers, doctors, and civil servants—to emigrate, leaving Ghana with a shortage of human capital as well.

Finally, inflation averaged 34.9 percent per year from 1970-82 compared with 10.8 percent in the rest of Sub-Saharan Africa. It was fueled largely by the need to print money to finance growing government deficits, and led to the lowering (of already low) real interest rates and to a tremendously overvalued exchange rate, which was held fixed for most of the decade. In an attempt to suppress the inflation, the government imposed a variety of price controls. This led to relative prices that were often wildly out of line, required extensive rationing of many goods (including, of course, foreign exchange), and caused black markets and smuggling to flourish.[2]

External Sector

In the years immediately after independence, Ghana's economy had been relatively open. For example, exports equaled 28 percent of GDP compared with 21 percent in all of Sub-Saharan Africa. But the constant dollar value of exports remained stagnant in the 1960s and declined at a rate of 5.3 percent per year in the 1970s to the point where, in 1982, exports equaled only 3.3 percent of GDP (annex 6.3, table A3.3).

Ghana's poor economic performance has made access to official capital inflows difficult, and private flows have been rare. Thus, foreign exchange for imports has been restricted to export earnings. As a result, imports have followed exports down, and were also only 3 percent of GDP by 1982. Further, petroleum accounted for 50 percent of imports, and only 30 percent were intermediate or capital goods (World Bank 1983, p.13). The lack of spare parts was such that in 1982, an estimated 70 percent of the transport fleet was out of commission (World Bank 1983, p.14).

Exchange rate policy largely accounts for the collapse of foreign trade. Taking 1973 as a base year, Chrisney (1985, table IV.15) estimates that by 1978 the cedi was overvalued by 250 percent. The government devalued the nominal exchange rate by about 58 percent that same year, but it did little to stem the appreciation of the real rate. By 1982, the World Bank (1983, p.3) estimates that the exchange rate was overvalued by 816 percent. Such drastic overvaluation obviously offers no incentives to export anything that could be consumed locally. Exporters even began to smuggle goods such as cocoa, which are not consumed to a great extent in Ghana, at the black market exchange rate, which ranged from 250 to 350 percent of the official exchange rate in the late 1970s, and soared to 4,000 percent of the official rate

---

2. For example, despite two rounds of OPEC price hikes on world markets leading to a 600 percent increase in real world prices, official real oil prices within Ghana were actually lower in 1980 than in 1972 (World Bank 1984b, p.14). This led to a black market, and a considerable amount of oil imported on the official market was re-exported on the black market.

by late 1982. This greatly reduced the flow of foreign exchange through official channels.

Imports, however, became extraordinarily cheap. Demand for imports at the official exchange rate far outstripped available foreign exchange, and the government was forced to control all imports strictly. Thus, in the 1970s it put into place a careful system of import licensing, price controls, and administrative allocation. As the exchange rate became increasingly overvalued, however, even the licensing system could not keep up with the demand for imports. Authorities were forced to resort to further gimmicks, such as controlling letters of credit issued to importers, and they also began to license more imports than available foreign exchange would permit, leaving some supposedly licensed imports without foreign exchange. In the end, only very small amounts of imports were possible, and those that were allowed were usually not goods with high scarcity values (such as spare parts). This contributed to the economy's poor performance overall.

Agriculture

Even though Ghana has a comparative advantage in certain agricultural crops, especially cocoa and timber, this sector suffered disproportionately in Ghana's economic decline and largely accounts for the collapse of exports.

Cocoa has always been Ghana's most important export, and is also a significant part of the GDP. Through the 1970s, cocoa accounted for 60 to 70 percent of all exports, so the decline in cocoa production of the 1970s explains much of the decline in export revenues. From a peak of 538,000 metric tons in 1965, production gradually declined to 394,000 metric tons in 1976, then dropped sharply to a mere 179,000 metric tons in 1983. The reasons for the decreased production are not difficult to find. Table 6.2 shows the real producer price the Ghana Cocoa Marketing Board (GCMB) paid to farmers. The real prices paid to farmers in the mid-1970s drop steeply, coinciding with the decline in production.

What accounts for the fall in producer prices? First, the overvaluation of the cedi throughout the period made it difficult for the GCMB, which receives its revenues in foreign exchange, to pay a high cedi price to farmers. Second, the GCMB itself became inefficient, leading to increased "marketing costs" (payments to GCMB). The World Bank has estimated that of GCMB's staff of 100,000, it really only needs half. Finally, the government has steadily increased the (implicit) tax on cocoa exports by holding producer prices down. Thus, in 1965, the year of peak production, producers received 68 percent of the revenues from the cocoa crop—the rest went for export duties and marketing costs—while in 1979, the producers' share had fallen to only 26 percent (World Bank 1983, p.12). In addition, the government's financial difficulties and the general foreign exchange constraint meant that extension services were no longer provided and that imports were difficult to obtain. Thus, by 1982, Ghana's cocoa production had fallen to 70 kg/ha, compared to 111 kg/ha in all of Sub-Saharan Africa (World Bank 1983, p.13).

The decline of cocoa production (and exports) is the most important problem for Ghana's agriculture, but it is certainly not unique. Despite the substantial contraction of cocoa exports, cocoa's share of all Ghanaian exports remained relatively constant, indicating that most exports had experienced a similar collapse. Thus, from 1970-80, the export volume of gold, Ghana's second most important export, fell 7 percent annually, and the export volume of timber fell 14 percent annually. Here too the poor incentive provided by the overvalued exchange rate, the inability to import key spare parts, and the general deterioration of the infrastructure (especially the railways) all contributed to the decline in these key exports.

The agricultural production of nonexport food crops fared little better than that of industrial crops. As tables 6.3 and 6.4 show, production of all food crops fell from 1970-82. Per capita food production fell an average of 2.9 percent per year from 1970-82.

Table 6.2 Cocoa Production and Cocoa Prices, 1965-86

Year	Cocoa production, Ghana (mt 000)	Cocoa price, Ghana[a]	Cocoa price, Togo[a]	Cocoa price Côte d'Ivoire[a]	Real cocoa price (1980 cedis)
1965	538	151.6	187.35	187.69	5,533
1966	401	197.7	351.04	519.04	6,377
1967	368	247.9	368.76	472.77	8,729
1968	415	278.5	497.64	498.96	9,072
1969	323	293.8	571.68	523.78	8,930
1970	403	300.5	523.12	489.05	8,864
1971	413	360.9	583.81	530.32	9,728
1972	454	385.0	588.03	538.60	9,413
1973	407	484.5	564.19	563.21	10,073
1974	340	577.9	675.92	894.85	10,074
1975	376	679.2	783.56	1,193.94	9,203
1976	394	976.8	1,055.54	1,556.65	8,479
1977	320	1,601.4	2,795.70	4,260.43	6,424
1978	271	3,308.1	4,632.04	7,730.57	7,667
1979	265	3,936.3	8,347.46	10,972.32	5,908
1980	296	5,333.5	17,232.23	21,866.14	5,334
1981	258	12,000.0	14,914.72	20,338.25	5,543
1982	224	12,000.0	30,203.59	40,271.46	4,536
1983	179	20,000.0	n.a.	n.a.	3,389
1984	159	30,000.0	n.a.	n.a.	3,640
1985	174	56,600.0	n.a.	n.a.	6,226
1986	219	85,000.0	n.a.	n.a.	7,791

n.a. = not available

a. All three prices in nominal cedis. Prices for Togo and Côte d'Ivoire were translated from CFA francs to cedis at the black market exchange rate.

Source: Cocoa production and producer prices: *Quarterly Statistical Digest* (various), cocoa prices for Togo and Côte d'Ivoire, May (1985).

Table 6.3 Ghana's Agricultural Production for Major Crops, Selected Years *(tons 000)*

Year	Maize	Rice	Millet	Guinea corn	Total cereals	Starchy staples
1970	482	49	141	186	858	6,007
1975	343	71	122	135	672	5,452
1980	382	78	82	132	674	4,349
1981	378	97	119	131	725	4,114
1982	346	36	76	86	544	4,431
1983	172	40	40	56	308	3,649
1984	574	66	139	176	955	6,150
1985	395	80	120	185	780	4,891
1986	495	80	140	190	905	n.a.

n.a. = not available
Source: World Bank (1987)

Table 6.4 Ghana's Agricultural Yields of Major Crops, Selected Years *(kg / ha)*

Year	Maize	Rice	Millet	Guinea corn	Average cereal yield	Starchy staples
1970	1,065	887	567	766	858	5,680
1975	1,074	906	613	650	834	6,078
1980	1,080	836	630	536	718	6,321
1981	1,016	836	758	662	860	5,997
1982	928	590	442	394	661	6,020
1983	430	1,000	229	255	369	4,918
1984	790	1,100	600	700	n.a.	n.a.
1985	1,000	920	540	740	n.a.	n.a.
1986	1,100	890	580	680	n.a.	n.a.

n.a. = not available
Source: World Bank (1987)

Public Finance and Monetary Policy

The fiscal performance of Ghana's public sector has been extremely poor and lies at the heart of Ghana's economic problems. Figure 6.1 shows that government deficits as a proportion of GDP were substantial throughout the 1970s and early 1980s. These deficits are the starting point for many of the problems that Ghana's economy faced in the period.

To begin with, because of the government's poor performance, it did not have access to private credit from either domestic or foreign sources. Consequently, it had to finance its deficits by borrowing from the banking system, especially the central bank. In essence, the government printed money to cover its deficits. This in turn led to high rates of inflation, which caused the overvaluation of the cedi and eroded real producer prices, leading to the agricultural sector's disappointing performance and the worsening balance of payments situation. Overall, the government's share of domestic credit rose from 49 percent in 1970 to 86 percent in 1982. Thus, the persistent budget deficits forced the government to absorb almost all the credit available in the economy, crowding out private borrowers and causing severe inflation.

This series of problems is not, of course, unusual. The cycle of deficits leading to monetary expansion leading to misaligned real prices (especially exchange rates) is quite common, but the extreme nature of the problem in Ghana led to some rather unusual phenomena. Figure 6.1 shows that, beginning in the late 1970s, government expenditure as a proportion of GDP, rather than increasing, began to decline sharply. The deficit persisted only because revenues also declined sharply. Indeed, an explanation of this begins with the decline in revenues, which was brought about by the decline in international trade (figure 6.2), the overvaluation of the cedi, and the general collapse of formal markets in the Ghanaian economy.

Figure 6.3 shows the real value of import and export (largely cocoa) taxes collected by the government. Both sources of revenue decline in the late 1970s. As we have already seen, cocoa production fell substantially through this period, so despite the government's increasingly high "tax" on cocoa implied by low real producer prices, overall tax revenue from exports declined. The reduction in imports required by the decline in exports reduced the tax base for import tariffs, leading to a decline in tariff revenues as well.

Apart from the reduction in volumes of imports and exports, the overvaluation of the cedi also contributed to the decline in real tax revenues. Taxes are levied on the cedi value of imports and exports. Because these values are not inflating with the rest of the economy, taxes based on them lose real value. Thus, while the cedi prices of domestic goods and services purchased by the government were inflating rapidly, the cedi prices of the exports and imports it taxed were not, leading to increased deficits.

In addition to losses in taxes on international transactions, revenues also declined as the structure of formal markets in the economy collapsed. Both smuggling and black market transactions are, of course, nontaxable, and both increased significantly during the period (see May 1985). Finally, significant delays in the actual collection of taxes, combined with rapid inflation, also reduced the real value of revenues when they were finally collected. Faced with substantial declines in revenues, the government was forced to reduce expenditures. Thus, at the same time that government deficits were causing persistent inflation, the real value of government expenditure was actually falling due to even greater declines in revenue.

Figure 6.1 Government Surplus, Revenues, and Expenditures as a Share of GDP

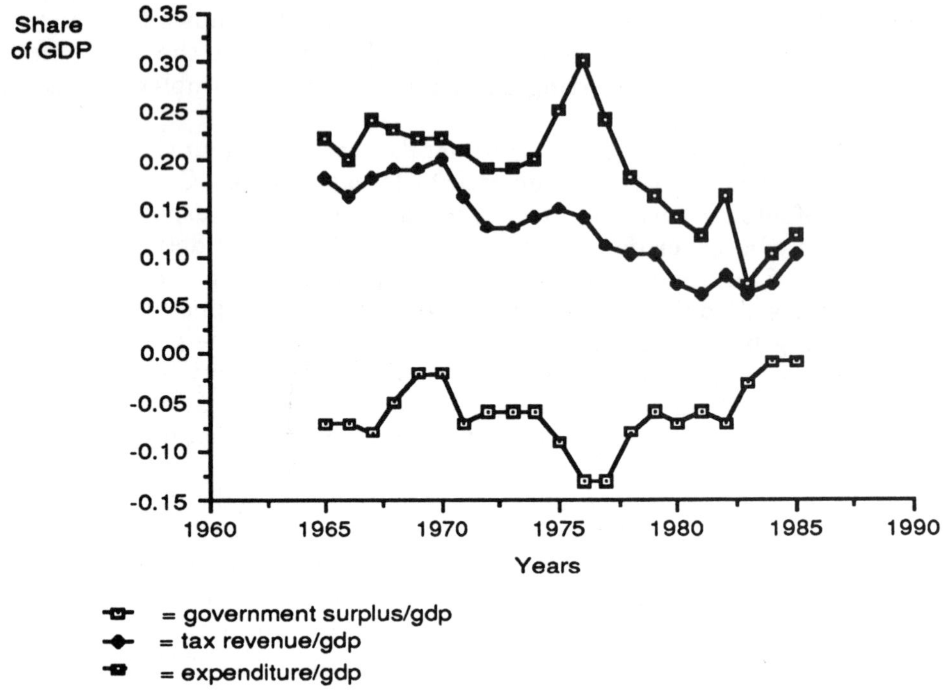

Figure 6.2 Real (1980 US$) Value of Exports and Imports

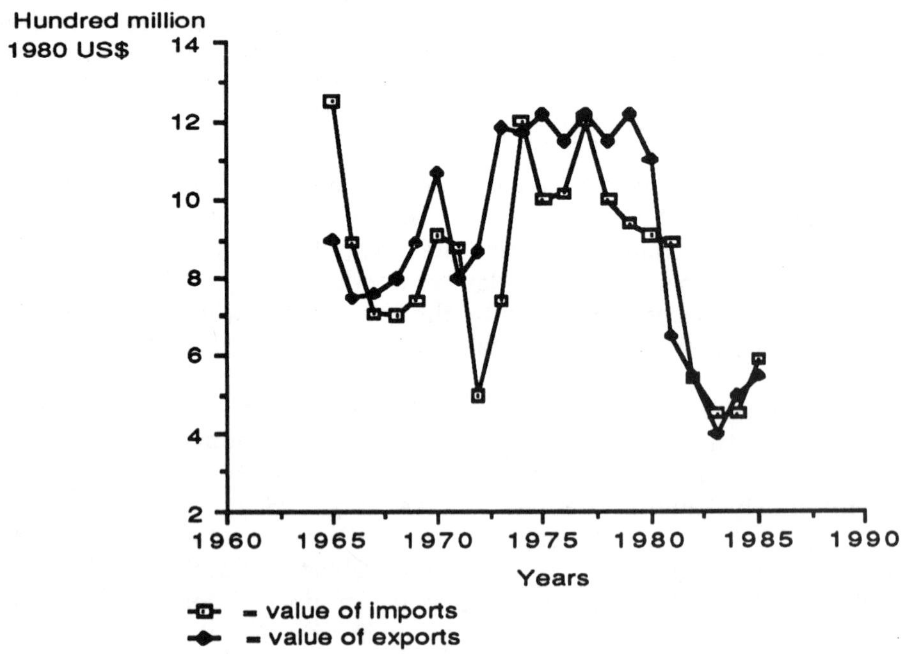

Figure 6.3 Real Value of Taxes Collected on Exports and Imports

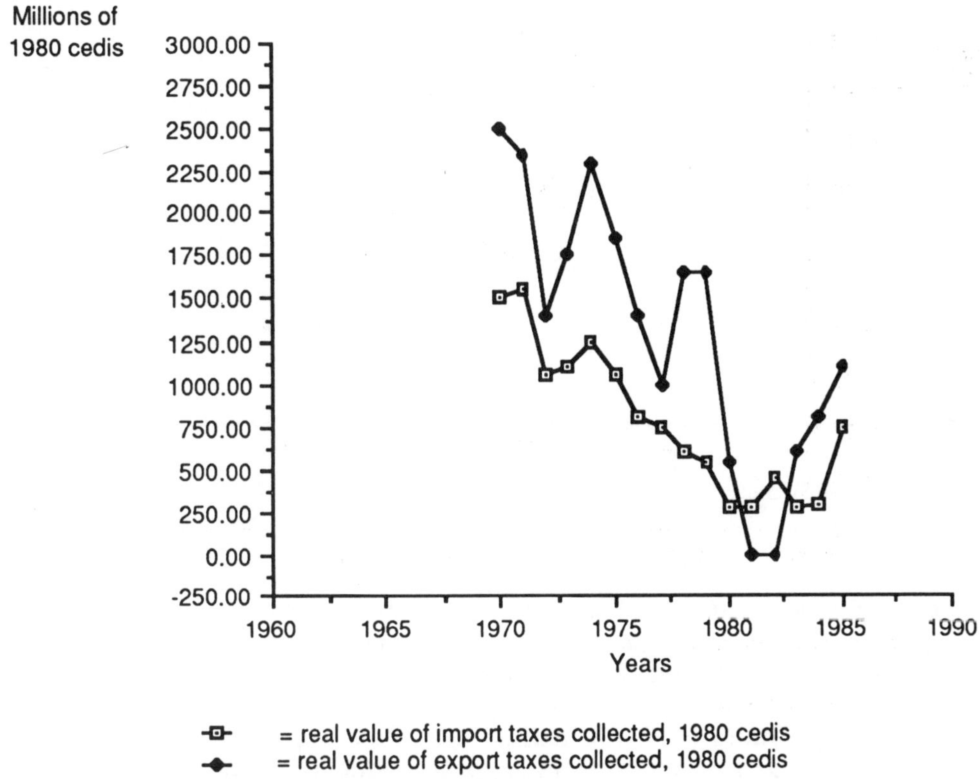

Economic problems led to political problems for a succession of governments, and a principal response was to dole out patronage in the form of government employment. Thus, despite an already overstaffed bureaucracy and increasing budgetary problems, civil service employment grew at 14 percent per annum between 1975 and 1982 (World Bank 1983, p.67). Given that even as early as 1972 almost 60 percent of the government's nondebt current expenditure was for wages, this rise in employment meant that either real wages or other expenditures had to fall. In the end, both did.

Development expenditures, typically 4 to 6 percent of GDP in the early 1970s, fell to 1.5 percent of GDP in 1982. Two areas severely affected included education and health. Expenditure on education averaged 3.4 percent of GDP during the 1970s (compared with 5.2 percent in all of Sub-Saharan Africa), and fell to only 1 percent of GDP in 1983 (World Bank 1985, p.74). Government expenditures on health declined from 1.4 percent of GDP in 1975/76 to 0.78 percent in 1979/80 and 0.32 percent in 1983.

Finally, the reduction in revenues forced real wages down, particularly for those holding higher-level administrative posts. Thus, while the real minimum wage for unskilled civil servants fell to only 32 percent of its 1977 value in 1983, a remarkable decline, for senior civil servants the reduction was even more severe, with 1983 wages being about 15 percent of 1977 wages in real terms (World Bank, 1985, pp. 67-69). Thus, the wage structure was compressed—senior civil servants earned only about twice as much as unskilled civil servants compared to a 10:1 ratio in the private sector (World Bank 1985, p.68). Wages fell so much overall that even mid-level bureaucrats found themselves below the poverty line (table 6.5).

Table 6.5 Average Monthly Real Wages for Civil Servants, Selected Years (*1977 cedis)*

Year	Unskilled	Semiskilled	Junior professional	Senior professional
1977	1,017	n.a.	n.a.	5,940
1980	322	398	1,273	1,808
1982	419	476	1,149	1,858
1983	329	355	668	877
1984	354	373	595	701
1985	719	737	1,043	1,188

n.a. = not available

Source: World Bank (1985), p.69

The salary reductions caused a flight of skilled labor from the civil service (and often from Ghana as well), and a general collapse of the government's routine functions. For example, the Ghana Water and Sewage Corporation had 90 engineers in 1979; only 20 remained in 1984. The same agency had *no* accountants by 1984. That same year, the Ghana Highway Authority's planning section had only one senior staff member and seven vacancies, and the education ministry lost up to 10,000 staff, including 13 percent of all teachers (World Bank 1984b, p.34). Those staff that remained often found that support services, such as telephones, typing, even stationery, were not available, and the low salaries required a high degree of moonlighting or out and out absenteeism.

Thus the government had, in many respects, ceased to function normally: support for education and health had all but disappeared; infrastructure was badly maintained; and even tax collection was inefficient. The policies that had ravaged Ghana's economy in the 1970s—large deficits that fueled rapid monetary growth, an overvalued exchange rate, widespread price controls and the consequent rationing of many goods, and low producer prices for agriculture—eventually caused the government itself to deteriorate.

In the early 1980s, three important shocks caused the Ghanaian economy to grind to a complete halt. First, the extremely favorable terms of trade that Ghana had experienced in the 1970s deteriorated rapidly in the 1980s. Calculating net barter terms of trade as the world price of cocoa divided by a nonoil developing country import price index, the World Bank (1983, p.9) finds that Ghana's terms of trade improved 50 percent between 1975 and 1979. While Ghana did not take advantage of this by increasing export volumes—indeed, they fell—the better prices did prop up export earnings. But the terms of trade then deteriorated about 12 percent per year from 1979-82, reversing Ghana's fortunes. Second, Nigeria expelled much of its migrant labor force, forcing roughly one million Ghanaian workers to return. Finally, the drought of 1981-83 severely reduced agricultural output, especially in the 1983 season, and contributed to widespread bush fires that reduced cocoa acreage.

As the economy collapsed, so did the government, and Flight Lt. Jerry Rawlings took power in a military coup d'état on the last day of 1981. Rawlings' government, the Provisional National Defense Council, made some attempt at stabilizing the economy in 1982, concentrating on the government budget. The government increased tax collection efforts and put in place severe expenditure controls. These measures helped control the deficit, which increased only 3 percent in nominal terms in 1982, and inflation, which at 22 percent was the lowest in eight years. However, the government clearly saw that the rapid decline in output and general deterioration of the economy meant that fiscal austerity was not enough. Throughout 1982 the government considered a major program that combined stabilization and structural adjustment measures. It opened negotiations with the IMF and the World Bank, and finally in April 1983, the government announced its economic recovery program (ERP). (For a more detailed account of Ghana's recent history see annex 6.1.)

The Economic Recovery Program

The ERP is not simply a package of policies implemented in 1983. It is a continuing effort to stabilize, rehabilitate, and restructure the Ghanaian economy. As such, it involves a wide range of policies, many of which have been adjusted since 1983 in reaction to their effects on the economy.

The goal of the ERP is to reverse the poor policies of the previous 10-15 years to reestablish economic growth and development. In particular, its main objectives are (a) to "get the prices right" by devaluing the exchange rate, increasing real interest rates, and decontrolling internal prices; (b) to reduce the fiscal deficit sufficiently to eliminate the need for printing money to cover it, thus reducing inflation; and (c) to liberalize the economy, including the foreign sector, by encouraging markets to function freely.

In addition to these typical policy changes, however, the ERP recognized that the badly run down state of Ghana's roads, railways, ports, water and sewerage installations, and telecommunications systems dictated sizeable investments to rehabilitate the basic infrastructure. The government deemed these investments to have a high rate of return because of their absolute necessity for re-establishing normal market functions, particularly for exports.

At the same time, however, the resources available to the government (and the nation as a whole) were extremely limited due to the rapid decline of tax and export revenues, and because of Ghana's lack of creditworthiness in international capital markets. For example, in 1983 the World Bank estimated that simply to restore capacity that had been idled by the lack of imports would require US$600 million in intermediate inputs per year. Meanwhile, the government only had US$650 million in foreign exchange, including an IMF loan of US$265 million (World Bank 1983, pp.53-55). Consequently, the government not only faced the problem of how best to implement a stabilization program, it also had to be highly selective in rationing its expenditure for structural adjustment. In an economy where investment is needed virtually everywhere (and likely to be profitable if carried out well), this is a particularly difficult situation.

During the ERP's first year, most of the policies were directed toward macroeconomic stabilization rather than investment in rehabilitation or structural change, though there was some early emphasis on rehabilitating export industries (see annex 6.2 for a timetable of important policy changes from 1983-86). This was partly because stabilization policies are easier to implement quickly, and partly because neither the government nor the economy as a whole could afford much investment expenditure. The stabilization policies focused on a variety of price changes, including decontrol of many domestic prices, and a sharp reduction in the fiscal deficit (which allowed the government to reduce the rate of monetary growth considerably). The most important price adjustment was in the exchange rate. In April 1983, the cedi was devalued from 2.75 to the dollar to a dual rate of 23.375 cedis per dollar and 29.975 cedis per dollar depending on the type of receipt.

According to the World Bank (1984b, pp.5-8), exporters of certain products, for example, timber and minerals, were allowed to retain from 10 to 30 percent of their foreign exchange earnings for purchases of productive inputs, giving them an even higher effective exchange rate. The government then gradually adjusted exchange rates upwards with the local inflation until they were unified at 30 cedis per dollar in October 1983, meaning that the cedi had been devalued by more than 1,000 percent in the first six months of the stabilization effort.[3]

With two exceptions—fertilizer and petroleum products—the government allowed importers to raise their prices to reflect fully the higher cedi cost of imports. Later in the year, fertilizer and petroleum prices were also increased substantially—900 percent and 500 percent respectively. In addition, the government also raised the charges for its services significantly. Railway freight charges rose 380 percent, urban water rates rose 150 percent, electricity tariffs rose 700 percent, road transport tariffs rose 165 percent, and so on. Deposit interest rates were raised from 8 percent to 11 percent and loan rates from 14 percent to 19 percent, though both remained well below the rate of inflation.

The government was forced to make these huge changes in many controlled prices because most official prices had been held constant in the face of very rapid inflation, making them extremely unrealistic. This also meant that the amount of initial price adjustments was difficult to assess. That is, it was difficult to guess what the appropriate *relative* prices ought to be after all prices had been increased, and the government made some mistakes in the calculations. To its credit, the government has continued to adjust controlled prices in an attempt to establish the appropriate relative prices, even though this is often politically unpopular. In many cases, the government "set" prices closer to opportunity cost simply by removing the price controls, which eliminated the black market and established an appropriate free market price directly. Indeed, by December 1983 only 23 items had absolute price controls, though a reference price system offered government "guidelines" for other prices.

As the ERP progressed, the price adjustments led to substantial changes in relative prices in favor of exports and Ghana's traditionally competitive industries. For example, from 1983-86, the real exchange rate recovered almost all of the deterioration it had suffered in the 1970s. Also, the ratio of the price of a metric ton of cocoa to the urban minimum wage—a rough measure of relative pay to Ghana's key

3. Despite this huge devaluation, the official exchange rate remained below the black market rate. The 1984 *World Currency Yearbook* reports black market rates for the cedi of 55 per dollar in May 1983, leaving the official rate at only about half the black market rate. By the end of the year, the black market rate had jumped to 97 cedis per dollar, more than three times the official rate. A second interesting aspect of the black market is that the black market exchange rate, which represents the marginal cost of foreign exchange in a rationed regime, actually fell when the first major devaluation of the official rate occurred (in April). This is apparently because a larger flow of foreign exchange through the official market lessened the demand for foreign currency in the black market, strengthening the cedi. It also suggests that the devaluation may not have been inflationary since the true scarcity price of tradable goods, as captured in the black market, actually fell.

agricultural export and the rewards for urban labor—rose sharply during the ERP, reversing the decline of the 1970s. Thus the ERP has, on the whole, corrected much of the dramatic shift in relative prices away from the agricultural and export sectors.

The second important policy initiative of the 1983 stabilization was a sharp improvement in the fiscal deficit, which fell from 6.9 percent to 2.5 percent of the GDP (which actually fell in real terms). Because imports and the GDP did not grow as expected, revenues actually fell as a proportion of the GDP, so the government reduced the deficit entirely by making difficult cuts in both current and capital expenditures. This allowed it to cut its borrowing from the central bank and to stay well within the credit limits established in its IMF stand-by arrangement (World Bank 1984b, p.9).

In all, the ERP's first year saw many radical policy changes, most of which were aimed at correcting the government's fiscal position and reducing or eliminating the widespread price distortions caused by controls.

Economic Performance, 1983

Despite the government's bold actions the economy's performance in 1983 was disappointing, yet much of this was due to a drought that persisted and worsened through the 1983 growing season. Agricultural output, which accounts for roughly half of the GDP, fell by 7.2 percent, while overall GDP declined by 4.6 percent.[4] At the same time, the drought pushed agricultural prices up substantially; the food component of the consumer price index rose 145 percent in 1983, pulling overall inflation up to 123 percent (annex 6.3, table A3.5).

The drought and several ensuing brush fires also contributed to another year of declining cocoa production, which fell by 11.8 percent in 1983 to a record low of 158 million tons. Economists estimate that this decline cost Ghana US$80 million in export receipts.

Not only did export revenues fall, net capital inflows were one-third of the initial ERP projections—US$113 million instead of an expected US$331 million. To some extent this reflected delays in disbursement of aid, but large shortfalls of official oil credits—only US$10 million of an expected US$139 million materialized—and supplier's credits to importers—US$30 million rather than the estimated US$192 million—cut the available foreign exchange significantly. The lack of foreign exchange forced a reduction in imports from the already unprecedentedly low 1982 level, which had important adverse effects on the economy.

Government revenues, which depend heavily on import taxes, declined slightly in real terms rather than increasing as the ERP had projected. This forced large expenditure cuts, including a 43 percent reduction in badly needed capital expenditures. As a result, much of the ERP's rehabilitation work—maintenance expenditures on infrastructure such as roads, ports, and railways—was left unfunded. This created a vicious circle: the decline in rehabilitation expenditure had a negative effect on exports. Many exporters who had had very favorable relative price changes in 1983, especially producers of minerals and timber, were

4. Even though it is difficult to distinguish between the effects of the drought and the effects of the ERP's policy changes, evidence that the poor growth performance was largely accounted for by the drought is provided by data on agricultural yields. Cereal yields fell 23 percent in 1982 and 44 percent in 1983. Yields of starchy staples were stable in 1982, but fell 20 percent in 1983 (World Bank 1983, table 7.06).

hampered in responding to these price changes due to a lack of spare parts and to poorly functioning railways and ports. As a result, noncocoa exports were US$86 million below the ERP's expectations in 1983, further constraining foreign exchange revenues.

The same type of shortage in rehabilitative investment was prevalent throughout the economy, in both the public and private sectors, and generally depressed the level of economic activity. From 1980-84, capacity utilization rates in the manufacturing sector were less than 20 percent, due largely to the lack of imported spare parts or inputs (see table 6.6). Imports of crude oil, an important energy source for transport and industry, declined by 62 percent because of a decline in oil credits and a refinery accident, and electricity production from the Volta dams fell 48 percent in 1983 because of the low water levels of the lake after three years of drought.

Table 6.6 Capacity Utilization in Selected Industries, 1978-85
(percent)

Year	Textiles	Wood processing	Vehicle assembly	Food processing	All manufacturing
1978	40.0	36.0	18.4	40.8	40.4
1979	32.0	36.4	16.7	22.9	33.1
1980	20.1	27.3	n.a.	n.a.	24.4
1981	20.0	37.6	n.a.	24.6	24.9
1982	10.0	20.0	15.0	n.a.	21.0
1983	6.8	25.3	4.0	25.0	14.7
1984	17.3	28.1	7.6	22.9	18.0
1985	19.7	32.5	19.9	31.2	25.0

n.a. = not available

Source: Quarterly Digest of Statistics, March 1987

It is evident that fate was not with the Ghanaians in 1983, making it in many respects an inopportune time to initiate an ambitious change in economic policy.[5] Given the poor economic performance of 1983, it would have been understandable if the government had abandoned its stabilization effort and run up a large, money-financed fiscal deficit in an effort to counter the adverse effect of the drought. To its credit, the government made the politically risky decision to stick with the ERP. As we have seen, the government held the budget deficit to 2.5 percent of the GDP by making large cuts in expenditures, allowing credit ceilings to be met. Furthermore, policies that followed the initial flurry of changes were generally consistent with the goals of stabilization, relative price adjustment to reflect scarcity values, and

5. Joseph Abbey has contested this point, arguing that the government actually *chose* to initiate the program during the drought so that it could deflect criticism of some of the program's adverse effects—especially price increases—by blaming them on the drought.

economic liberalization. In short, the government stuck to its guns in the face of extreme adversity.

This determination and the return of normal rainfall in 1984 represent the turning point in the success of the ERP. By maintaining the program under economically and politically difficult circumstances, the government gained credibility with the IMF, the World Bank, and bilateral donors who had shunned Ghana throughout the 1970s. As a consequence, gross official development assistance rose 78 percent in 1984 (Republic of Ghana 1985) as donors began to recognize that the ERP was a serious effort worth their support, and further increases followed in 1985 and 1986. As early as 1984, the World Bank had come to believe in the government's commitment and "went to bat" for it with other donors.[6]

Policies and Performance Since 1983

Ghana's stabilization policies continued along the same lines through 1986. Occasional devaluations occurred as the government attempted to move the official rate toward an equilibrium where import rationing was unnecessary. Thus, the cedi was devalued to 50 per dollar in December 1984, to 60 per dollar in October 1985, and to 90 per dollar in January 1986. Finally, in late 1986, the government adopted an auction system so that the exchange rate, which is determined on a weekly basis by market forces, is more or less at an equilibrium level. (See annex 6.4 for a detailed description of Ghana's auction system.)

Fiscal policy remained tight, with the deficit held to 2 percent of the GDP in 1984 and 1985, and government borrowing from the central bank held to 0.6 percent of the GDP, or about an 8 percent increase in domestic credit to the government (World Bank 1986). By July 1985, only eight items were subject to statutory price controls, and administered prices continued to be adjusted upwards in real terms, the most important being an 88 percent increase in the producer price of cocoa in May 1985.

The main change after the first year of the ERP was that with a return of normal rains spurring sharp agricultural growth, a fortunate increase in world cocoa prices, and the increase in foreign aid commitments, import flows could increase and the government could begin its rehabilitation programs for several key sectors of the economy. Payoffs were both immediate, since certain production bottlenecks were alleviated, and long-term, as the stage was set for structural adjustments whose benefits would come in the future. The results were impressive. Real GDP growth was 8.6 percent in 1984 and 5.1 percent in 1985 (see annex 6.3, tables A3.2, A3.3, and A3.6). Growth for 1986 is estimated at 5.3 percent (World Bank 1987, table 2.03). Thus, Ghana has experienced three consecutive years of economic growth for the first time since 1970.

As might be expected, the agriculture sector, which grew by 9.3 percent, led the 1984 growth. The return of the rains caused much of this growth, but industrial growth was also strong in 1984 at 8.6 percent, as was the growth in services at 6.4

---

6. For example, the introduction to a 1984 World Bank progress report on the ERP states:

> In sum, in less than two years, the government has wrought a major transformation in the country's overall economic environment...A severe drought, an unanticipated foreign exchange crisis, and the resultant high inflation have greatly complicated the management of this period of transition..Taking account of all these difficulties, it is, to say the least, highly praiseworthy that so much has been achieved thus far...it would indeed be tragic if this experiment were allowed to fail for lack of adequate external support and Ghana's economy were permitted to slip back down the dreary slope of decline. (World Bank 1984b, p. xii)

percent. Furthermore, the solid growth persisted in 1985 even though agricultural growth fell to 0.8 percent after the previous boom year. So, while part of the growth was due to a return of normal weather, a considerable part was also due to perseverance with the ERP and timely adaptation to changing conditions.

The performance of other macroeconomic indicators in 1984 and 1985 was also encouraging. Inflation fell to 40 percent in 1984 and 10 percent in 1985, helped by falling food prices in 1984 and by the government's greatly diminished use of the inflation tax.

The constant dollar value of merchandise exports rose by 29 percent in 1984, 12 percent in 1985, and 26 percent in 1986, allowing Ghana to fund a larger share of its increased imports from its own resources. Furthermore, the export recovery has been broad based, with every major export commodity showing increases in volume. Cocoa bean production, which was 159,000 metric tons in 1983, rose to 219,100 metric tons in 1986. Diamond exports rose from 425,000 carats in 1983 to 556,000 in 1986. Timber exports more than tripled from 103,000 cubic meters in 1983 to 329,000 in 1986, and manganese exports doubled in two years from 127,000 tons in 1983 to 263,441 in 1985. Even minor exports more than doubled in value from 1983 to 1985.

As table 6.7 shows, not all of these export goods posted production gains at the same time, both because the initial nominal prices determined by the ERP sometimes went awry in real terms, and because the repairs to infrastructure needed to move particular export goods to and from ports were completed at different times. But as it gained experience, the government adjusted prices and the rehabilitation program moved forward, yielding a broad based increase in exports and demonstrating the government's sustained commitment to establishing relative prices that reflect scarcity values.

After the sharp reductions in government expenditures necessitated by low revenues in 1983, government spending has grown steadily as a proportion of the GDP as the government has begun to perform its normal functions (see figure 6.1 and annex 6.3, table A3.4). Thus, overall expenditures grew from a low of 8.0 percent of GDP in 1983 to 12.3 percent in 1985, and development expenditures grew from 0.7 percent of GDP to 2.0 percent. (Note, however, that these figures are still well below the 18 to 25 percent and 4 to 7 percent ranges, respectively, for the 1960s and 1970s.)

Yet all of this has been accomplished without increasing the fiscal deficit, which has been held to less than 1.5 percent of GDP because of improved tax revenues (see table A3.4). Tax revenues have increased partly because of better enforcement of the tax laws, but largely because of the effect of successive devaluations on trade tax revenues. The devaluations increased the cedi value of exports and imports considerably, thereby increasing the traded goods tax base. The devaluations also allowed the government to increase producer prices for cocoa, which encourages more exports (and a larger tax base), and to reinstate a cocoa export duty. Finally, the increased flow of exports and foreign loans has allowed an increased flow of imports, again increasing the tax base for tariff duties.

Based on wide macroeconomic measures, the ERP appears to be succeeding. After more than a decade of declining output, imports, and exports and of rapid inflation, the economy has experienced three years of solid growth that has not been fueled by a large fiscal expansion. Indeed, the government's fiscal and monetary policies have been tight, helping to reduce inflation and restore local and international confidence in the Ghanaian economy. However, a host of unmeasured changes have also occurred. Store shelves are full. Trading has returned to legal markets. Government workers are back in their offices.

Telephones, roads, and water lines are being repaired and service is much improved. This is the broad sense in which the ERP is a success.

Table 6.7 Production Volume of Major Export Goods, 1970, 1980-86

Year	Cocoa (mt 000)	Gold (oz 000)	Diamonds (carats 000)	Manganese (mt 000)	Timber (m^3 000)	Bauxite (mt 000)
1970	403	n.a.	2,550	392	1,560	337
1980	258	353	1,149	250	600	225
1981	224	341	837	223	550	181
1982	179	331	684	160	410	64
1983	159	280	339	173	663	70
1984	174	289	346	267	758	49
1985	219	310	636	357	800	169
1986	n.a.	n.a.	556	332	n.a.	204

n.a. = not available

Source: World Bank (1984, 1986)

Furthermore, this has occurred even though Ghana started the ERP in a "worst case" situation. The World Bank (1983, p.4) reports that price distortions were worse in Ghana than in any other developing economy during the 1970s. Imports and exports had fallen to almost insignificant levels, as had government tax revenues. By 1983, formal markets barely functioned. And just as the stabilization program was initiated, Ghana was hit by a serious drought. In the face of such odds, it is remarkable that the ERP has achieved the results that it has.

Of course, any set of policy changes as radical and wide-ranging as the ERP cannot succeed without encountering problems. Two deserve mention here: liquidity and overstaffing.

Liquidity Problems

With the dramatic change in the exchange rate in 1983, firms that imported inputs found that their costs had risen sharply. To continue operations, the firms had to borrow much more money (in cedis) to finance their imports. However, in many cases banks doubted the firms' ability to repay loans and were reluctant to provide them.

Several factors contributed to this situation. First, no one knew initially whether the government would allow the firms to increase their prices sufficiently to cover the higher costs of imports. If not, they would be unable to repay the loans. However, the government did permit the price increases fairly quickly. Second, the Bank of Ghana maintained credit ceilings for individual sectors of the economy such that some sectors did not require all of their allocations while others were overly constrained. Third, the banks were not sure of the firms' profitability under the new circumstances. It was not clear, for example, that firms could maintain sales if they increased their prices enough to cover the higher costs. Moreover, firms that had been able to import inputs at artificially cheap prices due to the overvalued cedi had gained an implicit rent on those imports—the difference between what they paid and the domestic value of the good. This rent, which contributed to the firms' profitability and thus their ability to repay loans, was reduced or eliminated by the devaluation.

In more general terms, the great changes in relative prices meant that some firms that had been profitable under controlled prices might not be so in freer markets, while other firms would actually be more profitable. The trick for the banks was to figure out which were which. In the language of financial institutions, the banks need to distinguish insolvent firms—those that would not make a profit even if they received a loan—from illiquid ones—those that would make a profit (and repay) if they could get the necessary letters of credit. However, making these reassessments reliably is difficult in a rapidly changing economic environment. The result was that many firms that were merely illiquid, not insolvent, did not get loans, which reduced the flow of imports and constrained the pace of the recovery.

Depositors' lack of confidence in the banks has also hindered financial intermediation. The ratio of currency to M2 (the money supply, broadly defined) gives a measure of confidence in the banking system since it shows the proportion of monetary assets people hold as cash outside the banks. As table A3.7 (annex 6.3) shows, this ratio is high in Ghana and has fallen very slowly in the course of the ERP despite substantial increases in real interest rates on bank deposits. To some extent, the reluctance of depositors to shift out of currency into deposits reflects the continued uncertainty surrounding the government's financial policy, however, the government has also used records of bank deposits as a means of checking income for tax purposes, thus people with income to hide tend not to deposit it in a bank.

Thus far, the large inflow of foreign capital to Ghana has been sufficient to compensate for the banking system's inability to generate significant domestic finance. However, as the net inflow of foreign credit falls, Ghana's financial intermediation will have to improve to avoid serious credit constraints. While the government has taken some positive steps to encourage capital to move into the banking system,[7] Ghana's financial system remains very underdeveloped, a problem that will hinder the country's long-term development prospects.

Overstaffing

The overstaffing of Ghana's civil service presents the government with an important policy dilemma: on the one hand, the stabilization program requires tight control of government expenditures; on the other hand, restoration of the efficiency of the civil service requires higher real wages, as does the government's ability to retain relatively skilled civil servants needed to carry out the extensive administrative and evaluative work of the ERP.

The obvious solution is to lay off some civil servants and workers in the parastatal sector, while raising the remaining workers' wages. This, however, is a very difficult option to pursue politically, because the private sector may not be able to absorb all the excess labor currently on the government payroll. Even though the economy has been growing quite rapidly, the private sector has also been

7. For example, in 1987 the government "remonetized" the 50 cedi bills, with interest, that had been demonetized in 1978. (This was done to penalize smugglers and black market traders, who the government believed were the major holders of 50 cedi bills.) In addition, the government is now assuring potential depositors that information on bank accounts will remain private, but it takes time to build confidence in such assurances, and progress to date has not been great.

overstaffed. Thus, firms will not hire new labor until they absorb their own excess staff; a turning point that is difficult to predict.

Nevertheless, the government recognizes the importance of resolving this problem and has begun to address it by laying off some staff. As a start, the Cocoa Marketing Board laid off more than 30,000 "ghost workers," that is, fictitious people added to the payroll to pad other employees' salaries. The marketing board has also divested itself of several farms, and the 9,000 employees working on those farms have also been removed from government payrolls. Finally, the government has taken advantage of several well-publicized instances of misconduct to fire the guilty parties, particularly in the Educational Service.

These moves are "easy" in the sense that they are perceived as fair (in the case of ghost workers and misconduct, at least) and, with the exception of the misconduct dismissals, they do not leave the workers without an income. Thus, no significant political or social problems have been associated with these moves.

The government is planning similar changes elsewhere, and has begun at the State Fisheries Corporation and the Education Service. However, the government recognizes that even greater staff reductions are necessary, particularly if it is to address the problem of low wages in the civil service satisfactorily. Indeed, the wage increase of January 1986 almost upset the fiscal and monetary discipline critical to the ERP's success. The January wage increases turned out to be far too high to be supported by tax revenues, thus threatening to force the government to monetize a deficit for the first time in four years. In response, the government reduced the size of the announced increases and effectively devalued the exchange rate by adopting an auction system. (This latter change helped to increase tax revenues based on international trade.) By the end of 1986, the government budget was actually slightly in surplus, and the government had carried out two more difficult policy changes.

However, civil service salaries are still too low, and will probably remain low until the civil service is pared down to a reasonable size. The government must continue to balance employment, salaries, and the fiscal deficit. Given the sensitive nature of the problem, a satisfactory resolution may take years.

The Political Situation

While the focus of this paper is economic policy, at least some discussion of politics is in order. In particular, one cannot help but wonder why it is that after so many Ghanaian governments fell in the wake of attempts at economic stabilization, this government has survived and even prospered during four years of orthodox economic policies.

The widespread belief that a stabilization policy, especially devaluation of the exchange rate, inevitably leads to a coup in Ghana is based at least partly on a spurious correlation. A succession of Ghanaian governments held out until the bitter end before attempting any sort of stabilization policy, so that economic conditions were particularly bad when they finally did make policy changes (usually to gain "last resort" financial assistance from the IMF and/or World Bank). Thus, the governments introduced stabilization programs when conditions were ripe for a coup anyway, and the policy changes, especially devaluations, were a convenient excuse for overthrowing the government. Nevertheless, after this chain of events had repeated itself several times, many people viewed stabilization attempts, particularly devaluations, as the kiss of death for a government. What then, makes the ERP different?

First, Ghana's economy had deteriorated badly between 1978 and 1982, and everyone realized that things had to change. This made them more willing to accept the policy changes of the ERP, even if they were painful. In addition, the economy's rapid deterioration meant that many of the people who had benefited from the distorted economic policies in 1978 no longer did so in 1982. For example, as the amount of available foreign exchange dwindled, the number of people able to earn a large rent by gaining an import license decreased. Similarly, as the government budget shrank in real terms, fewer people benefited from government patronage. This reduced the size of the constituency that favored the *status quo*, again making policy changes easier.

Aside from the economic considerations, Rawlings came to power as a very popular figure, which gave his government a fair amount of political capital to expend on difficult decisions. This popularity was based on Rawlings' first coup in 1979 following the corrupt military governments of Acheampong and Akuffo. When Akuffo announced that there would be a return to civilian rule in 1979, people speculated that the new government would let those responsible for the corruption off the hook in exchange for the military's blessing.

This concern provided the excuse for Rawlings to lead a coup of junior officers. The new government summarily tried and executed several senior government and military officials—an impulsive show of violence rare in Ghana. Nevertheless, most people saw the executions as just, and Rawlings' as the man who "threw the rascals out." Rawlings' reputation as a sincere leader interested in the nation's welfare rather than in personal gain was enhanced by his announcement that elections would be held a mere three months after he took power. Dr. Hilla Limann was elected in September 1979, and Rawlings turned power over to Ghana's first civilian government in seven years.

The Limann government, however, proved to be somewhat tentative, both in terms of economic policy and in terms of eliminating corruption in the civil service.[8] The reluctance to make needed policy reforms, along with the decline in the terms of trade and the drought of the early 1980s, meant that the economy began to deteriorate badly under Limann, wiping out whatever popularity the government had started out with.

By the end of 1981, Rawlings again had a pretext for taking power, and once again his coup had widespread support. This time, however, Rawlings stayed on to govern. His government has been able to use its popularity to push through difficult policy changes. Furthermore, it has used the rationale that the "rascals" should be punished to put in place a variety of policies, particularly those aimed at squeezing rents (generally collected by those with political power) out of the system.

Nevertheless, his government's actions took courage. It could easily not have survived the policy reforms it introduced, particularly in 1983 when economic performance remained poor and the ERP's policy changes hurt many influential people. However, the government did survive. Even though it used up a fair amount of its political capital in the difficult period at the beginning of the ERP, the three years of solid growth since 1984 have helped build a general sense of confidence in

---

8. To some extent, this can be blamed on Rawlings himself, whose widely publicized statements that he would be "watching" the civilian government's behavior carefully made the government reluctant to take bold steps. Given the fate of the Akuffo government, this was understandable.

its policies.[9] This has rebuilt the government's political capital to the point where in mid-1987, it is difficult to imagine that a successful challenge to the government could be mounted without a dramatic change in economic conditions.

Lessons Learned

The policies and problems of the Ghanaian economy prior to the ERP were not uncommon, but they were unusually long lasting and extreme. Many other countries run large fiscal deficits, maintain overvalued exchange rates, and control key prices at unrealistic levels. Many other countries suffer the consequent problems of slow growth, high inflation, rationed goods, and pervasive black markets. Thus other countries may be interested in Ghana's experiences with the ERP's range and mix of policy actions, particularly since Ghana's problems were initially so severe.

The Costs of Procrastination

Even though governments often find it politically convenient to avoid or postpone economic stabilization by using price controls, import controls, and other ad hoc administrative methods, the long-run costs of this are high. In Ghana's case, 15 years of refusing to adopt appropriate stabilization policies destroyed an economy that had once had the most promising development prospects in Africa.[10]

Furthermore, prolonged procrastination makes the task of finally undertaking a stabilization program much more difficult. Thus, by the time Ghana began the ERP, it really needed to be a *recovery* program rather than a "simple" macroeconomic stabilization. In addition to standard macro policies (devaluation and fiscal balance), Ghana needed a tremendous amount of structural adjustment and rehabilitation. The government had to adjust hundreds of relative prices, rebuild infrastructure, and rehabilitate industries. In essence, it had to overhaul the entire economy.

Persistence

Economic recovery is also a very lengthy process. Even after four years of the recovery program and three years of solid growth, Ghana has not "recovered." Per capita income is still well below peak levels, capacity utilization is still low, parts of the bureaucracy remain terribly inefficient and lack skilled personnel, and several important services are inadequate. Despite the ERP's success, a country

---

9. The government's confidence in its own policies is shown by its pushing through difficult policy changes in recent years by carefully explaining to the public the problems it is trying to address and how its proposed policy changes would address them. The government then challenges others to propose better policies. The lack of takers makes it appear that the proposed policies, even though they may offend some special interests, are really necessary to address the problems cited. This kind of openness in the policy process has turned out to be very good public relations for the government. However, to a large extent, it is made possible because the government really does appear to conduct policy with an eye toward the national interest rather than the welfare of any particular interest group. This gives the government the "moral high ground" and makes it more difficult for those special interests who are hurt to object to policy changes.

10. Note that several Ghanaian governments, including Nkrumah's and Acheampong's, fell even though they did not make the "politically risky" decision to adjust.

simply cannot undo the damage of 15 years of inappropriate policies all at once. For economies as badly rundown as Ghana's, the policy changes associated with a stabilization/structural adjustment program must be persistent. Indeed, the impressive thing about the ERP is not so much the initial policy changes of 1983—many governments are forced into such changes in desperate circumstances—but the government's consistent adherence to the program.[11] It has continued to devalue the cedi, squeeze out economic rents, and maintain fiscal balance. After a shaky start, this determination and persistence are now paying off.

Flexibility

Overhauling a deteriorated economy requires flexible policy making. Any policy package that aims at wide-ranging changes in economic structure is bound to involve mistakes and miscalculations that the government must correct, luck (good and bad) that it must adjust to, and unforeseen complications that it must address. Thus, even though the government must consistently adhere to the overall policy goals of reasonable relative prices, fiscal balance, and improved economic efficiency, the actual policy tools used to pursue these goals and the way in which they are used may need to be changed with time.

Weathering the Storm

One of the ERP's more discouraging aspects is that the first year, 1983, went so poorly. Part of this was due to the drought, but it is not uncommon for things to get worse before they get better in stabilization programs; a problem that is more severe in badly rundown countries because the infrastructure is unlikely to be able to support the adjustment without significant investments, and because the initial inflow of essential imports is likely to be slow.

One way to put this problem in perspective is to recognize that dramatic changes in relative prices will lead to changes in the demands placed on infrastructure. For example, when real prices paid to manganese exporters double, mining companies will be keen to increase production and sales. However, this implies increased use of roads, railways, and ports. If the roads are impassable, the railways in poor repair, and the ports not dredged, manganese exports cannot increase despite the prices changes. As we have seen, this is exactly what happened in Ghana. Thus, countries engaging in economic stabilization programs must consider what improvements they might have to make in their infrastructure to meet the increased demands for its use, so that producers can actually achieve increased production and sales in response to price changes.

An inadequate flow of imports contributed both to the infrastructure problems, since many of the needed repairs required imported parts and equipment, and also to other delays in production response. Quite apart from the lack of foreign exchange availability (which was worsened by the drought), the bureaucracy also slowed down the flow of imports: aid money remained in the pipeline for long periods of time. Aid can, of course, help to relieve the foreign exchange constraint, increase the flow of

11. Conversations with government officials indicate a possible explanation for this persistence. The dire circumstances Ghana faced in 1983 made it obvious that recovery would not be rapid, yet the decision to begin the ERP was taken anyway, with government officials knowing full well that they would have to stick with it for an extended period before seeing any benefits.

imports, and rehabilitate the economy, but only if it is disbursed. The policy changes of the ERP changed the demands placed on the bureaucracy just as it changed the demands on the infrastructure. If planning officers, customs officials, and so on are unprepared for the surge in imports that could result from increased aid, the inflow of imports will be slowed and will constrain the recovery of the economy.

In Ghana, the import flow was further slowed by the inability of private importers to obtain cedi financing for imports. The large changes in relative prices meant that banks found judging the creditworthiness of potential borrowers difficult. Further, because they were required to make loans at negative real interest rates (at least initially), they were particularly averse to risky loans. Thus, because of the credit problems, imports by the private sector were often less than what had been licensed.

These problems delayed the positive response of the economy to the ERP's policy changes, and they underline the importance of being prepared to weather the storm in the initial stages of a major adjustment program. Indeed, if Ghana had abandoned the ERP after its first year, it would have been declared yet another failed stabilization attempt. Only by seeing the program through has Ghana begun to reap some benefits.

Establishing Credibility

In an economy like Ghana's, where imports have been rationed for years, import-intensive investments in infrastructure and capital rehabilitation are likely to be necessary for a structural adjustment program to succeed. Further, even though these investments will probably have high rates of return, exports are unlikely to be sufficient to fund even a small fraction of them. Indeed, these imports may be necessary to allow increased exports, as in the case of parts for Ghana's transport sector.

One might therefore think that the best way to sequence policy changes in a major structural adjustment would be to begin with a large initial injection of key imports funded by loans from donors, the IMF, and the World Bank. As already noted, the economic returns to these loans are likely to be high in the context of a program like the ERP, so it should be easy for the country to service the debt. They would also provide the initial push out of the downward spiral of inadequate imports leading to inadequate exports leading to low foreign exchange earnings leading to still lower imports. It certainly appears that the large, well-invested flow of foreign loans that developed in 1985 and 1986 could have improved the pace of the recovery if it had come in 1983 instead.

Yet expecting a recovery program to proceed along the lines just described is probably unreasonable. Neither the World Bank nor the IMF is inclined to provide large loans to economies with policy histories like Ghana's in 1982; bilateral donors are even more reluctant. Indeed, starting from significantly repressed macroeconomic disequilibria in the government budget and the balance of payments, stabilization policies to reduce such disequilibria to manageable levels are likely to require substantial cuts in aggregate demand. External lenders, understandably, may wish to feel more confident that the disequilibria are being narrowed before making larger loans that imply higher investment demand. Consequently, a government is likely to have to begin a stabilization/structural adjustment program with a still serious foreign exchange constraint, making early progress very slow or nonexistent. Any government considering such a program must therefore be prepared for a tough initial year.

A happier lesson follows from this: Ghana needed only about a year and a half to reverse its reputation among donors and to establish the credibility of the ERP as a serious stabilization and structural adjustment program. Ghana had gained the enthusiastic support of the World Bank as early as 1984, and the Bank not only increased its own commitments, it also helped to rally other donors to Ghana's cause. Thus, after the first year, support from the donor community was even greater than anticipated in response to what they perceived as a good faith, well-conceived effort at economic reform. Indeed, at the most recent meeting of the Consultative Group for Ghana, the government requested roughly US$575 million in foreign assistance for 1988, but was offered more than US$800 million!

Conclusion

Economists have debated at length the efficacy of the type of orthodox policies Ghana has adopted. Despite widespread skepticism, given sufficient time and political determination, these policies are working in Ghana. Devaluation has improved exports across the board; fiscal and monetary discipline have reduced inflation (even in the presence of large devaluations); and "getting the prices right" has brought forth supply responses—in cocoa, in food crops, and in industry. The results are all the more impressive because Ghana started in a worst case situation.

Of course, much still remains to be done. Even with steady growth at the current rates of 5 to 6 percent per year, for Ghana simply to recover to the level of per capita income it had achieved before the decline began will take many years. But there is a growing sense in the international community and in Ghana itself that policies are on the right track, that they will stay there, and that the economic recovery program will succeed.

Annex 6.1 Some Notes on the Historical Context*

The history of economic policymaking in Ghana from the 1960s provides the longest continuous record of a government's attempts to come to grips with a set of problems that are currently widespread in other African countries, namely the problems of fiscal and trade imbalances leading to increasing internal and external indebtedness and to inflation. Ghana is the classic example of what can happen to an economy over a long period if the government does not respond to these problems adequately: the infrastructure deteriorates progressively and human capital is lost through emigration, unemployment, and a deterioration in the quality of education, training, and health care.

Ghana's prosperity, the quality of its human resources, and its political leadership in the late 1950s and early 1960s made the country a model of what other African countries might aspire to become. One would never have expected that a country that got off to such an auspicious start would suffer such a reversal of fortunes. How does one account for Ghana's experience, in particular the delay of more than two decades in taking effective action?

The most noteworthy feature of the last three decades has been the number of changes of government—seven between 1966, when Nkrumah was removed, and 1981, when the current Rawlings regime took power. Twice military governments have passed control to civilian governments (to the Busia and Limman administrations); and military coups have occurred five times. From the very beginning, the reason offered for each coup was the same: the inability of the previous regime to deal with the country's worsening economic situation.

Nkrumah, 1957-1966. Nkrumah's political constituents were "the verandah boys," unskilled urban workers, market women, and small businessmen. Ghanaians regard his major legacies to be the opening of economic and social opportunities to the poor through the education system, and the creation, through the same system, of highly competent professional and intellectual classes. Many Ghanaians feel deeply indebted to Nkrumah's social policies. His overall economic policies have been characterized as socialist, collectivist, and statist.

Ghana got into serious balance of payments and international indebtedness problems in the very early 1960s because of a decline in cocoa prices and a growing fiscal deficit. In real terms, the government's budget nearly doubled during 1960-65 to finance social programs and subsidize parastatals. By 1963, the government's credit rating was so poor that it had to rely increasingly on supplier credits at exorbitants rates to finance new state enterprises and on international barter arrangements. In 1965, the government asked its main creditors to reschedule its debt, and they in turn suggested that the government approach the IMF. The IMF mission recommended a standard stabilization package of economic measures, including a retrenchment in the budget and the termination of subsidies to state enterprises and of the practice of financing new projects with supplier credits. The Nkrumah regime accepted these recommendations, but was overthrown before the formal meeting with creditors in London in December 1966.

The National Liberation Council (NLC), 1966-69. The NLC's record shows that from the outset, it understood clearly what had to be done to stabilize and restructure the economy. Six months after taking power, it devalued the cedi by about 43 percent.

* *Based on a paper by Amon Nikoi, former minister of finance, Ghana.*

It took significant measures to liberalize imports, to control expenditures in major spending ministries better, and to raise taxes. It met twice with its creditors in London (in December 1966 and October 1968) to reschedule medium-term debt. There was limited privatization of state-owned enterprises that was constrained by strong popular opposition to foreign participation in ownership and a lack of local entrepreneurs with sufficient capital. It took bold steps to reduce the very large number of redundant workers in the government, in parastatals, and in state farms and builders' brigades, most of whom were Nkrumah supporters.

The Busia Government (The Second Republic), 1969-71. General elections ushered in Busia's Progress Party in October 1969, led by moderate middle-class intellectuals and professionals. Its main constituents were the urban middle classes, businessmen, salaried workers in the private sector, the self-employed, and wealthy farmers. The party favored a radical reorientation of policy away from Nkrumah's socialism and statism toward liberalization and reliance on the private sector to realize economic development. Busia himself was a sociologist and the quintessential Oxbridge elitist. He was the first Ghanaian recruited into the Colonial Administrative Service in the late 1940s. Though nominally nonaligned in foreign policy, he seemed to be pro-West.

The government's economic policies were, for the most part, a continuation of the NLC's policies, with priority being given to macroeconomic policy, in particular the foreign trade sector, and to employment. The sectoral priority was agriculture and substantial support was to be given to irrigation, land clearing, insecticides, fertilizers, and marketing.

The Busia government was simply unlucky. Import liberalization led to a flood of imports at a time when the world price of cocoa continued to decline. The consequences were again a loss of reserves and an accumulation of short-term debt and arrears of payments. The situation was aggravated by an increase in debt service payments from an average of US$20 million for 1966-70 to an anticipated US$40 million in 1971. A further debt rescheduling was necessary and devaluation was desirable. The cedi was devalued on December 30, 1971, and on January 13, 1972, General Acheampong overthrew the Busia government.

The Acheampong Regime (The National Redemption Council), 1972-78. The circumstances surrounding the Acheampong coup had disastrous consequences for Ghana's economy. First, the government threw many civil servants and political figures into jail for their mistakes (primarily the devaluation), which many blamed on the Harvard group of advisers, the IMF, the World Bank, and on foreign advisers in general. This was a particularly painful episode for those who had to endure it and made further discussions of devaluation almost taboo.

As an ardent admirer of Nkrumah, and with strong support from students and Nkrumah's natural constituencies, Acheampong reversed the policies of the NLC and of the Busia regime. He revalued the cedi. For the next few years he worked hard to build a coalition of the army, trade unionists, and rice farmers using policy instruments. He reintroduced a system of import licensing and used it to reward his followers. Rice farmers benefited from subsidized seeds and fertilizers, and from government services. He introduced low-cost housing programs for workers and an enlarged role for parastatals. Army officers were provided with jobs in the parastatals and in the government. All of this required an expansionary fiscal policy that, in turn, brought about inflationary pressures and severe balance of payments problems. Acheampong introduced a wide range of administered prices through a price and incomes board, which only exacerbated the situation by creating scarcities, thereby increasing the subsidies required by parastatals and creating parallel markets. He was unable, because of his prior actions, to use the exchange rate as an instrument of policy. He did, nevertheless, initiate discussions with the IMF over stabilization policies. In a coup in July 1978, General Akuffo overthrew General Acheampong.

The Akuffo Regime, 1978-79. In the month following the coup, the Akuffo regime, approving the prior regime's work with the IMF, devalued the cedi by the artifice of introducing a new currency. This short-lived regime began to take tentative steps toward trade liberalization and greater flexibility in exchange rate management, but it lasted only 11 months and was overthrown in June 1979 by Flight Lt. Rawlings.

The First Rawlings Regime, 1979. The Rawlings regime halted the movement toward liberalization and flexibility in exchange rate management and reinforced the system of administered prices. Rawlings forced a very large number of senior civil servants into retirement, so many as to affect the operations of the government detrimentally. His major accomplishments during this period were the preparations that were made for the return to civilian rule, including the convening of a constituent assembly and the drafting of a constitution. The provisions of the constitution represent the last great civilian consensus on government and its priorities. Ghanaians wrote into their constitution: a mandate that government, subject to the availability of resources, provide "free and equal access to secondary and higher education." The constitution also reflects a consensus that the government should strictly regulate foreign participation in the economy, preserving large areas for Ghanaian citizens. There is a strong consensus on the efficacy of state enterprises and therefore opposition to privatization, particularly if foreigners are involved. In general, the consensus endorsed many of the principles followed by Nkrumah, but built unusually detailed provisions into the constitution to avoid a recurrence of the abuses. Parliament must approve all foreign borrowing by the government. Provisions were made for exceptionally close monitoring of foreign exchange transactions by a parliamentary committee. The governor of the central bank would disallow foreign exchange transactions he deemed contrary to the law.

The Limman Administration (The Third Republic), 1979-81. The new civilian government proceeded very cautiously to gain a broad national consensus before taking action. While agreeing in principle with the IMF and the World Bank on stabilization and structural adjustment measures that were needed, there was substantial disagreement on the timing of reforms. In particular, support for Bank and Fund recommendations for devaluation was lacking. In any event, the Ghanaian economy continued to deteriorate under the new and extremely cautious civilian regime. The civil service, already demoralized by the mass sackings of 1979 and by their loss of real incomes, was further reduced by voluntary departure. A growing number of government departments could no longer function.

The Second Rawlings Regime (The Provisional National Defense Council) (PNDC), 1981-. The second Rawlings regime seems to have had two distinct periods reflecting the ideological split that has characterized all postindependence governments. At the outset, the PNDC put forward a four-year recovery program that explicitly increased state control over the economy and proposed, among other things, a government monopoly over imports and exports. An architect of the plan was the former minister of finance under Nkrumah, Kwesi Amoako-Atta. The plan required substantial public resources, and the regime unsuccessfully sought support from the Soviet Union. But resources became very scarce during 1983 because of drought and the need to care for one million Ghanaian citizens who returned after being expelled from Nigeria. The government was forced by circumstances to set aside the four-year recovery program and announced a new economic recovery program in April 1983.

The ERP is an amazing document because it represents an almost complete reversal of the four-year recovery program and a return to the policies of the NLC and the Busia regimes. The support for the ERP derives from the NLC and Busia regime constituencies, as well as from the technocrats, professionals, middle-class salaried workers, and small business people as well as some students. The program's success depends upon this coalition holding together and upon dealing with some of the social cost of the program successfully, in particular, the unemployment problems caused by economic retrenchment.

Annex 6.2 Dates of Major Economic and Political Events

Date		Event
1957	March 6	Ghana gains its independence. Ghanaian pound established as legal tender.
1960	July	Exchange controls announced in response to payments crisis. Deflationary budget adopted.
	September	Dockworkers strike the major ports.
1965	January	Nkrumah calls a referendum on a constitutional amendment to establish a one-party state.
	July	Currency reform introduces the cedi as legal tender at an exchange rate of 0.855 cedis/US$, an effective devaluation.
1966	February	Nkrumah is overthrown by officers from the military and police force. The National Liberation Council, led by General Ankrah, is formed to govern the country.
1967	February	Currency reform introduces the new cedi as legal tender, at 1.02 cedis/US$.
1969	October	Civilian rule is re-established as elections are won by the Progress Party, headed by Dr. Kofi Busia.
	December	Many foreign residents working in Ghana are forced to leave in an attempt to ease unemployment.
1971	December	The cedi is devalued to 1.82 cedis/US$.
1972	January	Colonel I. K. Acheampong leads a coup and establishes a government by the National Redemption Council.
	February	The cedi is revalued to 1.15 cedis/US$. A price and incomes board is established. Widespread wage and price controls are introduced in an attempt to check inflation.
1975	April	The Investment Policy Decree requires full Ghanaian ownership of wholesale trading firms and partial Ghanian ownership of all other firms.
1978	July	General Akuffo overthrows Acheampong in a palace coup. Akuffo announces that civilian elections will be held in 1979.
1978	August	The cedi is devalued to 2.75 cedis/US$ as part of a stabilization program.

Date		Event
1979	June	Flight Lieutenant Jerry Rawlings leads a group of junior officers in a coup, postponing the elections.
	September	Elections are held and Dr. Hila Limann of the People's National Party is elected president.
1981	December	Rawlings again seizes power, forming the Provisional National Defense Council to govern the country.
1983	April	*Economic Recovery Program announced.*
		Devaluation of the cedi from 2.75 cedis/US$ to multiple rates of 23.375 and 29.975 cedis/US$.
		All controlled prices, including those of government services, increased substantially to pass through the cost of the devaluation.
		Tariff schedules are simplified to rates of 0, 25, and 30 percent.
		New taxes introduced on wealth (property and noncommercial vehicles), and taxes on rental income increased.
		Government begins an ongoing effort to improve tax collection.
	May	Cocoa producer price raised from 12,000 to 20,000 cedis per ton.
		Minimum wage raised from 12 to 25 cedis per day.
	October	Interest rates raised three to five percentage points.
		Exchange rates are unified and devalued to 30 cedis/US$.
		Retail prices of beer and cigarettes raised by 75 percent and 33 percent respectively, raising 800 million cedis in additional tax revenue.
	December	Price controls have been eliminated on all but 23 goods throughout the year.
		External arrears have been reduced by US$69 million to US$532 million.
1984	March	Exchange rate devalued to 35 cedis/US$.
		Public sector wages and salaries increased 40 percent.
	May	Cocoa producer price raised to 30,000 cedis/ton.
	June	Personal income tax rates lowered; taxes on cigarettes and beer raised.
	August	Exchange rate devalued to 38.5 cedis/US$.
		Interest rates raised by two percentage points.

Date		Event
1984	November	Exchange rate devalued to 50 cedis/US$.
	December	Throughout 1984, foreign exchange retention schemes are introduced for key exporters needing imported inputs. Timber exporters are allowed to retain 20 percent of their foreign exchange earnings; gold exporters, 35 to 45 percent; and exporters of other minerals, 20 percent.
		Discussions of improved management and retrenchment in key parastatals begin.
		External arrears reduced by US$300 million to US$232 million.
1985	January	Civil service wages and salaries doubled.
	April	Significant revenue initiative is launched, including increased taxes on beer, cigarettes, airport and casino services, gasoline, and special unnumbered licenses for imports. Many government fees are also increased.
		Deposit interest rates increased one percentage point.
	June	Cocoa price raised 50 percent to 56,600 cedis/ton; layoffs begin at Ghana Cocoa Marketing Board.
		Cotton and tobacco prices raised 100 percent and 50 percent, respectively.
	July	List of goods with controlled prices reduced to eight: imported rice, sugar, baby food, cement, textiles, drugs, matches, and soap.
		New investment code published guaranteeing repatriation of profits and capital (for foreign investors) and providing protection from expropriation.
	August	Petroleum prices increased further (by 20 percent in real terms).
	December	About 28 percent (or 16,000) Cocoa Board staff have been retrenched. By February 1987, 10,000 more will be removed from the payrolls.
1986	January	Minimum wage increased from 70 to 90 cedis per day.
		Wages and salaries of civil servants adjusted for inflation and to widen the ratio of top to bottom pay scales from 2:1 to 6:1.
		Exchange rate devalued to 90 cedis/US$; controlled prices adjusted to account for the devaluation.
	February	Foreign exchange retention rate for nontraditional exports raised to 35 percent.

Date	Event
April	Cocoa price raised 50 percent to 85,000 cedis/ton.
	Coffee price raised 50 percent.
August	Interest rates raised two percentage points.
	Foreign exchange auction introduced (see annex 6.2).
December	External arrears have been reduced to US$171 million.

Annex 6.3 Statistical Tables

Table A3.1 Real Minimum Wage and Real Exchange Rate Measures, 1965-85

Year	Real minimum wage	Real exchange rate (WPI)	Real exchange rate (GDP) deflator)
1965	n.a.	579.40	673.04
1966	n.a.	578.79	697.37
1967	n.a.	811.71	884.83
1968	n.a.	782.77	793.42
1969	n.a.	732.54	756.71
1970	n.a.	718.27	758.39
1971	n.a.	1,258.88	1457.30
1972	14.14	802.20	902.93
1973	13.11	755.11	727.46
1974	20.37	696.80	678.14
1975	15.65	585.06	595.14
1976	12.23	478.74	463.13
1977	10.96	303.42	290.92
1978	8.43	451.74	509.57
1979	6.11	368.14	338.34
1980	5.36	278.16	275.00
1981	6.91	172.79	200.74
1982	5.40	137.83	150.34
1983	5.05	682.65	726.72
1984	5.19	855.48	678.90
1985	7.96	783.95	520.92

n.a.= not available

Note: Real wage calculated as minimum wage divided by the gdp deflator; real exchange rate calculated as the exchange rate divided by either the wholesale price index or the gdp deflator times the U. S. wholesale price index.

Source: *Quarterly Digest of Statistics* (various) and *International Financial Statistics*

Table A3.2 Type of Activity and Proportion of GDP, 1970 and 1975-85

Year	Agriculture, of which	Cocoa	Industry, of which	Manufac-turing	Services, of which	Wholesale and retail trade
1970	0.47	0.14	0.18	0.11	0.31	0.12
1975	0.48	0.11	0.21	0.14	0.31	0.12
1976	0.51	0.08	0.19	0.13	0.31	0.13
1977	0.56	0.06	0.16	0.11	0.28	0.12
1978	0.61	0.07	0.12	0.09	0.27	0.13
1979	0.60	0.08	0.12	0.09	0.28	0.14
1980	0.58	0.05	0.12	0.08	0.31	0.17
1981	0.53	0.02	0.09	0.06	0.39	0.26
1982	0.57	0.01	0.06	0.04	0.38	0.27
1983	0.60	0.06	0.07	0.04	0.34	0.23
1984	0.49	0.03	0.11	0.06	0.40	0.28
1985	0.41	0.03	0.15	0.11	0.44	0.28

Source: World Bank (1987)

Table A3.3 National Income Accounts as a Proportion of GDP, 1965-85

Year	Consumption	Government	Investment	Exports	Imports
1965	0.77	0.14	0.18	0.17	0.27
1966	0.79	0.13	0.13	0.15	0.20
1967	0.77	0.15	0.12	0.18	0.21
1968	0.70	0.17	0.11	0.23	0.22
1969	0.73	0.14	0.10	0.22	0.21
1970	0.74	0.13	0.12	0.23	0.24
1971	0.79	0.13	0.12	0.21	0.28
1972	0.75	0.13	0.09	0.21	0.15
1973	0.76	0.11	0.08	0.21	0.17
1974	0.79	0.12	0.12	0.19	0.23
1975	0.73	0.13	0.12	0.19	0.18
1976	0.79	0.12	0.10	016	0.16
1977	0.77	0.13	0.09	0.10	0.12
1978	0.83	0.11	0.06	0.08	0.10
1979	0.83	0.10	0.07	0.11	0.11
1980	0.84	0.11	0.06	0.08	0.09
1981	0.87	0.09	0.05	0.05	0.05
1982	0.90	0.06	0.04	0.03	0.03
1983	0.94	0.06	0.04	0.06	0.09
1984	0.90	0.06	0.07	0.08	0.11
1985	0.84	0.09	0.09	0.09	0.11

Source: 1965-77, *International Financial Statistics* (March 1987 tape)
1978-85, World Bank (1987)

Table A3.4 Government Revenues and Expenditures as a Proportion of GDP, 1965-85

Year	Expenditures, of which	Development expenditures	Revenues and grants, of which	Export taxes	Import taxes	Surplus/ deficit
1965	0.30	n.a.	0.18	n.a.	n.a.	-0.04
1966	0.20	n.a.	0.16	n.a.	n.a.	-0.04
1967	0.24	n.a.	0.18	n.a.	n.a.	-0.06
1968	0.23	n.a.	0.19	n.a.	n.a.	-0.05
1969	0.22	n.a.	0.19	n.a.	n.a.	-0.02
1970	0.22	0.04	0.20	0.06	0.04	-0.02
1971	0.21	0.04	0.17	0.06	0.04	-0.04
1972	0.19	0.04	0.14	0.04	0.03	-0.05
1973	0.19	0.04	0.14	0.04	0.03	-0.05
1974	0.20	0.05	0.15	0.05	0.03	-0.05
1975	0.25	0.07	0.16	0.04	0.03	-0.09
1976	0.28	0.08	0.15	0.04	0.02	-0.12
1977	0.24	0.06	0.11	0.03	0.02	-0.12
1978	0.18	0.03	0.10	0.04	0.01	-0.08
1979	0.16	0.02	0.10	0.04	0.01	-0.06
1980	0.14	0.02	0.07	0.01	0.01	-0.07
1981	0.12	0.02	0.06	n.a.	0.01	-0.06
1982	0.16	0.01	0.09	n.a.	0.01	-0.07
1983	0.08	0.01	0.06	0.02	0.01	-0.02
1984	0.10	0.01	0.08	0.02	0.01	-0.01
1985	0.12	0.02	0.11	0.02	0.02	-0.01

n.a. = not available

Source: Quarterly Digest of Statistics (various)

Table A3.5 Prices, Wages, and Exchange Rates, 1965-85

Year	CPI	CPI inflation	GDP deflator	GDP deflator inflation	Official exchange rate (cedis/US$)	Black market exchange rate (cedis/US$)	Minimum wage/ (cedis/day)
1965	2.74	n.a.	4.43	n.a.	0.71	2.27	n.a.
1966	3.10	0.13	4.58	0.03	0.71	1.72	n.a.
1967	2.84	-0.08	4.68	0.02	1.02	1.61	n.a.
1968	3.07	0.08	4.97	0.06	1.02	1.79	n.a.
1969	3.29	0.07	5.51	0.11	1.02	1.65	n.a.
1970	3.39	0.03	5.84	0.06	1.02	1.69	n.a.
1971	3.71	0.09	6.12	0.05	1.82	1.82	n.a.
1972	4.09	0.10	7.07	0.15	1.28	1.56	1.0
1973	4.81	0.18	7.63	0.08	1.15	1.72	1.0
1974	5.68	1.18	9.82	0.29	1.15	1.54	2.0
1975	7.38	0.30	12.78	0.30	1.15	1.92	2.0
1976	11.52	0.56	16.36	0.28	1.15	4.35	2.0
1977	24.93	1.16	27.36	0.67	1.15	7.69	3.0
1978	43.15	0.73	47.42	0.73	2.75	10.00	4.0
1979	66.63	0.54	65.44	0.38	2.75	14.29	4.0
1980	100.00	0.50	98.86	0.51	2.75	11.11	5.3
1981	216.49	1.16	173.63	0.76	2.75	50.00	12.0
1982	264.76	0.22	222.06	0.28	2.75	120.00	12.0
1983	590.08	1.23	495.32	1.23	30.00	97.00	25.0
1984	824.13	0.40	674.48	0.36	50.00	135.00	35.0
1985	909.06	0.10	879.21	0.30	59.99	160.00	70.0

n.a. = not available

Source: CPI, official exchange rate, 1965-77 GDP deflator: *International Financial Statistics* (March 1987 tape)
1978-1985, World Bank (1987)
Black Market Exchange Rate: Pick (1978)
Minimum Wage: *Quarterly Digest of Statistics* (various)

Table A3.6 National Income Accounts, 1965-75
(millions of 1980 cedis)

Year	Consumption	Government	Investment	Change in inventories	Exports	Imports	GDP	GDP growth
1965	25,599.9	4,790.10	6,010.22	-67.78	5,671.30	8,857.2	33,124.0	n.a.
1966	26,231.3	4,324.57	4,302.72	-21.84	4,848.75	6,508.7	33,155.0	0.001
1967	24,911.9	4,811.32	3,720.75	-406.29	5,859.12	6,735.8	32,161.0	-0.030
1968	24,120.7	5,738.22	3,765.08	40.27	7,973.11	7,429.5	34,228.0	0.064
1969	26,449.6	5,166.64	3,535.07	743.27	8,103.47	7,759.0	36,239.0	0.059
1970	23,498.7	4,966.72	4,641.31	822.08	8,957.21	9,231.2	38,689.0	0.068
1971	32,235.2	5,307.21	5,078.59	702.18	8,769.14	11,251.3	40,841.0	0.056
1972	29,793.7	5,022.21	3,451.88	-622.47	8,233.59	6,054.9	39,824.0	-0.025
1973	34,757.7	5,006 .58	3,512.47	629.10	9,842.77	7,863.7	45,898.0	0.153
1974	37,373.4	5,794.40	5,651.83	539.72	8,839.26	10,733.4	47,455.0	0.034
1975	30,313.9	5,392.80	4,805.77	461.79	8,007.01	7,623.5	41,350.0	-0.129
1976	31,610.8	4,884.36	3,918.49	-379.01	6,265.91	6,400.4	39,894.0	-0.035
1977	31,566.7	5,149.04	3,833.46	679.72	4,279.30	4,710.5	40,794.0	0.023
1978	36,845.8	4,999.80	2,857.33	139.18	3,698.71	4,287.0	44,253.8	0.085
1979	35,857.5	4,436.34	2,902.04	-82.52	4,844.37	4,813.8	43,142.4	-0.025
1980	36,366.5	4,839.02	2,643.05	-205.33	3,669.73	3,968.1	43,345.9	0.005
1981	36,475.3	3,676.73	1,975.44	-62.78	1,989.26	2,226.5	41,827.4	-0.035
1982	34,954.1	2,523.20	1,374.86	-59.89	1,299.65	1,161.0	38,931.5	-0.069
1983	34,752.7	3,177.75	1,397.46	-4.24	2,268.80	3,437.7	37,154.7	-0.046
1984	36,171.9	2,527.88	2,749.09	9.64	3,199.95	4,286.9	40,371.6	0.087
1985	35,629.9	3,821.83	3,717.99	7.96	3,774.40	4,529.7	42,422.3	0.051

Source: 1965-77, *International Financial Statistics* (March 1987 tape)
1978-85, World Bank (1987)

Table A3.7 Money and Credit, 1965-86
(millions of current cedis)

Year	Currency outside banks	Monetary base	M2	Currency/ M2	Domestic credit	Government credit (net)	Government credit/ total credit	M2/GDP
1965	116	151	301	0.386	348	178	0.512	0.205
1966	116	156	315	0.366	406	205	0.504	0.208
1967	119	161	319	0.373	481	266	0.552	0.212
1968	125	168	352	0.356	537	315	0.587	0.207
1969	151	201	389	0.388	577	314	0.543	0.194
1970	151	231	427	0.353	600	291	0.485	0.189
1971	159	238	475	0.335	736	289	0.393	0.190
1972	239	352	668	0.358	828	358	0.433	0.237
1973	245	437	794	0.309	843	376	0.446	0.227
1974	336	594	1,005	0.334	1,254	584	0.466	0.216
1975	486	879	1,386	0.350	1,598	924	0.579	0.262
1976	707	1,249	1,903	0.372	2,429	1,573	0.648	0.292
1977	1,157	2,015	3,044	0.380	3,848	2,780	0.722	0.273
1978	2,122	3,720	5,131	0.413	6,454	4,523	0.701	0.244
1979	2,459	4,396	5,942	0.414	7,406	4,903	0.662	0.210
1980	3,521	5,742	7,949	0.443	9,494	6,518	0.687	0.185
1981	6,050	8,924	12,029	0.503	15,483	10,649	0.688	0.166
1982	6,957	10,211	14,837	0.469	18,827	11,057	0.587	0.172
1983	10,389	14,639	20,804	0.499	32,429	28,055	0.865	0.113
1984	17,631	21,828	31,962	0.552	48,723	37,459	0.769	0.117
1985	22,557	29,570	46,718	0.483	77,823	48,052	0.617	0.125
1986	32,357.6	47,249	69,112	0.468	n.a.	76,588	n.a.	n.a.

n.a. = not available

Source: International Financial Statistics (March 1987 tape)

Table A3.8 National Income Accounts, 1965-85
(millions of current cedis)

Year	Consumption	Government	Investment	Change in inventories	Exports	Imports	GDP
1965	1,133	212	266	-3	251	392	1,466
1966	1,201	198	197	-1	222	298	1,518
1967	1,165	225	174	-19	274	315	1,504
1968	1,198	285	187	2	396	369	1,700
1969	1,459	285	195	41	447	428	1,999
1970	1,664	290	271	48	523	539	2,259
1971	1,974	325	311	43	537	689	2,501
1972	2,106	355	244	-44	582	428	2,815
1973	2,652	382	268	48	751	600	3,502
1974	3,670	569	555	53	868	1,054	4,660
1975	3,873	689	614	59	1,023	974	5,283
1976	5,171	799	641	-62	1,025	1,047	6,526
1977	8,638	1,409	1,049	186	1,171	1,289	11,163
1978	17,473	2,371	1,355	66	1,754	2,033	20,986
1979	23,464	2,903	1,899	-54	3,170	3,150	28,231
1980	35,953	4,784	2,613	-203	3,628	3,923	42,853
1981	63,333	6,384	3,430	-109	3,454	3,866	72,626
1982	77,619	5,603	3,053	-133	2,886	2,578	86,451
1983	172,140	10,787	6,922	-21	11,238	17,028	184,038
1984	243,972	17,050	18,542	65	21,583	28,914	272,298
1985	313,262	33,602	32,689	70	33,185	39,826	372,982

Source: 1965-77: *International Financial Statistics* (March 1987 tape)
1978-85: World Bank (1987)

Table A3.9 Government Revenues and Expenditures
(millions of current cedis)

Year	Expenditures	Development*	Revenue and grants	Export taxes	Import taxes	Surplus/ deficit
1965	322.0	n.a.	257.5	n.a.	n.a.	-64.5
1966	297.0	n.a.	242.5	n.a.	n.a.	-54.5
1967	360.5	n.a.	276.0	n.a.	n.a.	-84.5
1968	397.5	n.a.	315.0	n.a.	n.a.	-82.5
1969	431.5	n.a.	384.5	n.a.	n.a.	-47.0
1970	496.0	96.2	444.0	146.2	86.1	-52.0
1971	533.5	106.1	435.0	144.7	96.9	-98.5
1972	545.5	99.9	405.0	101.9	74.9	-140.5
1973	651.0	132.7	485.0	134.65	88.0	-166.0
1974	950.0	227.7	694.0	231.5	127.4	-256.0
1975	1,315.0	363.7	839.5	237.0	135.6	-475.5
1976	1,810.5	539.20	1,005.5	232.1	154.5	-805.0
1977	2,651.0	666.3	1,266.5	281.2	209.1	-1,384.5
1978	3,730.5	727.6	1,996.0	757.2	297.80	-1,734.5
1979	4,482.0	667.3	2,775.5	1,077.3	358.0	-1,706.5
1980	6,193.5	992.4	3,092.5	476.8	400.1	-3,101.0
1981	8,624.5	1,158.5	4,019.0	14.5	607.8	-4,605.5
1982	13,611.1	1,280.2	7,654.7	2.1	1,074.1	-5,956.4
1983	14,755.0	1,354.0	10,241.0	2,934.3	1,972.0	-4,514.0
1984	26,694.0	3,994.0	22,641.0	4,974.0	3,159.0	-4,053.0
1985	45,765.0	7,303.0	40,312.0	9,172.0	6,591.0	-5,453.0

n.a. = not available

* This does not include projects funded directly by aid from foreign donors.

Source: Quarterly Digest of Statistics (various)

Table A3.10 Balance of Payments, 1965-86
(US$ millions)

Year	Exports (fob)	Imports (fob)	Current account	Balance of payments
1965	321.2	-439.4	n.a.	15.2
1966	280.3	-320.7	n.a.	-48.1
1967	284.2	-265.4	-84.9	-49.0
1968	304.4	-264.6	-56.1	1.5
1969	345.0	-295.3	-60.1	-18.6
1970	427.0	-375.1	-67.7	-8.0
1971	334.6	-368.2	-145.8	25.0
1972	384.3	-222.9	108.2	77.7
1973	585.0	-372.1	126.7	86.8
1974	679.0	-708.2	-171.5	-83.3
1975	801.0	-650.5	17.6	10.6
1976	779.0	-690.3	-74.0	-59.7
1977	889.6	-860.2	-79.7	61.1
1978	892.8	-780.3	-45.9	117.5
1979	1,065.7	-803.1	122.0	-17.1
1980	1,103.6	-908.3	29.2	-66.1
1981	710.7	-954.3	-420.8	11.1
1982	607.0	-588.7	-108.6	20.8
1983	439.1	-499.7	-174.1	-249.1
1984	565.9	-533.0	-61.3	-11.7
1985	632.4	-668.7	-165.5	-56.9
1986	773.0	-702.0	n.a.	n.a.

n.a. = not available
Source: International Financial Statistics (March 1987 tape)

Annex 6.4 Ghana's Foreign Exchange Auction

At the end of the second IMF stand-by agreement (August 1986), the Fund and the Government of Ghana disagreed about the appropriate size of the devaluation that was to be a precondition for a further stand-by. The disagreement was resolved by the adoption of a foreign exchange auction in September. The system lets market forces determine an equilibrium exchange rate and, to some extent, allows the government to place the "blame" for a devaluation on the private market.

Initially, the system used a dual exchange rate. The old official rate (90 cedis/US$) was applied to all sales of cocoa, all official grants, all purchases of oil, and some purchases of essential pharmaceuticals. All other purchases were made in the auction, and all other exports were credited at the rate established there. In February 1987, the rate was unified so that all foreign exchange transactions were conducted at the auction rate.

The procedure for allocating foreign exchange is as follows:

1. Potential bidders must obtain an import license that specifies how they will use the foreign exchange they wish to purchase. This allows the government to maintain the prohibition of some imports, just as it had under the fixed rate system. Nevertheless, as of July 1987, licenses were automatically granted for all productive inputs and about 40 percent of all consumer goods imports, reflecting the significant liberalization of imports.

2. Bidders then specify the quantity of foreign exchange (in U.S. dollars) they wish to purchase and their bid price. The bid is endorsed by the bidder's bank to ensure that the bidder has the proper cedi cover available, and submitted to the Bank of Ghana.

3. Each Friday, the bids for that week are ordered by the bid price. The highest bidder is granted his or her foreign exchange request in full, then the next highest, and so on, until the available foreign exchange for the week is exhausted. Each bidder pays his or her own bid price for the foreign exchange they buy.

4. The bid of the last successful bidder is called the marginal price. This price is then used for all foreign exchange transactions in the following week, including the payment of export receipts and all government purchases. The government does not bid in the auction, but it does pay the marginal price for all foreign exchange that it requires. This is important insofar as the temptation for governments to "tax" the auction by siphoning off large amounts of foreign exchange at cheap rates appears to have forced auction systems in other countries to collapse as buyers "rushed" the market, fearing that there would not be a steady supply of foreign exchange.

As table A4.1 shows, adopting the auction system resulted in a large initial devaluation: 42 percent the first week and 68 percent in the first five weeks, indicating that the cedi had been overvalued at 90 cedis/US$. However, from the fifth week on, the rate has been quite stable, depreciating only 3.3 percent in 20 weeks with little volatility (even in January when cocoa, oil, and pharmaceuticals were added to the auction). This stability, along with the general early success of the auction system, can be attributed to the government's steady macroeconomic management.

Table A4.1 Prices and Quantities in the Foreign Exchange Auction, September 1986-March 1987

Date	Marginal rate (cedis/US$)	Highest bid (cedis/US$)	Lowest bid (cedis/US$)	Total demand (US$ millions)	Total supply (US$ millions)
09/19/86	128	152	90	7.83	2.47
09/26	136	160	92	11.95	3.98
10/10	145	155	100	12.97	6.00
10/17	145	160	141	2.46	2.36
10/24	151	163	142	4.86	3.46
10/31	147	165	130	3.10	2.52
11/07	149	157	143	2.03	1.30
11/14	148	158	146	2.89	2.64
11/21	149	155	146	1.35	1.06
11/28	150	160	146	2.09	1.72
12/05	151	158	146	3.12	1.64
12/12	152	157	145	5.83	3.67
12/19	154	160	150	4.21	1.95
01/09/87	152	160	152	2.63	2.63
01/16	150	158	150	1.37	1.37
01/23	152	158	150	3.32	2.54
01/30	153	155	152	3.06	2.25
02/06	154	157	152	3.15	2.79
02/13	148	157	148	2.50	2.50
02/20	152	158	148	6.26	2.38
03/06	150	157	149	6.84	6.47
03/13	153	156	151	4.54	2.37
03/20	155	158	150	7.26	4.28
03/27	156	158	152	5.85	4.52
03/30	156	160	152	6.18	4.29

Source: Bank of Ghana

References

Callaghy, Thomas M. 1987. *The Politics of Structural Adjustment in Africa: Policy Initiation and Sustainability.* New York: Columbia University (draft).

Chrisney, Martin D. 1985. *Poverty, Equity, and Growth Issues in Ghana. 1950-1983.* Unpublished.

International Financial Statistics. March 1987. Washington, D.C.: IMF. Tape.

May, Ernesto. 1985. *Exchange Controls and Parallel Market Economies in Sub-Saharan Africa: Focus on Ghana.* World Bank Staff Working Paper No. 711. Washington, D. C. : World Bank.

Pick, Franz. 1978. 1976-1977: *Pick's Currency Yearbook.* New York: Pick Publishing Corp.

Quarterly Digest of Statistics. Various. Accra: Government of Ghana Printing Office.

Republic of Ghana. 1985. *Progress of the Economic Recovery Program, 1984-86, and Policy Framework, 1986-88.* Report for the Third Meeting of the Consultative Group for Ghana, Accra.

Roemer, Michael. 1984. "Ghana, 1950-80: Missed Opportunities." In Arnold C. Harberger (ed). *World Economic Growth.* San Francisco: Institute for Contemporary Studies Press, pp. 201-225.

World Bank. 1983. *Ghana: Policies and Program for Adjustment.* Report No. 4702-GH. Washington, D. C.: World Bank.

World Bank. 1984a. *World Development Report.* Washington, D. C.: World Bank.

World Bank. 1984b. *Ghana: Managing the Transition.* Report No. 5289-GH. Washington, D. C.: World Bank.

World Bank. 1985. *Ghana: Towards Structural Adjustment.* Report No. 5854-GH. Washington, D. C.: World Bank.

World Bank, Consultative Group for Ghana. 1986. *Status Report.* Washington, D.C.: World Bank.

World Bank. 1987. *Ghana: Policies and Issues of Structural Adjustment.* Report No. 6635-GH. Washington, D. C.: World Bank.

7

Botswana: Macroeconomic Management of Commodity Booms, 1975-86

Catharine B. Hill, Department of Economics, Williams College
D. Nelson Mokgethi, Ministry of Finance and Development Planning, Botswana

Botswana is well endowed with mineral resources. The mining and quarrying sector, primarily diamonds, accounted directly for about half of GDP in 1985/86 (preliminary figures, Statistical Bulletin, March 1987),[1] (table 7.1). Diamond exports were approximately 70 percent of total exports in 1986. In addition, mineral revenues have accounted for a large proportion of total government revenues every year since 1975/76. In 1985/86, mineral royalties and dividends, mineral taxes, and other revenue attributable to the mineral sector made up more than two-thirds of the government's recurrent revenue. In addition, government tax receipts from income and corporate profits are up when the mining sector is doing well. However, variability in and uncertainty about the income from this sector create difficult macroeconomic management problems for the government. Reliance on diamond receipts presents the government with several economic policy choices. One choice concerns the rate at which diamonds should be mined and sold. A second choice, the one discussed here, is the appropriate policy response to booms and busts in the diamond sector.

During the 1970s, many developing countries experienced booms in their commodity export sectors, which produced large windfall gains. Mexico, Nigeria, and other oil-exporting developing countries experienced four-fold increases in the price of their oil exports. Coffee prices rose in the mid-1970s, leading to export booms in Colombia, the Côte d'Ivoire, and Kenya. Many of these countries have since, however, experienced balance of payments problems and debt crises. Debt difficulties arose because of the way the windfall gains were used, as well as from decreases in commodity prices since the 1970s. Windfall gains resulted in increased government spending, and even in borrowing against future expected export receipts to increase current expenditure further. Real exchange rates tended to appreciate, reducing the competitiveness of other traded goods. When the commodity price rises proved to be temporary, the countries had accumulated large debts and painful adjustment was necessary (World Bank 1985, pp. 56-57). To reestablish external balance, they adopted expenditure reducing policies, causing either slower or even negative GDP growth rates.

Botswana has avoided many of the economic problems that have plagued other primary commodity exporters by adopting appropriate, stabilizing, macroeconomic policies in response to variable diamond receipts. Guided by two objectives—

We would like to thank Charles Harvey for his valuable comments on an earlier draft.

1. This understates the mining sector's contribution to GDP because it ignores indirect effects, some of which (government GDP) are significant.

avoiding having to adopt a package of austerity measures to decrease imports and encouraging diversification—Botswana has not experienced severe balance of payments crises as a result of fluctuations in the price of its main commodity export. The policies adopted have included avoiding excessive increases in government expenditure during boom periods, instead building up international reserves and government balances at the central bank to be used when the boom ended. These policies, combined with management of the nominal exchange rate, have helped Botswana avoid real exchange rate appreciation.

Table 7.1 Real GDP and Contributions of Major Sectors, 1977/78-1985/86

Year	Total GDP (P millions)	Growth rate (%)	Agriculture (P millions)	Growth rate (%)	Government (P millions)	Growth rate (%)	Mining (P millions)	Growth rate (%)
1977/78	549.4	n.a.	86.8	n.a.	80.5	n.a.	171.4	n.a.
1978/79	615.1	12.0	86.6	0.2	90.4	12.3	169.1	-1.3
1979/80	701.5	14.0	83.3	-3.8	92.6	2.4	210.7	24.6
1980/81	761.8	8.6	75.0	-10.0	104.7	13.1	260.6	23.7
1981/82	743.3	-2.4	71.8	-4.3	113.9	8.8	222.1	-14.8
1982/83	920.5	23.8	60.1	-16.3	122.9	7.9	393.3	77.1
1983/84	1,106.0	20.2	50.9	-15.3	136.5	11.1	533.4	35.6
1984/85[a]	1,170.9	5.9	48.0	-5.7	156.2	14.4	560.6	5.1
1985/86[a]	1,315.6	12.4	48.0	0	165.7	6.1	673.2	20.1

n.a. = not available

Note: Pula are in constant 1980 prices.

a. Provisional

Source: Statistical Bulletin, March 1987, Volume 12, No. 1.

Extreme vulnerability from several other sectors as well as the diamond sector, may partially explain the cautious and ultimately appropriate policy decision adopted by Botswana. Botswana also had the advantage of having watched other countries make mistakes. The government often cites the negative effects of "import strangulation" in countries that have managed booms badly as a justification for its reserve accumulation policies. Finally, Botswana's political stability has certainly played a role. In countries where the government's power is precarious, excess spending and suboptimal saving may result from interest group pressures.

The Botswana Economy and the Diamond Sector

The Botswana economy is extremely open. Merchandise exports and imports each accounted for over 50 percent of GDP in 1985. The three main export commodities are diamonds, copper and nickel matte, and meat, accounting for 76 percent, 9 percent, and 7 percent respectively of total export receipts. Botswana's imports are concentrated by market: almost 75 percent come from the Common Customs Area (Lesotho, South Africa, and Swaziland).

Botswana's economy is therefore highly dependent on exports from the mining sector, which, in turn, is dominated by diamonds. DeBeers started diamond exploration in Botswana in 1955. The first discovery in 1967 led to the Orapa mine. A second find in 1969 led to the Letlhakane mine. The third source of diamonds is at Jwaneng, where production started in 1982. All three mines are joint ventures between the Botswana government and DeBeers, through the government's 50 percent ownership of Debswana. Botswana's output is sold through the DeBeers Central Selling Organization (CSO), as negotiated in five-year marketing agreements.

Diamonds have become increasingly important to Botswana during the 1980s. Diamond production has more than doubled since 1980, mainly as a result of the opening of the Jwaneng mine. The diamond sector's contribution to GDP and GDP growth rates has, however, been variable. Booms have occurred when the new diamond mines have come on line. When new mines open, foreign exchange earnings and government revenues quickly increase to a much higher level than before. During the transition, growth rates shoot up, but thereafter level off. Such booms occurred when each of the three mines opened.

Botswana has also experienced several booms and busts in the diamond sector when unexpected price changes have occurred in the diamond market or when the quality of diamonds mined has proved different from that expected. For example, between 1976/77 and 1979/80, actual diamond production in carats was close to levels predicted in the National Development Plan 1976-81, however, sales values were much higher because of unexpectedly large annual price increases, ranging from 20 percent to 35 percent (Republic of Botswana 1977, p. 186).

The world diamond market collapsed during the early 1980s. Among the causes were recession in the major industrial countries and the collapse of a speculative boom in diamonds. The unit value for diamond exports dropped over 20 percent in 1981 and a further 12 percent in 1982. Diamond exports fell from P238 million (US$305 million) in 1980 to P135 million (US$162 million) in 1981. The CSO was unable to sell all the diamonds it was acquiring from producers while maintaining the cartel price. As a result, the CSO imposed export quotas on producers, forcing producers to increase their stockpiles. The quota was imposed in November 1981 and remained in force through 1984. Botswana's quota increased with the opening of the Jwaneng mine in 1982, because the quota is approximately equal to Botswana's share of the total supply of diamonds available to the CSO. As a result, diamond exports increased to P243 million (US$248 million), in 1982, despite the continued fall in diamond prices.

Diamond prices and exports have since recovered. In 1983, unit values rose by 44 percent and export receipts increased to P464 million (US$406 million). By 1986, diamond exports had reached P1,130 million (US$615 million) (see tables 7.2 and 7.3).

Table 7.2 Total Exports and Major Export Commodities, 1975-86 (*pula millions*)

Year	Total	Diamonds	Copper-Nickel Matte	Meat and Meat Products
1975	105.0	32.1	22.0	36.5
1976	153.2	37.5	51.8	43.0
1977	151.6	46.8	39.8	41.2
1978	183.5	75.5	50.1	27.6
1979	355.4	183.5	60.7	63.8
1980	391.5	237.8	81.0	28.2
1981	332.4	134.8	79.7	60.5
1982	467.4	243.2	64.5	79.5
1983	696.7	463.9	65.8	79.1
1984	857.1	616.0	68.8	62.4
1985	1,385.1	1,049.0	119.9	97.5
1986	1,599.3	1,130.5	121.1	n.a.

n.a. = not available
Source: Statistical Bulletin, various issues.

Table 7.3 Diamond Prices: Unit Value Index, 1978-85 (1977=100)

Year	Index	Percentage change
1978	145.8	45.8
1979	200.7	37.2
1980	220.1	10.0
1981	175.9	-20.1
1982	154.3	-12.3
1983	222.0	43.9
1984	296.2	33.4
1985	470.0	58.7

Note: The index is not pure price changes. It is calculated as the value of diamond exports divided by physical volume in carats. The prices of the various grades of diamonds vary from one selling to the next (there are generally one or two CSO sales per month), so to say that the world price of diamonds rises or falls by any percentage is really a weighted average for the various grades of diamonds. Second, the weighted average for Botswana depends on the particular quality mix of stones that Botswana happens to export in any given year. During the years when Botswana was not selling all its diamond production, it was stockpiling a higher proportion of its highest quality gems. When it started selling from the stockpile in recent years, the unit value index rose both because diamond prices were rising across the board, and because the quality mix of Botswana's exports was rising due to the high quality gemstones coming out of the stockpile.

Source: Republic of Botswana (1985, p. 27); *External Trade Statistics* (various issues); *Statistical Bulletin* (various issues).

The Effects of Booms on the Economy

A temporary boom in an economy's export sector can give rise to a variety of economic effects elsewhere in the economy, a number of which may be unwelcome. A boom generates changes in the economy that tend to offset the boom's effects on the balance of payments. In particular, the increased export receipts will tend to appreciate the real exchange rate, and thus lead to a loss of competitiveness and output in other tradable goods sectors. When the boom ends, the country's external position may be no better, or even worse, than before the boom.[2]

A boom can affect the real exchange rate through several channels. First, higher incomes that result from the boom can increase domestic demand for both tradables and nontradables. In the nontradable sector, increased demand will result in higher prices. If the prices of tradables are fixed on world markets, then their price relative to nontradables in the domestic market will fall. Second, the price boom will initially shift the balance of payments toward surplus, leading to an increase in international reserves. This can lead to an increase in the monetary base of the banking system. If the domestic money supply does increase, the result is likely to be an increase in both imports and domestic inflation.[3]

Through these channels, the real appreciation of the exchange rate will work to reverse the effect of the boom on the balance of payments. The competitiveness of the traded goods sectors of the economy that are not experiencing the boom will be decreased. If the prices of nonboom traded goods are set on world markets, they will decline relative to the boom sector and the nontraded goods sector. Resources will move out of other tradable goods sectors into both nontradable goods and the boom-tradable goods sector. At the same time demand will shift toward tradables and will be met by increased net imports. This is the "Dutch disease" phenomenon of countries that experience a boom in their export sectors (Corden and Neary 1982).

A boom may result in pressure for both nominal and real wages to rise. High income in the boom sector and increased government revenue may create pressures for increases in real wages in these two sectors. These wage increases in turn may spill over into other sectors, increasing real wages for unskilled workers. If this happens, it will bias investment decisions away from labor-intensive sectors, decreasing the growth of employment opportunities. The rise in wages further decreases the competitiveness of traded goods in the economy relative to nontraded goods. Traded goods prices are fixed on world markets, so an increase in wages squeezes profitability. In contrast, prices in the nontraded goods sector can rise to offset increased costs.

---

2. Booms in the diamond sector have been temporary in Botswana in two different ways. New mines have resulted in increased growth rates of diamond revenues, GDP, and government revenues that are not sustainable. Also, unexpected price changes have led to higher diamond revenues than previously expected. This paper will focus on booms of the latter type. With only minor modification (temporary increases in growth rates rather than levels), the analysis applies to both types of boom.

3. In some countries, the above pressures toward real appreciation have been exacerbated because fiscal deficits have actually increased rather than declined. If financed by borrowing abroad, international reserves and the domestic money supply can increase further, putting more pressure on the real exchange rate. In addition, import restrictions or tariffs are sometimes eliminated in response to an export price boom as the balance of payments constraint eases. Also, again because the balance of payments constraint is relaxed, the currency may be revalued to slow inflation by lowering the domestic prices of imports.

The Costs of Assuming a Temporary Boom is Permanent

If the boom is only temporary, as most commodity booms are, but the government acts as if it were permanent and allows the effects discussed above to take place, including real exchange rate appreciation and increasing wages, then balance of payments crises, instability of income growth, and wasted resources are likely to result.[4]

If the boom in export receipts is only temporary, adopting policies to avoid the decline in profitability of other tradable goods sectors is the appropriate response. In the absence of perfect capital markets, resources will be reallocated toward nontradables and the boom sector. If the boom is temporary, resources will be wasted in the form of transition costs, perhaps taking the form of unemployed resources, as resource allocation responds to the changed profit conditions. Even if private agents realize that the boom is temporary and decide not to reallocate resources, profitability will decline in the nonboom tradable sector. If financial markets do not allow borrowing against future earnings, then the nonboom tradable sector may decline.

If policymakers assume that a temporary commodity export boom is permanent (whether implicitly or explicitly), increased expenditures by the government, producers, or consumers can also lead to increased instability in income and balance of payments crises in the medium or long run. If the boom in the export sector is permanent, real future GDP is higher and higher expenditure levels are justified. If it is temporary, however, any rise in expenditure levels will not be sustainable. Instability in expenditures will create an additional source of instability in income. In addition, if increased expenditures lead to increased imports, both through increased demand and real exchange rate appreciation, an unsustainable balance of payments position will result.

The Appropriate Policy Responses to a Temporary Boom

The appropriate policy response to a temporary boom (Cuddington 1986 a,b) is to avoid the macroeconomic effects and structural changes that would only be appropriate for a permanent price increase. First, current spending should be kept in line with expected long-run revenues, not with short-run receipts. The difference between the appropriate level of current spending and actual current income (temporarily high because of the boom) should be saved. Increased savings, in turn, should be allocated between domestic investment and foreign assets. Finally, keeping the real exchange rate from appreciating will avoid unnecessary and unjustified resource reallocations away from the nonboom traded goods sectors, and any accompanying transition costs.

The Choice Between Savings and Consumption

Turning to these policies in more detail, when temporary booms in the export sector lead to increased income, the government can increase welfare by spreading the increased consumption that such a boom allows over time. The appropriate behavior for a country is the same as it would be for an individual who experiences a

4. If the rise in prices in the boom sector is permanent, the changes in relative prices and competitiveness bring about an efficient reallocation of resources (see Corden 1983, Edwards 1984).

windfall gain. The windfall gain in income allows an increase in consumption. The individual can consume the entire windfall immediately, or alternatively, the increased consumption can be spread over the individual's remaining life time, with consumption increasing by a smaller amount in any given year. If the marginal utility of consumption declines with the level of consumption, an individual's utility will be higher if the increased consumption is spread over time. In other words, stabilizing consumption levels raises welfare. The same logic applies to a country that has experienced a windfall gain. When a country's income increases temporarily, the appropriate response is to save a large percentage of the windfall rather than to consume it.[5] If consumption is increased more than this, future consumption will have to be reduced. This variability in consumption can lead to macroeconomic instability and reduce welfare.

The Allocation of Savings

Once the government determines the appropriate level of savings, the next step is to allocate the savings. The main options include increasing official reserves (while sterilizing the effects on the domestic monetary base), increasing domestic capital investment, decreasing outstanding external debt, and increasing private sector holdings of foreign assets (if allowed). Each of these actions is a form of net saving for the economy.

The choice between paying back debt and increasing official reserves depends on the relative interest rates. If the expected cost on outstanding debt is greater than the return available on international reserves, then outstanding debt should be paid back.[6]

Increased saving should be invested domestically only if profitable compared to investing in foreign assets. An important consideration is the economy's absorptive capacity for new investment. A too rapid rate of increase in domestic investment during booms can easily decrease the rate of return by increasing labor costs, creating bottlenecks that raise costs, or by causing other types of inefficiencies in project implementation. A too rapid rate of increase in investment can also overload the government's administrative capacity to analyze projects. Projects

5. Cuddington has proposed the following for what should happen to consumption: "So as to avoid the problem of overspending, a simple rule of thumb can be employed: limit the increase in national consumption expenditures to the annuity-equivalent of the windfall gain" (Cuddington 1986a, p.6). An unexpected windfall gain increases a country's wealth. Higher wealth permits increased consumption. If consumption increases by the rate of return on the increased wealth, then the country can sustain this increased consumption level indefinitely.

6. Note that a country can default on its debt. Thus, the default option on debt acts like a form of insurance and effectively reduces its cost. If debt is repaid, this option no longer exists. This increases the incentive to increase international reserves rather than pay back debt. If countries are credit constrained or expect to be credit constrained in the future, increasing external commercial borrowing may actually be appropriate during the boom. If credit constraints and the cost of credit decline during booms, increasing commercial borrowing today while the cost is low or credit is available and then saving these funds for future use may make sense. A problem with this strategy is that even larger government reserves (held for future use) would lead to greater pressure for government to award larger wage increases, expand government development expenditures or services, and so on, now contributing to an inappropriate savings policy. Note that in Botswana's case, concessional borrowing became harder to get as a result of the boom in diamond exports. This offset part of the boom's benefits.

with low rates of return may slip through, or even worse, projects may be chosen and implemented for "corrupt" rather than technical reasons.

The Effects on the Domestic Money Supply

The boom will result in an increase in international reserves. To avoid inflationary pressures and real appreciation, the effects of higher international reserves on the domestic money supply should be sterilized. If the government receives the windfall (either directly or by taxing it away from the private sector), and saves it in the form of foreign assets, then the monetary base will not increase as a result of the boom. If the windfall accrues to the private sector and it can accumulate foreign assets, the increase in international reserves need not lead to an increase in the monetary base.

If the boom does lead to an increase in the monetary base, the government or the central bank should offset it. The central bank can offset the increase by using available monetary policy tools. Alternatively, the government can run a government surplus or a smaller government deficit than what it had targeted before the boom appeared. Sterilization can be difficult. Offsetting open market operations may not be possible, given the limited development of financial markets. Running a government surplus or reducing the government deficit by increasing taxes or cutting expenditures or expenditure growth rates can also be difficult to implement.

Deciding Whether a Boom is Temporary or Permanent

An obvious question that the government must answer before deciding on the appropriate policy response to a boom in the export sector is, therefore, whether an unexpected increase in commodity prices is temporary or permanent. In some cases, deciding whether a price change is permanent or temporary may be easy. Coffee prices moved upwards in 1986, leading to windfall gains in coffee-exporting countries, because of the Brazilian drought. In the absence of further shocks, the other coffee-exporting countries should have expected Brazilian production to recover and should thus have treated the price rise as temporary.

In the case of diamonds, projecting future prices is more difficult. Given uncertainty about future prices, countries may want to err on the side of caution on the grounds that the costs of assuming a boom is permanent when it is actually temporary are greater than the costs of saving more than is optimal. If the government assumes a boom is permanent when it is not, expenditure levels and imports will increase to unsustainable levels. When the boom reverses itself, expenditures and imports will have to be reduced, with the likely result being recession and lost output. If, however, the government assumes that a permanent boom is temporary, the cost is the difference between the rate of return on international reserves and the return to domestic consumption or investment forgone.

Given uncertainty, a country should not save so much that it is never caught short of international reserves when its export prices decline unexpectedly. Saving in this form involves an opportunity cost, which must be weighed against the probability of an unexpectedly sharp decline in prices and export earnings catching the country short of savings.

This distinction between a world of certainty and a world of uncertainty is the same that an individual faces when looking at the demand for cash balances.

Given total certainty about both income and expenditures, an individual can decide exactly how much cash to hold and never be caught short. If there is uncertainty about either income or expenditures, an individual will hold precautionary balances, the optimal quantity of which will depend on the opportunity costs of holding cash balances, the expected probability of being caught with too little cash, and the cost of being without enough cash or access to credit. Always having enough cash will never be optimal.

For a country that faces uncertainty about future commodity prices, an unexpectedly large drop in export earnings will result in a need for adjustment, even if the country was following an optimal savings policy. Just as for an individual, for a country to always hold enough international reserves will never be the best policy.

Botswana's Macroeconomic Policy Responses to Export Booms and Busts

Several objectives have guided Botswana's macroeconomic policy response to commodity price variability. A primary objective has been to avoid external debt problems and stabilize growth.

> Government's judgments on external and internal balance must be fairly long-sighted. There are serious costs to the economy if adjustments to restore balance have to be sudden and sharp. A sudden credit squeeze when the balance of payments worsens, for example, should if possible be avoided by planning a smooth path of credit expansion that anticipates balance of payments trends. Similarly, if the level of resources available to Government suddenly increased, it is better to plan a steady but sustainable increase in expenditures than to go on a short-lived spending spree that inevitably exceeds domestic production capacities and results mainly in increased imports. Regular revision of economic forecasts and anticipation of the trends they show can make a stop-go-cycle much less likely (Republic of Botswana 1980, p.67).

A second objective has been to promote exports other than diamonds and more general economic diversification. In addition to several microeconomic programs to promote diversification, the government has managed the exchange rate to avoid real appreciation. As already discussed, a booming sector can result in real appreciation, which makes other tradable goods less competitive. Import-competing industries and nontraditional exports are put at a disadvantage.

The government has pursued these objectives during boom periods by adopting policies that avoid the Dutch disease problems. In the first instance, the government has maintained sustainable expenditure levels during booms, primarily saving the windfall gain by running government surpluses. The government has continually attempted to run up reserves in good years in order to be able to run them down in bad years, and thereby stabilize the growth of public expenditure, and therefore the domestic economy. This avoids having to cut government expenditures in bad years, which would contribute to instability in income by working in the same direction as the decline in export earnings. This policy also contributes to avoiding real appreciation by not adding to inflationary pressures, both by not adding directly to demand for domestic resources, as well as by not increasing the domestic money supply during the boom.

In addition to not spending too much and avoiding inflationary pressures, the government and the Bank of Botswana have managed the nominal exchange rate to avoid real appreciation and to promote the traded goods sector of the economy, in an attempt to promote diversification.

The Government Budget

The government has two primary sources of revenue: customs revenues and mineral revenues (most from diamonds) (table 7.4). Botswana receives customs revenues from the South African Customs Union. Receipts depend on Botswana's imports and the agreed revenue-sharing formula. Time lags are built in, so that revenues received in any year depend on imports two years earlier, making this source of revenue unchangeable in the short run. In the past, despite the dependence on past imports, customs revenue was not entirely predictable because of a lag in the availability of reliable data on imports. Currently the data lag is closer to one year, so the government has advance information on the size of these revenues.[7]

Table 7.4 Government Recurrent Revenue, 1966 and 1974-86
(pula millions)

Year	Mineral revenues	Other property income	Customs pool revenues	Nonmineral income tax	Other revenue	Total
1966/77	0	0	1.1	2.2	2.9	6.2
1974/75	8.2	1.6	30.4	10.4	12.0	62.6
1975/76	23.4	2.8	24.6	13.2	15.5	79.5
1976/77	17.2	3.2	15.4	14.4	21.4	71.6
1977/78	24.0	3.5	37.8	17.6	18.0	100.9
1978/79	38.8	6.2	49.8	20.9	21.7	137.4
1979/80	76.6	8.7	80.2	24.3	23.6	213.4
1980/81	101.1	3.9	102.0	38.4	25.3	270.7
1981/82	77.0	27.5	104.3	41.6	32.4	282.8
1982/83	99.5	35.4	114.3	58.3	62.6	370.1
1983/84	193.8	37.4	156.8	78.9	44.5	511.4
1984/85	376.5	79.5	155.8	87.2	56.0	755.0
1985/86	581.2	196.1	149.2	93.6	65.3	1,085.4
1986/87[a]	782.2	195.0	193.5	119.1	100.8	1,390.6

a. Estimate
Source: Financial Statements, Tables and Estimates of Consolidated and Development Fund Revenues (various issues); *Statistical Bulletin* (various issues)

7. To the extent that there were surprises in the level of customs revenues, they were usually larger than previously expected. A current issue of concern is that the two-year lag implies an interest free loan from Botswana to South Africa.

The second source of revenue is from diamonds. Revenues from diamonds are determined by long-term agreements with DeBeers, whereby profits are split between DeBeers and the government. The contracts between DeBeers and Botswana are not public information. These agreements do not eliminate variability in this source of revenue, but they do limit the government's short-run flexibility in raising revenue. Uncertainty about diamond export receipts therefore directly creates uncertainty about government revenue. Also note that customs revenue is closely linked to major new projects in the mining sector. When a large amount of construction is being done in the mining sector, imports are high because of increased demand for imported inputs. In addition, any increased labor income resulting from expansion of the mining sector leads to further increases in imports (Lewis and Mokgethi 1983, pp. 76-77).

Fiscal policy has been consistent with and guided by the government's objectives of avoiding external debt problems and stabilizing growth. Government expenditures are based on long-term expectations of revenues. When export receipts from diamonds, and therefore government revenues, increase, government expenditures do not rise directly to any significant degree. Instead, the government builds up its foreign exchange reserves and balances at the Bank of Botswana to draw on in the future when revenues are low.

Government savings can be measured by the recurrent budget surplus. As tables 7.5 and 7.6 show, the government has increased its savings as revenue has risen. Revenue has cycled around its trend several times since 1973/74 (figure 7.1). The government has responded to variability in revenues, from both minerals and the customs union, by building up its liquid assets when revenues are high relative to trend. This allows the government to maintain a fairly constant growth in real expenditures over time (Lewis and Mokgethi 1983, p. 85). In 1979/80, the government saved most of the increased revenue, resulting in a higher recurrent surplus. Then, in 1981/82, when mineral royalties and dividends declined by P36 million, the government recurrent surplus declined by P24 million while expenditure levels were maintained. Over a slightly longer horizon, the government's recurrent surplus as a percentage of GDP has risen from 7 percent in 1978/79 to 25 percent in 1985/86, with the latter figure far beyond what the government expected in the sixth National Development Plan. The plan projected a government recurrent surplus of P336.9 million, compared to an actual surplus of P612.9 million. The government now considers the continued unexpectedly large build-up of foreign exchange reserves and government revenues in 1985/86 and 1986/87 as justification for some increased development expenditures. It is focusing on projects that will help eliminate some bottlenecks in the economy, and therefore contribute to continued development.

In 1981/82, Botswana experienced an unexpected decline in export earnings from its diamond sector. When the balance of payments went into deficit in 1981 and the country's international reserves started to decline, the government adopted policies to reverse this decline. Botswana's need to adjust to this shock is not evidence that the country had followed inadequate savings policies earlier on. As argued earlier, even if a country is accumulating optimal reserves, an unexpectedly large decline in export earnings will catch the country short of savings, which will necessitate adjustment.

Thus, the government adopted a package of adjustment policies. After an increase in bank lending of almost 50 percent in 1981, the banks agreed to limit increases in lending to 8 percent in 1982, later raised to 15 percent (Harvey 1985, p. 32). The prime lending rate was increased from 11 percent in 1981 to 14.5 percent in

1982, wages and salaries were frozen, and the pula was devalued by 10 percent (Harvey 1985, pp. 32-39). In addition, the government attempted to reduce the projected increase in government expenditure and to increase taxation.

Table 7.5 Government Revenue and Expenditure, 1966/67 and 1974/75-1985/86 *(pula millions)*

Year	Total recurrent revenue	Total recurrent expenditure	Recurrent surplus/ deficit	Development expenditure
1966/67	6.2	10.3	-4.1	3.7
1974/75	62.6	37.0	25.6	32.8
1975/76	79.5	49.5	30.0	35.5
1976/77	71.6	68.0	3.5	37.6
1977/78	100.9	75.8	25.1	44.4
1978/79	137.4	101.6	35.8	79.0
1979/80	213.4	128.6	84.8	98.3
1980/81	270.7	170.4	100.3	121.4
1981/82	282.8	205.9	76.9	121.3
1982/83	370.1	233.6	136.4	160.4
1983/84	511.4	297.9	213.4	140.7
1984/85	755.0	378.0	377.1	209.7
1985/86	1,085.3	472.4	612.9	247.5

Average annual real growth rates 1975/76-1985/86

Recurrent expenditure	14.5%
Development expenditure	11.8%
Recurrent revenue	18.5%

Source: Statistical Bulletin, various issues.

The idea behind using a number of policy adjustments was to spread the impact over the whole economy. Relying on one policy tool would have meant a more drastic change to obtain the required results. The government adopted these policy changes quickly. The thinking was that taking moderate policy actions well in time was better than waiting until the situation was so serious that policy actions would have had to be much more extreme.

The size of the decline in the diamond market suggested that revenue growth would be less than previously expected. Therefore, the drop in diamond revenues and government revenues was considered more than just short-term variability. This change in the previously expected trend justified reducing previously planned expenditures; however, the rate of increase in recurrent expenditure slowed only marginally, while the rate of increase of development expenditure actually increased in 1982/83. The government used cash balances to finance these increases.

Table 7.6 Comparison of Government Budget and Projections, 1979/80-1984/85
(pula millions at 1979/80 prices)

Year	Total revenue		Recurrent expenditure		Development expenditure		Budget surplus or deficit	
	Proj.	Actual	Proj.	Actual	Proj.	Actual	Proj.	Actual
1979/80	219.2	249.1	120.6	121.9	76.2	87.1	+5.2	+21.1
1980/81	232.5	268.1	136.4	145.6	83.3	91.2	-23.5	-1.5
1981/82	224.6	252.0	146.8	156.2	93.3	85.3	-40.5	-14.7
1982/83	241.3	278.8	169.8	160.6	90.2	112.3	-43.5	-14.9
1983/84	285.0	371.9	177.3	178.4	93.9	93.7	-21.7	+68.5
1984/85	325.2	447.2	201.4	207.4	92.8	121.2	+2.9	+84.3
Average percentage growth per annum	+8.2	+12.4	+10.5	+11.2	+4.0	+6.8	--	--

-- = not applicable
Source: Republic of Botswana (1980; 1985, p.33)

Figure 7.1 Real Government Expenditures and Revenues, 1975/76-1985/86
(pula millions at 1979/80 prices)

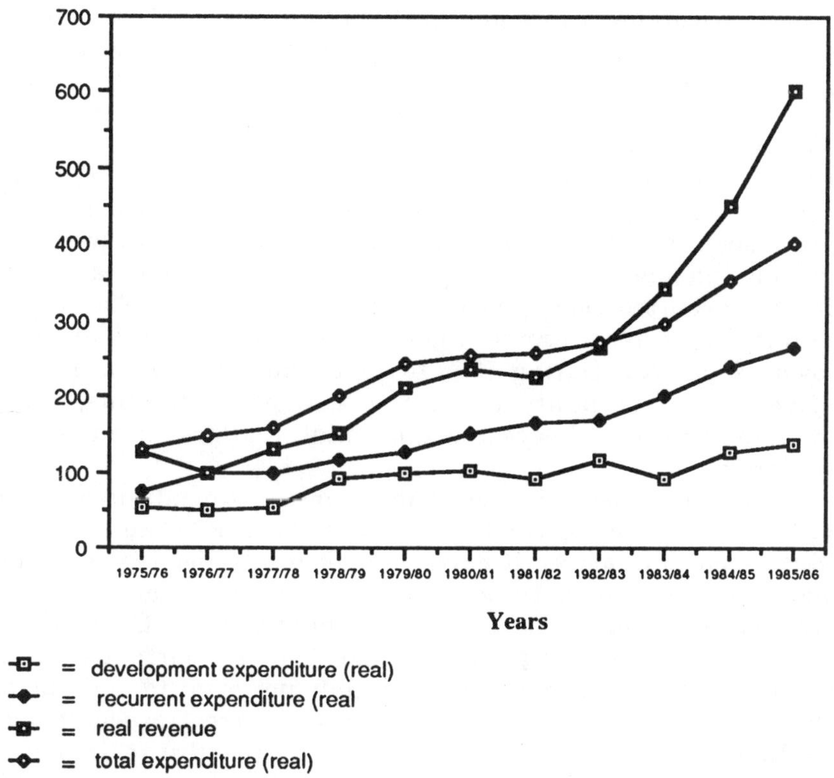

In the end, the government did not increase taxes. Raising taxes in Botswana is not easy, because mining and customs union revenues are determined by contracts that are not negotiated every year. Income taxes were not raised on equity grounds, because as part of the adjustment package, wage earners were already forgoing expected nominal wage increases. (In fact, the wage freeze implied falling real wages.)

So, although the unexpected and large decline in diamond exports called for the government to reduce net expenditures, this was not accomplished. Part of the explanation is that doing this quickly is difficult, and by the time the government could make changes, the crisis had reversed itself: the decline in diamond exports proved to be temporary.

Other elements in the adjustment package, as well as changing international conditions, helped slow the deterioration in the balance of payments. For example, the government set limits on the amount of credit that commercial banks could extend to the private sector. Since government net expenditures did not slow much during this period, the private sector shouldered most of the adjustment. If the crisis had persisted, however, the government would have had to adjust as well.

With improving external conditions, Botswana ran a government budget surplus of P188 million (US$121 million) in 1984/85. In 1986/87, the surplus is estimated at P413 million (US$225 million).

During the current plan period (National Development Plan Six 1985-91), the government budget was expected to move into deficit toward the end of the plan period. However, government revenues during the first two years were much larger than expected, and the crossover point has been pushed out to the seventh plan. The deficit projected for the future, although postponed, is still a worry. In the absence of major new revenue sources, maintaining expenditures in line with receipts would imply a cut in the growth rate of government expenditures. The government recognizes that some expenditure and revenue adjustment will be required.

As discussed earlier, the government has followed the policy of saving and dissaving in response to booms and busts. Some people in Botswana have asked whether saving has been excessive and whether the increase in recurrent expenditure has been too slow, given the size of the booms. The average annual percentage increase in real recurrent government expenditures during the 1980s has been over 12 percent. During 1975 to 1985, the average real increase was 13 percent. Given the uncertainty about the sources of revenue, erring on the conservative side, which in this case is quite high real growth rates in any event, may be appropriate.

Several factors limit faster increases in recurrent expenditures, including their already rapid rate of increase. The first factor is the link between the development budget and the recurrent budget. Recurrent expenditures depend in part on the level of development expenditures. Development projects lead to increased recurrent expenditures on such items as salaries and maintenance. Given the absorptive capacity limits on development projects, some type of recurrent expenditures are also constrained. The government would certainly not want to undertake otherwise undesirable development projects just to increase recurrent expenditures. A second factor that limits faster increases in recurrent expenditure in Botswana is a shortage of skilled manpower. Faster growth of government recurrent expenditures, or development expenditures for that matter, could have reduced the supply of skilled labor to local governments, parastatals, and the private sector even more.

Given the optimal level of saving, the government has to decide how to allocate it between international reserves and domestic investment. When the government saves the windfall gains, should it invest them domestically or in external assets? Government investment as measured by development expenditure has been based on long-run revenues, as has recurrent expenditure. The real growth rate of development expenditure has averaged almost 7 percent during the 1980s and over 12 percent between 1975 and 1985 (tables 7.5, 7.6). Development expenditure has been fairly volatile, however, partly as a result of the lumpy nature of the major investment projects undertaken. Between 1979/80 and 1984/85, real development expenditure increased at a higher rate than projected under the fifth plan's scenario of slower growth in the mineral sector: 6.8 percent versus 4 percent. The higher growth rates partly reflect favorable developments in the mineral sector from 1982, and partly higher than expected expenditures related to the drought. In any case, development expenditures have not been increased above planned levels by anything near the increase in revenues above expected levels. So the government has mostly saved unexpected gains in the form of international reserves, and not increased domestic investment through increases in previously planned levels of development expenditures.

In view of Botswana's limited absorptive capacity, the government's choice for allocation of savings seems appropriate. The government has felt that increasing development expenditure much beyond planned levels would depress the rate of return below what can be earned on alternative assets, in particular, international reserves.

During booms, increasing investment beyond levels already planned for could involve costs. The return to investment could decline by raising the costs of labor and other inputs, and by creating unexpected bottlenecks and thereby reducing efficiency. The rising cost of labor is of particular concern in Botswana because of the shortage of skilled manpower. Pushing investment beyond previously planned levels could also easily result in the adoption of investment projects with low returns, if for no other reason than because even if profitable investment opportunities exist, identifying them quickly may not be possible.

Increasing investment above trend during booms can add to aggregate demand at a time when the appropriate macroeconomic response may be to undertake countercyclical expenditure policies. Postponing investment until the boom subsides could help stabilize income growth. In Botswana, however, because the government does not automatically spend more when its revenues rise and DeBeers does not automatically spend more in Botswana when its profits increase, the boom does not directly affect aggregate demand. In addition, employment and workers' incomes in mining are very stable even during booms: only the quantity and quality of diamonds sold and the earnings of DeBeers and the government are affected. As a result, the worry about investment projects adding to aggregate demand is much less serious in Botswana than it may be in other countries.[8]

The current boom has continued long enough that the government is currently reconsidering its allocations to international reserves and development expenditures. As of October 1987, Botswana had accumulated reserves equal to 21 months of import cover, which the government considered excessive (table 7.7)). During the fall of 1987, Parliament approved a proposal to consider a number of "major economic development initiatives" that would use a portion of the accumulated reserves for big investments in areas that are major bottlenecks to development.

8. The difference between booms and new mines coming on line is important here. When major new mineral projects are undertaken, demand can increase substantially because of the lumpiness of projects and the size of such projects relative to the national economy.

Table 7.7 International Reserves and Months of Import Cover, 1976-86

As at end of	Pula millions	US$ millions	SDR millions	Months of import cover[a]
1976	65.1	74.9	64.4	4.3
1977	82.8	100.0	82.3	4.1
1978	124.5	150.3	115.4	4.9
1979	210.7	267.1	202.7	5.8
1980	255.0	343.4	269.2	5.7
1981	223.0	253.4	218.1	4.0
1982	310.8	292.9	265.6	5.3
1983	457.2	395.7	377.5	6.8
1984	736.7	472.2	481.9	10.1
1985	1,644.9	784.0	715.0	17.3
1986[b]	2,200.5	1,197.5	981.0	20.6

Note: International reserves include IMF reserve tranche and SDRs.
a. Reserves at year end divided by average monthly imports during the year.
b. Provisional.
Source: Bank of Botswana (1986).

The Balance of Payments and International Reserves

Botswana left the rand monetary area in August 1976 and introduced its own monetary system and its own currency, the pula. Between 1976 and 1980, foreign exchange reserves increased each year, from P65 million (US$75 million) in December 1976, to P255 million (US$344 million) in December 1980. Increasing mineral revenues and cautious government expenditure policies allowed this build-up. The justification for building up international reserves is the same as that for building up government balances: it is a way to save windfall gains from mineral revenues for use when export receipts decline. When the government saves by running recurrent surpluses, the part not invested domestically adds to international reserves. International reserves permit smoothing of imports over time as export earnings vary. If reserves are not built up during booms, the government would have either to borrow or reduce imports when diamond export earnings declined, by expenditure reductions and/or other policies.

As discussed earlier, in 1981/82 Botswana was hit by a severe depression in diamond markets. Diamond prices dropped at the same time that the volume of diamond exports fell drastically because of the marketing agreement with DeBeers. For several months, Botswana did not export any diamonds. Foreign exchange reserves fell rapidly as they were used to pay for imports (table 7.8). Previously accumulated reserves allowed continued imports while the government devised a policy response. In 1980, reserves equaled five and a half months of imports, whereas the average for developing countries at that time was three to four months of imports. This is an important benefit of a cautious policy. Instead of having to respond under pressure with drastic, fast-acting policies, the government has some time for more thoughtful decision making. If Botswana had not previously accumulated reserves, a more severe crisis would have ensued.

On its own initiative, the government adopted a stabilization program in 1982, having decided that adjustment was unavoidable. The reason was that the 1981/82 decline in diamond receipts, and therefore in government revenues and reserves, was unexpected. Foreign exchange reserves did not accumulate as rapidly as forecast, largely because of the deterioration in Botswana's terms of trade (table 7.9). As a result, accumulated reserves were inadequate to avoid a drop in expenditure. As discussed earlier, this does not imply that previous policy was not optimal. Insuring against worst case shocks is not optimal. The opportunity costs of having done so would have outweighed the expected costs of having to adjust to the worst case shock.

Table 7.8 Balance of Payments, 1977-86
(pula millions)

Year	Total goods and services	Total transfers	Current account	Capital account	Overall balance	Change in international reserves
1977	-56.8	79.3	21.5	2.1	15.3	17.9
1978	-105.0	67.2	-37.8	70.5	32.8	42.2
1979	-75.5	105.0	29.5	70.3	93.4	85.0
1980	-160.5	99.2	-61.3	90.7	42.2	45.4
1981	-287.5	116.3	-171.2	91.3	-60.8	-32.0
1982	-181.1	119.9	-61.2	103.3	66.5	85.9
1983	-135.2	137.3	2.1	105.3	138.1	148.1
1984	-118.4	132.0	13.6	144.0	165.1	279.5
1985	81.0	170.4	251.4	238.6	501.1	887.7
1986	125.0	184.0	309.0	222.0	565.0	541.3

Notes: Overall balance includes net errors and omissions. Change in external reserves includes adjustments for exchange rate changes.
Source: Statistical Bulletin (various issues), Bank of Botswana, *Annual Report* (various issues)

The large, unexpected drop in export earnings meant that some adjustment was necessary. The extent of adjustment depended on expectations for the future, in particular, whether the decline was temporary, implying a small windfall loss and less adjustment, or permanent, thereby implying a much larger loss. As there was little evidence that the recession would end quickly enough for Botswana to avoid running out of foreign exchange, the government decided that immediate adjustment was necessary and preferable to waiting until reserves fell even further (Harvey 1985, p.31).

Table 7.9 Balance of Payments Forecasts and Outcome, Fifth National Development Plan
(*months of import cover represented by foreign exchange reserves at year-end*)

Year	Forecast[a]	Outcome
1979/80	6.7	5.5
1980/81	8.0	4.4
1981/82	7.8	4.7
1982/83	7.3	5.2
1983/84	7.1	7.0
1984/85	7.1	9.2

a. This set of projections assumes slow growth in the mineral sector.
Source: Republic of Botswana (1985, p.32)

If the government had had perfect information about the future, it might have preferred a smaller contraction. Diamond prices recovered in 1983: the unit value index for diamonds increased 44 percent between 1982 and 1983. In addition, the Jwaneng mine started production in mid-1982, increasing export earnings. Although the government expected production to start at this time, the quality of the diamonds mined exceeded forecasts. Botswana also experienced an improvement in its terms of trade as a result of exchange rate changes. Botswana's exports are priced in dollars, while most of its imports are priced in rand. With the rand depreciating against the dollar in real terms (table 7.10), Botswana's exports could purchase greater amounts of imports.

With the recovery of diamond prices, in 1984 Botswana ran a balance of payments surplus of P165 million (US$129 million) and a trade surplus of P122 million (US$95 million). World diamond sales continued to increase in 1985 and 1986, as did Botswana's diamond exports. The balance of payments surplus was a record P501 million (US$265 million) in 1985 and P565 million (US$303 million) in 1986, partly because of the pula's depreciation against the dollar. As a result, foreign exchange reserves rose from P737 million (US$472 million) in December 1984 to

P1,645 million (US$783 million) in December 1985, and reached P2,201 million (US$1,198 million) by the end of 1986. At the end of 1986, reserves equaled almost 21 months of imports, having equaled 7 months of cover in 1983 (Bank of Botswana 1986, p.26).

Table 7.10 Bilateral Real Exchange Rates, 1977-86
(percentage changes in real exchange rates) (+ = real depreciation of the pula)

Year	Pula/ Rand	Pula/ Zimbabwe$	Pula/£	Pula/ other European currencies*	Pula/US$
1977	-7.4	-10.8	9.2	-3.2	-11.7
1978	1.5	-6.9	5.6	9.9	-0.1
1979	1.4	0.5	6.0	-6.8	-4.9
1980	4.2	-7.0	4.4	-23.1	-7.1
1981	-8.3	1.6	-9.2	-5.7	12.5
1982	10.7	6.4	0.0	7.7	15.3
1983	-3.0	0.7	-7.3	-11.2	0.8
1984	-14.7	10.0	-3.9	10.5	30.7
1985	13.1	23.7	65.5	63.9	29.0
1986	10.5	-11.2	-16.1	-0.1	-18.8

Notes: A positive percentage indicates real depreciation of the pula.
* = proxied by the pula/deutschmark rate.
Source: International Financial Statistics (various issues)

In addition to accumulating reserves, the government discussed the benefits of repaying the balance remaining on a commercial Eurodollar loan taken out in 1982. It decided that as the rate of return on the foreign exchange reserves was higher than the rate of interest on the loan, paying the loan back early would not be advantageous. By 1985, the situation had changed enough that in the end, the government paid the loan off ten months ahead of schedule.

Initially, neither the Bank of Botswana nor the Ministry of Finance and Development Planning considered the large reserve accumulation excessive. The government justified the reserve accumulation on the grounds that projections of future export earnings suggested that this level of surplus would not continue: projections of mineral production indicated growth of only 3-1/2 percent per annum during the next few years, resulting from the Jwaneng mine reaching full capacity, and therefore no longer contributing to rapid growth rates. Diamond and nickel-copper matte exports were projected to remain constant in real value at 1985/86 levels through the remainder of the decade.

With continued reserve increases, the government now considers its reserve accumulation to be excessive and is considering some major new economic development initiatives. However, it will continue to maintain large international reserves. The government expects to draw down reserves in the future to pay for imports, and thus to avoid having to impose austerity measures when export receipts decline. Given volatility and uncertainty in diamond prices and in the U.S. dollar/rand exchange rate, Botswana's vulnerability to events in the region, as well as the high growth rates of expenditure, a policy of maintaining large international reserves has its advantages.

Monetary Policy and the Exchange Rate

In general, Botswana has used monetary policy to reinforce its strategy of saving and increasing international reserves during booms, so as to sustain expenditure and growth during less good times. Monetary policy consists of controlling the exchange rate, changing domestic interest rates, and setting limits on the growth of commercial bank credit. The Bank of Botswana, in conjunction with the Ministry of Finance and Development Planning, is responsible for monetary policy, as well as supervision of domestic financial institutions.

Exchange Rate Management. In 1976, Botswana adopted its own currency, the pula, and created the Bank of Botswana. Initially, the pula was pegged to the dollar. In June 1980, the government decided to peg the pula to a basket of currencies, including the rand and the five SDR currencies. Since then, the government and the Bank of Botswana have changed the basket's composition, as well as the rate at which the pula is pegged.

Botswana's management of its exchange rate has been guided by several objectives, not always consistent. The government is committed to supporting diversification of the economy. By avoiding real appreciation of the pula, local producers of traded goods can compete more successfully with imports and in export markets. This objective of exchange rate management is entirely consistent with the government's policy of accumulating international reserves during boom periods. Allowing the real exchange rate to appreciate during booms would reduce reserve accumulation by reducing net exports.

When the real exchange rate is used as a tool to promote diversification, the pula/rand exchange rate is very important for several reasons. First, the largest percentage of imports (75 percent) comes from South Africa.[9] Second, Botswana's major export, diamonds, is priced in dollars and sales are controlled by agreement. Changes in the exchange rate affect the pula value of exports and government revenue, but not the value of foreign exchange earnings from diamond exports. Alternative measures of the real exchange rate, both bilateral and multilateral, are presented in tables 7.10 and 7.11.

At the same time that diversification has been a goal, the government has at times used revaluation to moderate imported inflation by reducing the pula price of imports. Between 1977 and 1980, when the pula was pegged to the dollar, it was

9. This overstates the proportion of imports that become less competitive when the nominal pula exchange rate appreciates relative to the rand. Many imports from South Africa originate elsewhere, or have a high import content. If the rand depreciates relative to other currencies at the same time it is depreciating relative to the pula, the rand price of these goods increases. This will offset the effects of any pula/rand appreciation on competitiveness.

revalued three times. This was a period when domestic price stability objectives dominated the diversification goal. In 1977, South Africa adopted several policies that increased the cost of imports in Botswana (Harvey 1985, p. 23). A revaluation of 5 percent was adopted to offset the effects of these price increases on incomes in Botswana. At the time, almost all manufactured consumer goods were imported. To the extent that the nominal exchange rate offset higher rand prices, the effects on local producers of traded goods was small. In addition, Botswana had very few local producers of traded goods at the time. The government recognized that the revaluation could decrease incentives for such a sector, but inflation and income distribution objectives dominated. It was felt that other factors more important than the exchange rate constrained local producers of traded goods. Also, it was hoped that revaluation would lead to lower inflation, which in turn would lead to smaller increases in nominal wages. In the end, domestic price increases would be smaller than otherwise and offset some of the effects of revaluation on competitiveness.[10]

Table 7.11 Multilateral Real Trade Weighted Exchange Rates, 1977-86
(percentage change in real exchange rate) (+ = real depreciation of the pula)

Year	Import weights	Export weights	Total trade weights
1977	-7.6	-5.7	-6.7
1978	0.1	-6.1	-3.4
1979	1.2	-5.3	-2.1
1980	2.7	-17.0	-6.7
1981	-7.0	-1.5	-4.7
1982	9.4	8.3	8.9
1983	-2.8	-6.6	4.4
1984	-10.8	14.3	-0.1
1985	16.1	47.3	31.2
1986	6.0	-5.9	-0.5

Notes: Weights were calculated using Botswana's import, export, and total trade shares with its trading partners.
Sources: International Financial Statistics, (various issues), *Statistical Bulletin,* March 1987.

The pula was revalued again in 1979 and 1980 by approximately 5 percent against the dollar each time. Again, the objective was to keep down the inflation

10. Some people went so far as to argue that domestic prices would fall by an amount equal to the revaluation and that there would be no effect on competitiveness. For this argument to hold, revaluation must lead not only to a fall in the pula price of traded goods prices, but also in nontraded goods prices. This can happen if real wages are constant, implying a drop in nominal wages as a result of revaluation. The drop of nominal wages must be passed through to lower nontraded goods prices.

rate. Despite the revaluations, the real pula/rand exchange rate actually depreciated by small amounts during these years (tables 7.10, 7.11, and 7.12).

During 1981, Botswana's real exchange rate appreciated about 8 percent against the rand. The pula was pegged to a basket including the rand and the SDR, and as the rand depreciated relative to the currencies in the SDR basket, the pula appreciated relative to the rand. At the time, Botswana's inflation rate was about equal to that in South Africa. The pula price of most imports into Botswana from South Africa therefore fell. This was not a good time for import prices to fall, however, as it would hurt the balance of payments as well as moves toward diversifying the economy. A real pula/rand appreciation would hurt import-competing sectors as well as "nontraditional" exports (exports other than diamonds, copper-nickel matte, and beef), most of which were exported to South Africa. Botswana had successfully encouraged these sectors though such policies as the Financial Assistance Policy, and did not want to undo the progress achieved.[11]

Table 7.12 Bilateral Nominal Exchange Rates (End of Period), 1976-86

Year	Pula/Rand	Pula/Zimbabwe$	Pula/£	Pula/DM	Pula/US$
1976	1.000	1.404	1.480	0.368	0.870
1977	0.953	1.281	1.579	0.394	0.829
1978	0.953	1.227	1.685	0.453	0.829
1979	0.954	1.170	1.755	0.456	0.789
1980	0.995	1.176	1.769	0.379	0.742
1981	0.920	1.223	1.680	0.391	0.880
1982	0.986	1.154	1.713	0.447	1.062
1983	0.946	1.045	1.676	0.425	1.156
1984	0.785	1.037	1.803	0.496	1.560
1985	0.821	1.279	3.034	0.854	2.101
1986	0.842	1.094	2.710	0.948	1.838

Source: *International Financial Statistics*, various issues.

11. The Financial Assistance Policy was instituted in 1982 to increase the economy's productive base and to expand employment opportunities. Government funds are channeled to new or expanding ventures that promise reasonable returns and new jobs. The assistance is temporary (Republic of Botswana 1985, p. 239).

During 1982, when the balance of payments was moving into deficit and international reserves were falling, the pula continued to appreciate against the rand, as it had done during 1981. In an attempt to slow down the decrease in international reserves, the government devalued the pula 10 percent against the rand, which offset the appreciation of the previous year. In 1982, the real exchange rate depreciated over 9 percent. By this time, in contrast to the late 1970s, small "nontraditional" export and import-competing sectors had arisen. Most of these goods competed primarily with South African goods. The devaluation, therefore, contributed to keeping this sector competitive. Awareness of the effect of the real exchange rate on diversification contributed to the decision to devalue.

In the last several years, the government has managed wages and the exchange rate so as to avoid overvaluation of the real exchange rate. During 1984, the real pula/rand exchange rate appreciated by about 15 percent because of the weakness of the rand, given the basket to which the pula was pegged.

In January 1985, the pula was devalued 15 percent against the basket of currencies to restore the competitiveness of domestic traded goods. At the same time, the weights in the basket were changed to increase the rand's importance. The policy was reversed later in the year because of uncertainty about the rand. During 1985, the pula depreciated against the dollar and other currencies, while it appreciated against the rand, but not enough to offset the January devaluation.

The pula continued to depreciate relative to the rand in real terms in 1986. Inflation was about 10 percent higher in South Africa than in Botswana at the same time that the rand appreciated in nominal terms against the pula.

Countries undergoing export booms will experience pressures for real exchange rate appreciation. Since 1980, Botswana has managed its nominal exchange rate to avoid real appreciation. Because the government considers the current boom in diamond export earnings to be temporary, this is the appropriate policy response. Note the relationship between exchange rate and international reserve accumulation policies. If the real exchange rate is allowed to appreciate, the trade account worsens, offsetting the effects of the boom on the balance of payments surplus, and therefore on international reserve accumulation. Again, this is only an equilibrium phenomenon if the boom is permanent.

The Money Supply. When countries experience export booms and increasing international reserves, high powered money will increase, leading to increased imports, inflationary pressures, and real appreciation through price increases. All of these effects will act to reverse the initial improvement in the balance of payments. Botswana has partly avoided this problem by using changes in government surpluses to sterilize the effects of changes in foreign exchange reserves on the domestic money supply.

Table 7.13 shows the contributions of the external sector and the government to changes in M3 over time. The external sector has over time exerted an expansionary effect on the money stock, which has been offset by a decline in net domestic credit. This is explained in turn by increases in claims by the government on the banking system. When the government follows the appropriate saving policy during booms, the monetary effects are minimized.

As an example, in 1985 the net expansionary effect of the external sector on the money supply was around P400 million.[12] The government budget, in contrast,

12. Net foreign assets of the banking system rose by P855 million in 1985. Almost half of this was the result of gains from revaluation resulting from depreciation of the pula during 1985.

reduced the growth rate of the money supply. The government ran a large surplus, and government deposits at the Bank of Botswana increased by P260 million. In 1986, the external sector exerted an expansionary effect on the money supply of P600 million. The government again offset this. Its claims on the banking system rose by P622 million.

Table 7.13 Changes in M3 and Causal Factors, 1979-86
(pula millions)

Item	1979	1980	1981	1982	1983	1984	1985	1986
Net domestic credit	-8.2	0.4	75.6	-33.0	-47.6	-119.5	-241.8	-605.5
Government deposits with the banking system	-20.4	-11.0	29.2	-37.1	-76.2	-181.0	-260.0	-622.0
Net foreign assets of the banking system	87.9	42.0	-37.3	94.7	144.6	298.4	855.6	600.9
Other items (net)[a]	-16.2	20.1	-56.6	-36.6	-22.9	-136.5	-445.9	78.9
Change in M3	63.5	62.5	-18.3	25.1	74.1	42.3	167.9	74.3

Note: Signs denote effect on the money stock.
a. Changes in other items (net) largely reflect contra entries to revaluation gains or losses in the international reserves of the Bank of Botswana because of changes in the pula exchange rate.
Source: Bank of Botswana (various issues)

Large increases in the money supply during booms are a worry because, through inflation, they can contribute to real exchange rate appreciation. Botswana has avoided this problem by appropriate government savings policies and nominal exchange rate management.

Wage Policy

The government's income policies are consistent with its overall macroeconomic policy. As discussed above, the government wants to promote diversification and increase employment. The government realizes that increasing real wages will reduce efforts to increase employment and promote investment.

A boom in one sector puts pressure on wages to increase as labor is attracted to the booming sector. These wage increases can spill over into other sectors of the economy, raising their costs. In nontraded goods sectors, higher costs can be passed through to higher prices. In traded goods sectors, higher prices will result in reduced competitiveness. Since prices are fixed on world markets, higher wage costs reduce

The -P445.9 million in "other items (net)" is primarily a contra entry to these revaluation gains. See Bank of Botswana, *Annual Report*, 1985, pp. 11-12.

profitability. So higher wages will result in a larger nontraded goods sector at the expense of the traded goods sector and less labor-intensive techniques throughout the economy as a whole. Again, if the boom is permanent, this reallocation of resources is appropriate. If the boom is temporary, avoiding resource reallocation and declining nonboom sectors will be appropriate. If wages rise during the boom, they will need to fall when the boom subsides. If wages are not very flexible, unemployment may result instead.

In an attempt to encourage diversification, the government has used income policies to avoid real appreciation. The government's income policies are "voluntary," but the government is ready to enforce its policies through statutes if the voluntary approach fails. The government controls wages for skilled manpower (in the government and private sectors), minimum wages for unskilled employees, and cost of living adjustments (Republic of Botswana 1985, p 67.)[13] From 1976 to 1980, salaries commissions undertook biennial reviews of government salaries. These commissions recommended appropriate cost of living adjustments and salary structures. As a result, percentage increases varied from one category of job to the next. In 1980, the government decided to undertake full-scale reviews of the salary structure only every four to five years, with annual cost of living reviews. The first cost of living increase took place in August 1981 and was a flat 7.5 percent increase. This was approximately one half the inflation rate, implying a fall in real wages. Despite the institution of cost of living adjustments, the government was not guaranteeing fixed or increasing real wages. At the time of the first cost of living adjustment, the government announced: "There is no guarantee that there will be an increase every year. There may be years when the economic circumstances of the country dictate that there be none or even that there be a decrease in salaries" (*Report of the Fourth Salaries Review Commission* 1985, p. 11).

In 1982, in response to balance of payments problems, no increase was granted. According to the Fourth Salaries Review Commission, between August 1980 and September 1985, cost of living adjustments fell short of inflation by 25.5 percent (*Report of the Fourth Salaries Review Commission* 1985, p. 10). Table 7.14 summarizes the average wage increases that resulted from the various salary structure and cost of living reviews, as well as changes in the cost of living index over time. During the first half of the 1980s, real wages tended not to increase. As table 7.15 shows, real minimum wages remained approximately constant from 1982 to 1986.

Commerce and Industry

In addition to its macroeconomic policies, the government has adopted several microeconomic policies aimed at encouraging diversification, for example, the Financial Assistance Policy for manufacturing and noncattle agriculture. These policies are, however, the subject of another paper. Note that it would be difficult for these policies to overcome the effects of a massively overvalued exchange rate on competitiveness.

---

13. For important qualifications concerning expatriates, see p. 67, paragraph 3.82. The government recognizes the difficulty of attracting any skilled expatriates needed if they were subject to the same income policies as the domestic labor supply.

Table 7.14 Salary Increases and Increases in the Cost of Living Index, 1976-87

Year	Increase (percent)	Comment	Increase in cost of living index[a] (percent)
1976	20 average[b]	Chiepe Commission	12.0
1977	None	—	12.2
1978	50 average	Mmusi Commission	12.5
1979	None	—	7.7
1980	22 average	Meswele Commission	14.3
1981	7.5 flat	Cost of living adjustment	14.6
1982	None	Cost of living adjustment	14.6
1983	8 flat	Cost of living adjustment	12.7
1984	10 flat	Cost of living adjustment	8.3
1985	6 flat	Cost of living adjustment	6.5
1986	17 average	Gasennelwe Commission	10.4
1987	10 flat	Cost of living adjustment	10.8

a. The inflation figure listed for 1976 is the rate of inflation from December 1974 to December 1975—on the assumption that a Salaries Commission that published its recommendations in 1976 had the previous year's inflation rate available to it.

b. All averages are estimates only.

Source: *Statistical Review* (various issues)

Table 7.15 Real Minimum Wage Rates
(Thebe / hour, 1980 prices)

Sector	1982	1983	1984	1985	1986
Manufacturing, service, and repair trades	34.4	34.0	34.9	33.5	35.4
Building, construction, exploration, and quarrying	34.4	34.0	34.9	33.5	35.4
Hotels, catering, and entertainment	34.4	34.0	34.9	33.5	35.4
Garages, motor trade, and road transport	34.4	34.0	34.9	33.5	35.4
Wholesale distributive trade	31.3	30.5	30.9	29.9	32.0
Retail distributive trade	31.3	30.5	30.3	29.3	33.5
Government (industrial class)	44.5	44.0	44.7	43.1	47.5

Source: Bank of Botswana, 1986

Have the Government's Policies Succeeded?

The government's overall macroeconomic policy has been consistent with avoiding balance of payments crises and with encouraging diversification. As already discussed, the government has managed international reserve accumulation, government expenditure, the exchange rate, and wages with these goals in mind.

Have these policies yielded the supposed benefits? The government has avoided balance of payments crises. The required adjustment in 1982 was the result of an unexpectedly large decline in diamond earnings and was less severe than would have been necessary if the government had not previously accumulated reserves. In 1986, international reserves equaled over 20 months of imports. This should certainly help Botswana avoid balance of payments problems in the near future.

GDP growth has been high and less variable than income from mining. The government has stabilized the growth rates of its expenditures, thereby contributing to this stability, and has avoided declines in GDP as a result of severe balance of payments crises. Real GDP growth per annum averaged 13 percent between 1979/80 and 1984/85, while nonmineral GDP increased an average of 5-1/2 percent per year (Republic of Botswana 1985, p.53, table A.2.17).

In general, the evidence suggests that diversification is progressing. Nontraditional exports have grown as rapidly as other exports maintaining their share of total exports at around 12 percent. Manufacturing had the fastest rate of employment growth from 1979/80 to 1984/85, almost twice as fast as projected in the fifth plan (Republic of Botswana 1985, p.32). For the sixth plan, the government used lower import coefficients of private consumption to reflect increased production in Botswana of consumer goods and services (Republic of Botswana 1984, p.34).

The Reasons Behind Botswana's Success at Managing Booms and Busts

Many countries do not handle temporary booms in export earnings well. Windfall gains in export earnings often lead to increased spending and increased imports. Saving does not increase in the form of either foreign assets or domestic investment by an appropriate amount given the temporary nature of the windfalls. Instead, public spending increases and governments borrow against expected future export receipts that often do not materialize when the boom subsides. As a result, many countries that experienced windfalls in the 1970s have since run into serious debt servicing difficulties.

Why do countries find it so difficult to respond to windfall gains? Part of the explanation is that commodity prices are difficult to forecast, and determining the appropriate macroeconomic policy is more difficult under uncertain conditions. Second, most governments are under heavy pressure to spend. In a developing country, the government may find accumulating large stocks of foreign assets very difficult politically when demand for both current consumption and investment expenditure is high. In many countries these political pressures make optimal saving during boom periods impossible. When governments do not know for certain that prices will fall in the future, they will be under strong pressures to err on the side of optimism about future price trends.

There is some debate about whether adopting appropriate policies is easier or harder if the government receives the windfall gain rather than the private sector. If the boom accrues to the private sector, the government can either tax it away to raise savings or devise policies to encourage the private sector to save it in an appropriate way. If the private sector is not allowed to accumulate foreign assets, the resulting increase in international reserves will lead to an increase in the monetary base. The government must sterilize this effect if it wants to avoid inflationary pressures and real exchange rate appreciation. Sterilization, however, can be difficult. If the government receives the windfall gain, the appropriate macroeconomic response may be less complicated in theory. However, many governments that have received windfall gains have managed their booms disastrously. Several explanations for this exist. Governments find avoiding increased expenditures during booms difficult. The expenditures can take many forms, including increased parastatal deficits and overpriced government contracts with the private sector.

Another possible negative effect of the government receiving the windfall is that when the boom ends, the government can more easily postpone adjustment by borrowing from the central bank or abroad, which ultimately may make adjustment more costly. In addition, when the government finally cuts back on its expenditures, the cuts may take debilitating forms, such as neglecting maintenance and cutting everything except salaries. As a result, the country ends up in worse shape with the boom than it would have been without it.

Botswana has avoided many of the negative economic effects of a booming export sector that other countries have been unable to avoid. One reason may be Botswana's overall vulnerability. The country is landlocked, and therefore depends on transportation routes through other countries. Among the major risks facing Botswana cited in the sixth plan was "the possibility of supply decreases or inability to obtain access to markets due to unfavorable development in other countries...risks of this nature are very real in Botswana's circumstances, and it is precisely because of such risks that Botswana needs to maintain a reasonable level of contingency reserves" (Republic of Botswana 1985, p. 41).

In addition, another major export earner, copper-nickel matte, has also proved vulnerable to external events. With reduced world demand, world prices have fallen. Nickel prices fell 22 percent in 1986, while copper prices fell 3 percent. As a result exports fell from P120 million (US$65 million) in 1985 to P99 million (US$53 million) in 1986 (Bank of Botswana 1986, p. 19). Meat and meat products—Botswana's third largest export commodity—is vulnerable to both drought and foot and mouth disease. Also, customs union revenue is not perfectly predictable. All these sources of uncertainty make following a cautious policy on international reserve accumulation politically easier.

Another explanation of why Botswana has been able to accumulate foreign assets is that real GDP, real government recurrent expenditure, and real development expenditure have all been growing at very high rates. The mineral sector has generated so much foreign exchange and government revenue that government expenditures could grow very fast and still not use up all the additional reserves. Accumulating savings must be easier when real income and spending are increasing rather than when more obvious sacrifices in current expenditures are required. (Nonetheless, the government has experienced pressure to expand its expenditures even faster, and could have tried to undertake additional projects or activities, perhaps projects and activities with very low rates of return.)

Several other factors may have contributed to Botswana's successful management of its diamond export booms. First, it has had the advantage of experiencing booms later than many other developing countries and has seen the effects of mismanagement. This may have contributed to Botswana's success, but is not in itself a sufficient explanation. Many other countries mismanaged commodity booms in the late 1970s and the 1980s that had either watched other countries mismanage booms earlier or had mismanaged booms within their own countries.

The second factor concerns the timing of Botswana's first bust. In the early 1980s, with the Jwaneng mine, forecast as one of the most profitable diamond mines in the whole world, coming on line, the government experienced considerable pressure to increase its spending even faster than planned. Some people cautioned against too fast an increase on the grounds that the opening of Jwaneng would increase foreign exchange earnings and government revenues to a higher level than before, but thereafter those revenues would increase in real terms only to the extent that diamond prices rose faster than the price of imports. Given the uncertainty in diamond prices, this would not be a reasonable assumption. So faster growth rates of government spending would not be sustainable in the long run. In the end, the opening of Jwaneng coincided with a bust in the diamond market. If it had coincided with a boom, the pressures for faster expansion of government expenditures would have been very difficult to resist. The lesson that diamond markets are volatile came very quickly, so that the country did not have time to make any major mistakes.

The third factor is Botswana's political stability and quality of leadership. Countries with unstable governments may find saying no to pressures from special interest groups to increase spending more difficult. Increased spending in response to political pressures may have short-run political benefits that outweigh any negative effects on the economy later on. Botswana also has the advantage of having an ex-minister of finance as president.

Given the political commitment to follow appropriate economic policies, setting up a system within the government whereby key officials have access to sound economic advice on macroeconomic policy can contribute to success. As Harvey (1986, p. 34) put it:

> It is striking that in...Botswana...senior technical advisors devoted a lot of time to setting up a framework for macroeconomic policy and to explaining it to the relevant politicians (and other key people), well *before* the immediate need to make decisions arose, as well as at the time that decisions had to be made.

Lessons

For a country to be endowed with a resource that is valued highly in world markets can be a benefit. However, it is not sufficient for strong growth performance. If badly managed, both unstable growth and external debt crises can result. Recent experiences of oil-exporting, middle-income, developing countries demonstrate this. Botswana has avoided many of the problems that other developing countries have been unable to avoid.

Macroeconomic policies can help offset any undesirable effects of temporary commodity price booms. One lesson that can be learned from Botswana's experience is that in the face of variability in and uncertainty about the value of a major export sector, erring on the cautious side and assuming that any increase is temporary and any decline permanent is better. Most pressures in the economy, particularly on the government, will be to reach the exact opposite conclusion: that increases are permanent and declines temporary. The costs of assuming a boom to be permanent when it is not may include balance of payments crises and unstable growth. However, the costs of assuming the boom to be temporary when in fact it is permanent will be increased savings at the expense of increased expenditures.

Another lesson is that adjusting to shocks quickly rather than postponing adjustment can have benefits. The necessary changes are smaller, which can reduce the short-term costs of adjustment. The package of adjustment policies adopted in Botswana in response to the bust in the diamond market in the early 1980s is a good example. Another example is Botswana's frequent but relatively small adjustments in the pula exchange rate over the last decade.

Anticipating and planning for future shocks can also help prevent crisis situations from arising and result in better economic performance. In Botswana, not only were reserves accumulated in expectation of future declines in diamond export growth rates, but the government thought through the effects of different adjustment policies that could be used if needed. As a result, when the bust occurred in the early 1980s, adjustment was easier than it would have been otherwise.

Although some of the reasons why Botswana was able to manage commodity booms and busts successfully are not applicable to other countries, these lessons are relevant for other countries. They apply not only to other countries trying to manage variable export earnings, but also to countries subject to other types of external shocks as well.

References

Bank of Botswana. 1986 and various issues. *Annual Report.* Gaborone, Botswana: Bank of Botswana.

Bank of Botswana. Various issues. *Bulletin.* Gaborone, Botswana: Bank of Botswana.

Bank of Botswana. 1985. *Tenth Anniversary 1975-1985.* Gaborone, Botswana: Bank of Botswana. July 1.

Colclough, Christopher, and Stephen McCarthy. 1980. *The Political Economy of Botswana, A Study of Growth and Distribution.* Oxford: Oxford University Press.

Corden, W.M. 1983. "The Economic Effects of a Booming Sector." *International Social Science Journal.* Volume 35, No. 3, pp. 441-54.

Corden, W.M., and J.P. Neary. 1982. "Booming Sector and De-Industrialization in a Small Open Economy." *Economic Journal.* Vol. 92, pp. 825-48.

Cuddington, John T. 1986. *Managing Coffee Export Booms.* Washington, D.C.: May 12 (processed).

Cuddington, John T. 1986b. *Commodity Booms, Macroeconomic Stability and Trade Reform in Colombia.* Washington, D.C.: January 24 (processed).

Davis, Jeffrey M. 1983. "The Economic Effects of Windfall Gains in Export Earnings, 1975-1978." *World Development.* Vol. 11, No. 2, pp. 119-139.

Edwards, Sebastian. 1984. "Coffee, Money and Inflation in Colombia." *World Development.* Vol. 12, Nos. 11/12, pp. 1107-1117.

External Trade Statistics. Various issues. Gaborone, Botswana: Central Statistics Office, Ministry of Finance and Development Planning.

Financial Statements, Tables and Estimates of Consolidated and Development Fund Revenues. Various issues. Gaborone, Botswana: Republic of Botswana, Government Printer.

Harvey, Charles. 1981. *Papers on the Economy of Botswana.* London, England: Heinemann Educational Books.

Harvey, Charles. 1985. *The Use of Monetary Policy in Botswana, in Good Times and Bad.* Discussion Paper 204. Brighton, England: Institute of Development Studies. May.

Harvey, Charles. 1986. *Successful Macroeconomic Adjustment in Three Developing Countries: Botswana, Malawi and Papua New Guinea.* Washington, D.C.: Economic Development Institute of the World Bank.

Lewis, Stephen, R. 1984. "Development Problems of the Mineral-Rich Countries." *Economic Structure and Performance:* Essays in Honor of Hollis B. Chenery. San Diego: Academic Press.

Lewis, Stephen R, and D.N. Mokgethi. 1983. "Fiscal Policy in Botswana 1966-1981." In M.A. Oommen, F.K. Inganji, L.D. Ngcongco (eds). *Botswana's Economy Since Independence.* New Delhi: Tata McGraw-Hill.

Mmusi, P.S. "Budget Speech, 1986." Republic of Botswana.

Republic of Botswana. 1977. *National Development Plan, 1976-81.* Gaborone, Botswana: Ministry of Finance and Development Planning.

Republic of Botswana. 1980. *National Development Plan 1979-85*, Gaborone, Botswana: Ministry of Finance and Development Planning.

Republic of Botswana. 1983. *The Mid-term Review of NDP V.* Ministry of Finance and Development Planning. Gaborone, Botswana: Republic of Botswana, Government Printer. August.

Republic of Botswana. 1985. *National Development Plan 1985-91*, Gaborone, Botswana: Ministry of Finance and Development Planning.

Oommen, M.A., F.K. Inganji, L.D. Ngcongco. 1983. *Botswana's Economy Since Independence*. New Delhi: Tata McGraw-Hill.

Report of the Fourth Salaries Review Commission. 1985. Republic of Botswana. December.

Statistical Bulletin. March 1987 and various earlier issues. Gaborone, Botswana: Central Statistics Office, Ministry of Finance and Development Planning.

World Bank. 1985. *World Development Report.* Washington, D.C.: World Bank.

World Bank. 1985. *Economic Memorandum on Botswana.* Report No. 5238-BT. Washington, D.C.: World Bank.

Conclusions

Earl L. McFarland, Jr., Department of Economics, Williams College

This study is not based on a statistical analysis of hundreds of development projects or dozens of structural adjustment programs. It is based on a mere handful of cases that were not selected at random, but specifically chosen. The purpose of the study is to look closely at a small number of successful African development projects, programs, and policies, to see if they yield insights that might have a broader validity.

Thus we do not claim to have discovered any universal truths. However, we do think that the case studies provide some lessons that extend beyond the individual examples cited. We hope that readers will approach these case studies in this spirit, and will look for insights that might be applicable in other settings.

The case studies in this volume suggest a number of important implications. A discussion of these follows.

Learning from Experience

All the case studies illustrate the importance of learning from experience. From the simple Oxfam project to control rainfall runoff with rock bunds in Burkina Faso, to the complicated macroeconomic management programs in Ghana and Botswana, the people carrying out the project or program learned from their mistakes and successes during the process and made modifications accordingly.

If countries were merely replicas of each other, learning from experience would be less important. Any country could copy whatever worked well in any other country, and the results would be the same. However, because countries differ from each other, transfers of successful techniques or programs from one country to another generally require significant adaptation to local conditions.

In the case of the Oxfam project, the initial idea of an imported earthen basin technology for growing tree crops failed to be useful in Burkina Faso. Instead, project personnel working closely with local farmers discovered that an adaptation of that technology—constructing simple rock bunds on hillside terraces—was not only very effective in controlling soil erosion, but was simple and cheap to construct and maintain. Similarly, the spread of the innovation depended on farmers' ability to learn from the successful experience of other farmers.

The gravity-fed piped water scheme in Malawi involves a more complicated technology than the bunds, but village labor can nevertheless largely construct and maintain the water systems. The basic system was designed by an engineer working closely with local villagers, and evolved over time as experience suggested improvements, such as switching to locally produced pipes that were both better and cheaper than the imported pipes initially used. The spread of the innovation depended heavily on additional villages learning from the successful experience of villages that, with government help, had constructed and were maintaining their own piped water supplies.

In the onchocerciasis control program in West Africa, the project staff learned that the original coverage was not broad enough to eradicate the fly, and they had to expand the program's geographical scope. They also had to make technical modifications in the sprays over time.

In the case of horticultural exports in Kenya, after some private initiatives suggested encouraging possibilities, the government established the Horticultural Crops Development Authority in 1967. The authority quickly learned how to perform best its function of fomenting horticultural development: which activities were best left to the private sector, such as the pricing of products, and which activities it could best perform itself. The government learned how responsive farmers can be to economic incentives and what types of government support are most effective in encouraging the desired responses in the horticultural sector. As the program evolved, the Horticultural Crops Development Authority determined what services to provide to organize shipping and to ensure that exporters met quality standards. Kenyan producers and exporters found out partly from foreign investors from the importing countries about market opportunities and requirements in those countries, and partly from the Horticultural Crops Development Authority and the International Trade Center.

The strategy of the export processing zone in Mauritius arose from a realization of the dangers of continued dependence on sugar exports, and the limited scope for import substitution in manufacturing given the economy's small size. The incentives initially provided were an attempt to learn from the experience of other countries that had set up export processing zones. As the program evolved, however, policymakers altered, and continue to alter, a wide range of policies to achieve the results they want. Indeed, if the government had failed to modify the incentive structure during the slow growth period of 1977-82, the program might not be considered today to have been successful. Similarly, if the government's more recent policies aimed at attacking the problems of product and market specialization and weak linkages with the rest of the economy, and at narrowing the differences in incentives between firms producing for the domestic economy and firms in the export processing zone are not effective, the EPZ program may ultimately be judged to have failed—unless policymakers manage to find other policies that do solve those problems.

Ghana's history between 1970 and 1982 provides ample evidence that allowing an exchange rate to become more and more overvalued over time, and tightly controlling most key domestic prices in the face of increasing shortages, can only make the domestic economic situation worse and eventually bring economic development to a halt. From a national point of view, the economic costs of such policies in the long run are considerably higher than the short-run economic and political costs of structural reform programs.

Since 1983, Ghana's economic recovery program has required policymakers to adapt their policies as conditions changed in a very fluid situation that might easily have seen the leadership return to the very policies that had caused the problems in the first place. The IMF and World Bank's willingness to help make considerable external resources available to Ghana represents in itself the result of a learning process in the international community, which now seems to accept that many structural adjustment programs are much less likely to succeed without substantial and long-term external financial assistance.

Both the Mauritius and Ghana studies illustrate a pattern that can be generalized as follows:

1. A government implements a set of policies to achieve specific objectives.

2. With time, the policymakers see that the policies either do not quite achieve the objectives, or that as they achieve these objectives, other problems arise.

3. The government modifies the original policies and/or implements additional policies.

4. The modified policies in turn cause new problems to arise.

5. The government must again revise the policy set, and so on.

This makes it clear why learning from experience is so important. At any point in the chain outlined above, if the new policies fail to solve satisfactorily the problems that have arisen, the program will be judged a failure. For the program to succeed, it must continue to adapt and solve problems as they arise during implementation.

Ghana's economic recovery program has encountered many opportunities for failure. From 1983 to the present, policymakers in Ghana have continually had to adapt their policies to keep the program on track. Two good examples are exchange rate policy and cocoa pricing policy. Having observed the disastrous effects on the economy of prolonged and exaggerated overvaluation of the cedi and excessively low producer prices for cocoa, policymakers set out to correct those mistakes. They had to devalue the cedi many times between 1983 and 1986 in the search for the "correct" exchange rate, and finally, they took the even bolder step to a foreign exchange auction. The search for the "correct" producer price for cocoa also required many sharp increases in that price during the same period.

The large expansion of foreign exchange earnings and government revenues from Botswana's mineral sector has occurred only in the last decade. As a relative latecomer to mineral wealth, Botswana has had the advantage of learning from the often unhappy experiences of other developing countries with commodity booms and busts. This made resisting pressures to increase government spending dramatically during the boom phase of the cycle easier, although disagreement between those policymakers who wanted to increase spending faster and those who wanted to resist such pressures still existed. The government was able to adopt a strategy aimed at smoothing the impact of variable mineral earnings on the economy, by avoiding expanding government expenditures at the same rapid rate as revenues were expanding during booms. Instead, the government used some of the revenues to build up foreign exchange reserves, and managed the exchange rate so as to encourage exports and import-competing investments.

The timing of the boom and subsequent bust also played an important role. As the boom continued, those policymakers who favored faster increases in government expenditures gained support. When the world diamond market crashed in 1981 and 1982, this reinforced the arguments of the more cautious policymakers. Government spending policies that had been justified largely by the experience of other countries were seen to be prudent in the light of Botswana's own experience.

All the case studies illustrate the importance of learning from experience and of being flexible in adapting policies as difficulties arise. The studies also suggest that the more complex the project or program, the greater the opportunities for failure. This is merely an observation, not a recommendation to select only simple projects or programs. The more complex the project or program, the more likely it is to have multiple objectives, some of which may conflict with each other. In such cases, the first set of policies selected is unlikely to achieve satisfactory outcomes, and problems that call for policy modifications are more likely to arise. In macroeconomic programs (such as those in Mauritius, Ghana, and Botswana), this complexity is particularly easy to see. Without the ability to learn from experience and to adapt policies flexibly, failure is almost guaranteed.

In this respect the pragmatism demonstrated by Mauritius and Ghana since 1982 and by Botswana has much to recommend it. If a government is able to consider the whole range of possible solutions to a given problem, without ruling some possible policies out of bounds, this pragmatic approach clearly facilitates learning from experience.

Government Concentration on Tasks That It Can Do Well

One of the basic principles in economics is that of comparative advantage: the idea that two parties can both benefit if each concentrates on producing that commodity in which it is relatively more efficient and then trades with the other. One can also apply this principle to the decision about which activities are best carried out by the government and which by the private sector.

Part of the decision is relatively easy. Some activities only a government can provide. National defense is one example. Formulation and implementation of macroeconomic policy is another. However, a wider range of activities could be carried out either by government or by the private sector, and here the principle of comparative advantage is applicable.

The piped water case study from Malawi provides an interesting example. The government was apparently efficient at drilling boreholes, but less efficient at maintaining them. Borehole technology is too complicated for villages to maintain themselves, and private borehole maintenance is not available. As a result, boreholes sometimes go for months without repair when they break down. One of the major advantages of the gravity-fed piped water system is that villagers can do most of the construction and maintenance themselves. The cost to government (and the economy as a whole) is reduced, and the system's reliability is increased. Since government resources are limited, but surplus village labor exists, the gravity-fed system makes much more efficient use of resources than the borehole system.

The study of horticultural exports in Kenya offers a good illustration of a government agency, the Horticultural Crops Development Authority, that has made judicious decisions about its activities. The authority has used the sweeping powers entrusted to it in 1967 selectively. It has played a major role in research and extension, in some aspects of marketing, and in quality control, but it has not used its powers to set prices. Instead it has allowed market prices to determine profitability, and this incentive has led to an extraordinary increase in horticultural production and exports. The private sector has carried out the direct investment and produced the output, while the government has provided the basic infrastructure and the Horticultural Crops Development Authority has provided the sector with a wide variety of supporting services. The division of activities according to comparative advantage is clear.

The export processing zone in Mauritius is another example of investment and production carried out by the private sector, but in response to a broad framework of government policies designed to provide economic incentives for export promotion. Moreover, in Mauritius the basic knowledge required to penetrate export markets was initially provided by foreign private investors who were already active in those markets. Mauritian private investors responded to the initiatives demonstrated by the foreigners, and to the incentives and support services provided by the government.

In both Ghana and Botswana, the government used a wide range of macroeconomic policy tools (for example, exchange rate policy, fiscal policy, monetary policy, wages policy) to elicit the responses that it wanted private producers to make. In Ghana, pricing policy was also a major element of the program.

Thus, since governments have limited resources and cannot do everything well, they will often do best to concentrate on those activities they can do well. This approach often involves using various indirect policies to affect economic incentives, and then allowing the private sector to respond to these incentives. In addition, governments must then be flexible in adjusting incentives until they get the results they seek.

Economic Incentives and Getting the Prices Right

The dramatic response of horticultural producers in Kenya, and the rapid growth of manufactured exports from the export processing zone in Mauritius and of cocoa and timber exports from Ghana demonstrate the power of market incentives. In Kenya and Ghana, the government provided basic infrastructure and support services, and in Mauritius, the government provided a comprehensive package of economic incentives. These actions increased the profitability of private investment in those sectors, and producers' response was impressive.

The nature of recent problems of the export processing zone also show how incentives can shape results, for example, duty free imports have led to import-intensive exports and relatively few backward linkages with the domestic economy. In addition the structure of the incentives attracted principally textile and garment producers oriented toward export markets in specific countries. These results led policymakers to alter the previous incentives to encourage diversification of products and markets.

The response of farmers in Burkina Faso to the higher incomes attainable with the bund system also illustrates the same point. The reduced risk and increased output made possible by the bund technology, as well as the low cost in terms of materials required and the farmers' own labor time, provided a powerful economic incentive to adopt the new technology. As a consequence, use of the technology has spread largely by word of mouth without the need for a large body of government extension workers, and farmers have been willing to bear the costs of their investment on their own.

The Ghana case study offers a vivid example of the devastating impact on an economy of getting the prices wrong and keeping them wrong with extensive controls for an extended period of time. Reduced profitability discourages new investment and productive capacity declines. Shortages become more and more acute, queues of consumers fight to purchase the shrinking supplies of goods at controlled prices that find their way through official channels, and more and more goods flow through illegal markets at much higher prices. Most of the consumers who were supposed to benefit from controlled prices end up either paying exorbitant prices on illegal markets or doing without.

The Ghana experience also illustrates the powerful contribution that getting prices much closer to right can make in getting a disrupted economy back on track. At the same time, it illustrates that getting the prices right may not be a sufficient condition. With basic transportation so poor and foreign exchange for needed inputs so scarce, initially major export products had no way to get to foreign markets. Structural problems had to be dealt with before market incentives could have substantial effects. This study therefore provides strong support for both the "get the prices right" school and the "structural obstacles" school.

Appropriate Technology and Consulting with Beneficiaries

The advantages of relatively simple technology are evident in both the gravity-fed water system in Malawi and the Oxfam bund project in Burkina Faso. Technology that villagers can implement and maintain themselves can have lower recurrent costs for government, greater reliability, and greater learning benefits for the villagers themselves.

The technology involved in the onchocerciasis project in West Africa, however, is very advanced and uses much costly capital equipment. In addition, implementation is coordinated over wide geographical areas by technicians and administrators in a unique intergovernmental organization. Involvement of the project beneficiaries is not required for the project's success. They are simply recipients of the project's benefits. Cases where the active involvement of a project's beneficiaries are not crucial to its success are probably quite rare.

The lesson here is the oft-cited one that the level of technology should be appropriate for the circumstances. The Malawi and Burkina Faso projects are good examples of the effectiveness of simple technology, while the onchocerciasis project shows that relatively advanced technology may be appropriate in other instances.

The Malawi and Burkina Faso projects also illustrate how the development of the technology in cooperation with the villagers contributed greatly to the success of both programs. Both were done with the people affected, not for them or to them. The nature of the project and its desired goals determine how important it is to work with the project beneficiaries, but government implementation of projects on behalf of a target group without adequate consultation with them always runs the risk of leaving recipients at the margin of the development process. It also increases the likelihood of inappropriate project design, with adverse effects on project costs and benefits, and reduces the possibility of learning from experience for both the government and the project beneficiaries.

Expanding Exports

An important implication of the Kenya and Mauritius cases is that if the government's supportive and incentive policies are judiciously designed and well implemented, developing countries can penetrate even extremely competitive export markets.

In Mauritius, starting with an economy in which sugar was the dominant export and existing manufacturing was for import substitution behind high protective barriers, the establishment of an export processing zone with a range of incentives expanded manufactured exports from zero to half of total exports in 15 years. The export market for textiles and garments is one of the most competitive in the world, yet Mauritius was able to expand production, exports, and employment in this sector dramatically before hitting barriers to further expansion in some importing countries' markets. By the time such exports became the target of quotas in some markets, Mauritius was ready to move on to other products and other markets.

Kenya's impressive expansion of exports of horticultural products also faced intense competition in European markets. Nevertheless, Kenyan producers successfully penetrated these markets as the varieties of products and their quality were adapted to market demands.

These two studies do not support the pessimism about possibilities for nontraditional exports that developing countries sometimes express. The advantage of being a small player in the world market comes into play here. Most developing countries are unlikely to be large enough producers of any single commodity to run into export market limitations before they have achieved significant benefits from export expansion. Even at that stage, diversification into different geographical markets and different commodities may enable them to escape the limitations a single commodity faces.

External Assistance

External assistance contributed in a variety of ways to several of the development cases analyzed here.

The structural adjustment reforms in Ghana would have been much more difficult to carry out without substantial external resources to help the country weather the transition from the stage when the formal economy was barely functioning, to the stage when markets began to perform their normal roles again. Initially Ghana faced such a shortage of foreign exchange that it could not afford to purchase the imported inputs that it needed to restore the infrastructure or to increase the output of exports. The country was unable to increase its foreign exchange earnings until it had more foreign exchange. External assistance helped to break this vicious circle. By reducing the short-term costs of structural adjustment, the assistance also helped the government to undertake the program and still hope to survive long enough to reap the longer-term benefits.

The case of the export processing zone in Mauritius illustrates a number of other ways in which external resources can be useful. First, foreign investors provided additional resources for investment. Second, foreign investors supplied needed managerial and production expertise and technology. Third, and perhaps most important, the foreign investors brought with them knowledge about the demand in foreign markets and how to meet it. External resources were important in the same three ways in the case of horticultural production and exports in Kenya.

Oxfam was the initial catalyst in the bund project in Burkina Faso. Similarly, the WHO provided the critical initiative for implementing the onchocerciasis program in West Africa, and in bringing together the governments concerned in the intergovernmental organization carrying out the campaign to suppress the disease. Foreign resources in the form of technical experts and administrators, as well as financing, have been instrumental in finding technical solutions to the problem.

Timely Adjustments in Macroeconomic Management

Ghana, during its downward spiral from 1970 to 1982, is a vivid illustration of how bad things can get when timely policy adjustments are not made because of policymakers' unwillingness to face the short-term economic and political costs. The government allowed the cedi to become more and more overvalued to avoid making all imports more expensive and increasing the cost of living. But the more overvalued the cedi became, the larger the devaluation that would have been required, and the bigger the short-term shock to the economy. Yet if policymakers were reluctant to devalue by 20 percent at one point, they must have been even more reluctant to devalue by 80 percent later on. Policymakers' hesitation to devalue in the hope that export earnings would simply pick up on their own or that other policy measures would make devaluation unnecessary is understandable.

Initially, increased tariffs and quotas on nonessential imports kept expenditures on imports under control, and foreign exchange rationing allocated foreign exchange to those goods and services judged the most essential for development. For a while these measures kept the growing scarcity of foreign exchange manageable. As the currency became more and more overvalued, however, the export sector's profitability suffered and export earnings declined. Falling export earnings increased the need for more tariffs and quotas and ever more stringent foreign exchange rationing. As exports earnings fell and imports had to be reduced, government revenues (much of which came from taxes on imports and exports) also declined, increasing the government's budget deficit and monetary expansion.

During the vicious downward spiral, policymakers got locked into bad exchange rate policy because the short-term costs of devaluation got worse the longer the authorities waited. Hindsight reveals that the best time to devalue would have been early on, when the short-term costs were much less. Thus, the lesson here is that a small devaluation early on, or even a series of devaluations spread over time, is much easier to handle, both economically and politically, than a huge devaluation carried out in desperation only when there is no longer any room to maneuver.

Botswana has consistently followed a policy of adjusting macroeconomic policy variables by relatively small amounts frequently, rather than waiting until large changes were required. This is perhaps clearest with respect to the exchange rate. The government has revalued and devalued the pula many times during the last ten years, but always by 5 to 10 percent. This has helped to keep both the public and policymakers aware that the exchange rate is a policy variable, not a constant, and has also kept the short-term costs of adjustment low.

In Botswana, the basic elements of timely macroeconomic management of the diamond boom and bust were using part of the rising diamond revenues during the boom to build up foreign exchange reserves, and responding promptly when the bust occurred by adjusting policies for the exchange rate, bank lending, interest rates, public sector wages, and (to a lesser extent) budget expenditures and taxes. The action taken during the boom made the prompt policy adjustment to the bust easier and more effective.

When Botswana instituted a whole package of policy responses to the bust in 1982, the government decided to make small changes in a number of key variables even though the foreign exchange situation might have corrected itself within a year or two. The government did not want to run the risk of having to institute much more drastic changes later on. By adjusting a number of key variables, the government was able to keep the changes smaller and spread the effects more widely across the economy.

Political Decisions and Leadership

Economic policy decisions by governments are inevitably intertwined with political considerations, and distinctive political and cultural factors often affect particular governments' decisions. What insights can we draw from these case studies that may facilitate bolder and more appropriate economic policy decisions? The Ghana and Botswana experiences are most revealing.

During the downward spiral in Ghana, economic conditions were generally bad and getting worse. The political situation was also chaotic, with many changes of government, often by military coups. Under such circumstances policymakers are likely to feel insecure and to focus primarily on short-run costs and benefits. The desire to retain eroding political support runs counter to the need for timely policy adjustments, since these often have substantial short-run costs. Policymakers focus on possible short-run costs rather than on larger economic and political benefits that might occur only over time.

The political situation in Botswana was quite different when the diamond bust occurred. Past economic trends had been favorable, and the party that controlled the government had won a series of national elections since independence. The government's political security, and its expectations that it would still be in power in five years, made it more concerned about the longer-run consequences of policy actions or inactions.

What can be done in the perhaps more common case of a government with weaker political support and a high discount rate on longer-term economic benefits? One possibility is that, against the odds, a political leader who is far-seeing and bold may also have the political skills to redirect attention to longer-run goals and strategies, and to ride through the short-run political costs of basic policy changes. Another possibility is that the situation may eventually get so bad that a new government comes to power with a mandate to make sweeping policy changes. If the new government manages to last long enough to reverse the downward spiral, the political dilemma may be resolved.

The international community may help to resolve this political dilemma by recognizing that governments will often have great difficulty in bearing the short-run economic and political costs of reform programs. Making external resources available, as in the economic recovery program in Ghana, may be critical for accelerating the transition period and reducing these short-run costs to bearable levels.

Implications of the Case Studies: A Final Comment

Whether we are talking about an individual or a society, progress is bound to be slow and erratic unless people can learn from experience. Repeating the same mistakes over and over again, or repeating the same mistakes that other countries have made, is a terrible waste that developing countries can ill afford. Similarly, neglecting the implications of other countries' successful development policies is a wasted opportunity.

A mistake that governments can easily make in formulating economic policy is to underestimate the power of economic incentives. Economists do not deny that other important incentives motivate individuals: the need for self-respect, love of family, loyalty to friends, patriotism, and many others. What economists do stress is that interacting with these other incentives, economic incentives are also very strong and influence greatly the outcome of governments' policy actions. Too often one sees governments exhorting their citizens to do one thing, while giving them strong economic incentives to do just the opposite. Economic development requires a sustained long-term effort, and economic incentives have much more staying power than exhortation.

At the same time, a mistake that economists can easily make when considering economic problems in a particular country at a particular time and suggesting appropriate economic policy measures, is to focus almost entirely on the economic effects of the problems and the policies. Yet a country and its government pursue political and social as well as economic aims, and decision making about which policy measures to adopt to deal with pressing economic problems often involves trade-offs among likely economic, political, and social effects. Although economists' basic responsibility when analyzing problems and policy options is to clarify their economic effects, relevant economic policy analysis at a particular time in a particular country calls for taking into account political and social considerations as well.

The country case studies in this volume are encouraging. A variety of countries have achieved substantial successes in a range of development activities, from simple to complex. The experiences in these successful development projects, programs, and policies deserve serious attention. How and why did they work out particularly well? What are the implications for development efforts in other settings? Surely insights from such relatively successful experiences can be instructive for economic policymakers facing development problems elsewhere.